Karen:

"Life is not measured by what you gather, but what you scatter into the lives of others."

— Helen Walton

Enjoy..

SPIRITUAL
LEADERSHIP

MOVING

PEOPLE

ON TO GOD'S

AGENDA

SPIRITUAL
LEADERSHIP

HENRY & RICHARD
BLACKABY

BROADMAN
& HOLMAN
PUBLISHERS

NASHVILLE, TENNESSEE

Ten-Digit ISBN: 0–8054–1845–8
Thirteen-Digit ISBN: 978–0–8054–1845–3

Published by Broadman & Holman Publishers
Nashville, Tennessee

Dewey Decimal Classification: 253
Subject Heading: LEADERSHIP

Unless otherwise noted, Scripture quotations are from the New
American Standard Bible, © the Lockman Foundation, 1960,
1962, 1963, 1968, 1971, 1972, 1973, 1975, 1977; used by
permission. Quotations marked NIV are from the Holy Bible,
New International Version, copyright © 1973, 1978, 1984
by International Bible Society.

Library of Congress Cataloging-in-Publication Data

Blackaby, Henry T., 1935–
Spiritual leadership: moving people on to God's agenda / Henry & Richard
  Blackaby.
    p. cm.
  ISBN 0–8054–1845–8 (hb)
  1. Leadership—Religious aspects—Christianity. I. Blackaby,
  Richard, 1961– II. Title.

BV4597.53.L43 B57 2001
253—dc21

2001025289

12 13 14 15 16 17 11 10 09 08 07 06

Dedication

I dedicate this book to my children: Richard, Thomas, Melvin, Norman, and Carrie. All five have become effective spiritual leaders in their own right and have made their parents extremely proud!

Henry Blackaby

I dedicate this book to the emerging generation of spiritual leaders, including my own three children, Michael, Daniel, and Carrie, who want their lives to make a difference in God's kingdom and who are willing to adjust their lives to God's agenda in order for that to happen.

Richard Blackaby

Contents

Preface

HAVE YOU EVER OBSERVED A WEAK, declining organization teetering on the brink of disbandment? Then a new leader arrived, and everything changed dramatically. Perhaps you have been a part of such an experience. You may have had little hope for the survival of your organization. Then along came a leader who mobilized people into action, and you were astounded at the difference. Results previous leaders had failed to achieve in ten years, the new leader accomplished in six months!

What happened? Was this not the same collection of people with identical problems and limitations? How did it languish under one leader and flourish under another? The difference had little to do with the problems or the limitations. It had everything to do with good leadership. The fact is, some leaders are successful no matter what challenge they take on, while others suffer chronic failure and mediocrity.

Over the years we have seen this phenomenon occur repeatedly. We have been intrigued by the contrast between weak and strong leaders. We have become convinced that all organizations have potential for growth and success; the key is effective leadership. We have invested many years in developing and encouraging leaders. We spend a great deal of time with emerging leaders at the front end of their careers—men and women who wonder if they have the necessary skills to lead people effectively. We regularly counsel discouraged leaders who struggle with feelings of failure and regret because they have not realized their hopes and dreams. We often hear from troubled executives who have achieved notable worldly success but who feel their lives are making little difference in God's kingdom.

The world is disoriented to what makes a truly successful leader. The Bible has much to say to leaders. We have examined the Scriptures, and we have scrutinized the lives of effective leaders in light of God's Word. In doing so, we identified several clear, biblical principles that lead to effective leadership. We have shared these truths around the world, and we have seen men and women return to their leadership roles with renewed vigor and vision. As they have applied God's methods of leadership, they have met with profound results.

Bookstore shelves overflow with leadership theories, and we are familiar with many of these works. Why add our voice to the throng? We believe crucial leadership truths are being overlooked. Secular writings can provide helpful insights for Christian leaders, and this book will purposefully interact with such works to highlight some of their strengths. We will discuss secular leaders who demonstrate characteristics of healthy leadership. Nevertheless, we are concerned that many Christian leaders are reading secular books and are accepting their teachings uncritically. Much secular leadership theory is based on presuppositions that may appear sound yet promote ideas contrary to the Scriptures. They leave God out!

Secular and spiritual leaders may use similar methods, but there are dimensions to spiritual leadership not present in secular leadership. Spiritual leaders who simply follow secular methods may experience some degree of success, but they will not rise to the higher level of leadership possible for true spiritual leaders. This book will distinguish between general leadership principles and spiritual leadership principles.

Our main goal in writing is to help Christian leaders. We have talked with hundreds of discouraged men and women who were ready to resign their leadership positions, but they retained a heartfelt desire to serve God effectively . As we helped them examine the Scriptures to discover God's agenda, leaders from all walks of life have found encouragement and direction for their lives and their organizations. We are not writing primarily to those in full-time Christian work, although those in vocational ministry will certainly benefit from the truths we discuss. The guidelines we present are for *all* Christians who seek to be spiritual leaders. Holding a leadership position in a Christian organization does not make one a spiritual leader. Spiritual leadership is not an occupation: it is a calling. Christian businesspeople, physicians, educators, politicians, and parents—all ought to be spiritual leaders. More and more people in "secular" occupations are taking their calling as spiritual leaders seriously, and they are impacting the world and extending God's kingdom.

Only when we understand leadership in light of God's calling on our lives will we be equipped to lead effectively. According to the Bible, God is not necessarily looking for leaders, at least not in the sense we generally think of leaders. He is looking for servants (Isa. 59:16; Ezek. 22:30). When God finds men and women willing to be molded into his servants, the possibilities are limitless. People are looking for someone to lead them into God's purposes God's way. They need leaders who truly believe God will do what he says. People will follow spiritual leaders who understand God's agenda and who know how to move them on to it.

As you read this book, we pray you will accept the challenge to be that man or woman God is seeking to use. We hope you will experience the incredible joy and satisfaction of knowing God is using your life as his instrument to build his kingdom and to change your world.

Acknowledgments

As always, we are grateful to our wives. We could not have written this book were it not for the loving, supporting life-partners God has graciously given us. Much of who we have become as spiritual leaders can be attributed to the investment they have made in our lives. Marilynn has steadfastly been a joyful partner in ministry with Henry for forty years. Lisa, once again, served as our primary editor, investing countless hours to ensure the book says what we mean to say! We greatly appreciate John Beckett, who thoughtfully studied our manuscript and made invaluable suggestions. We appreciate Gerry Taillon, National Ministry Leader of the Canadian Convention of Southern Baptists, who provided thoughtful insights into the practice of spiritual leadership. "Mack" McQuiston has been very encouraging and helpful to us in our effort to assist Christian CEOs. His aid in enlisting CEOs to fill out our leadership survey is heartily appreciated. We are also indebted to friends Alan Braun, senior pastor of Abundant Life Christian Fellowship, Ross Lincer, Student Services Director at the Canadian Southern Baptist Seminary, and Bob Shelton, the Pastor to Pastors in the Canadian Convention of Southern Baptists. These three men carefully read the manuscript and gave candid, insightful feedback. And finally, to the many pastors and leaders from all walks of life who have told us their stories, shared their struggles, and allowed us to celebrate their victories: You have greatly enriched our lives!

CHAPTER ONE

The Leader's Challenge

Mike sat in stunned silence, alone in the boardroom. He had appointments to keep, but they seemed irrelevant now. He remained frozen in his chair, trying to process the events of the previous hour. Mike was CEO of a software company. He was a young man—in his early thirties—bright, creative and good at his job. Moreover, he was a committed Christian with a strong work ethic. He'd always considered his faith to be an asset to his career. But the morning's executive team meeting had shattered that assumption. What began as a routine weekly meeting escalated into an acrimonious dispute, revealing a pervasive undercurrent of resentment toward him—more specifically toward his Christian beliefs. It seems a clear line had been drawn in the sand, with his executive team demanding he choose between his faith and his business.

First, the vice president for human resources announced a revision to the company benefits to include coverage for therapeutic abortions in the health policy. He urged Mike to herald the new policy as a public relations tool.

Then Barbara from Marketing announced a new advertising campaign, one that deliberately misrepresented the facts. Mike felt he had no choice but to veto both recommendations. That's when the floodgates opened and his colleagues' hostility spewed out. His staff seemed united on one thing—that his agenda for the company did not match theirs. Mike was bewildered. He had a talented staff who knew their fields. Yet the majority were nonbelievers and several were disdainful of the

Christian faith. Was there anything he could do? He worried about legal issues if he stood by his convictions on certain social issues. It had never been easy taking a stand for his faith at work, but he'd always tried to be obedient to Christ through his job. Now it just didn't seem possible. Maybe he should face the reality that his job and his faith could not co-exist, and resign.

Pastor Edwards could barely withhold his tears. He could still hear the deacons' voices as they walked down the hallway, away from his office. The group had arrived unexpectedly and lambasted him, blaming him for all the church's problems. And problems there were—lots of them! Two years ago Edwards had enthusiastically accepted the call to serve as pastor of the church, fully aware of some of the difficulties. After all, every church has issues. He was young and his faith was strong. He sincerely believed that prayer, biblical preaching, and loving guidance would bring the ailing church back to health. But now things were actually worse. Landmines seemed to explode under him no matter where he stepped. Several families requested more modern music in the services and he willingly obliged. In doing so he inadvertently alienated several others who were now withholding their tithes as well as their service in the church until the music was changed back to the style they enjoyed. One of the deacons was rumored to be in an adulterous relationship. An attempt to confront him had set the entire deacon body up in arms. They accused Edwards of witch hunting. They argued that this man had great influence in the community; they pointed out the sad truth the church could ill afford another public scandal. When Edwards proposed hiring a part-time youth pastor, a battle erupted. Various interest groups in the church clamored for more ministry—for seniors, for choir members, for college students, for the divorced, and for children. Even his preaching had come under fire—too long, not enough humor. Edwards had been growing weary under the stress, but he remained strong in his belief that, if he persevered, the problems would eventually sort themselves out. That was before this visit. Their words cut like a knife: "As representatives of this church, we feel obliged to tell you we can no longer follow your leadership. Perhaps you should begin circulating a resumé to other churches. There are churches out there who might appreciate your style of leadership. . . ." The pastor held his face in his hands. What more could he have done? He had worked to the point of exhaustion for this church. He had sacrificed time with his wife and children, spending most evenings at church meetings, counseling people in distress, or visiting potential members. He knew where the church should be heading, but he simply could not get the people to support him. He felt like a total failure.

LEADERSHIP: THE CHALLENGE

Leadership. Everyone experiences it, or the lack of it, in their daily lives. Those called to lead can find doing so a daunting task. Those expected to follow can experience frustration when their leader is unable to lead and their organization seems to be going nowhere. Struggling leaders may agonize in the knowledge that others resent them and blame them for their organizations' failures. Countless discouraged leaders would probably quit their jobs today, but they need the income. Besides, they fear the same problems would engulf them in their new jobs. Discouraged, Christian leaders carry the added, albeit misguided, burden that they are failing not only their people but their Lord. They feel guilty because they lack the faith to move their organization forward yet the same fears prevent them from leaving their leadership positions for jobs where they might be more successful. Is there any hope for the countless numbers of leaders who are not experiencing the fulfillment and reaching the potential God intended for them? If anything can revolutionize today's Christian leaders, it is when Christians understand God's design for spiritual leaders.

The twenty-first century provides unprecedented opportunities for leaders to impact positively their organizations. However, the new millennium also brings unforeseen challenges to leaders. The digitalized nature of the twenty-first century has created increasing expectations among followers, and the unrelenting advance of technology has made communication both a blessing and a curse. E-mail and cell phones provide instant access to leaders. In times past, people would write letters or send memos to their leader and then wait for days, or even weeks for a reply. People accepted such delayed responses as a matter of course.

Past leaders could take time to ponder their decisions and to consult with advisors before sending a response. Today's technology, however, has radically changed the dynamics of communication. The moment someone sends an e-mail they know that within minutes they could (and therefore should) receive a reply. Busy leaders can return from a lunch appointment to discover a dozen new e-mails and as many voice-mail messages waiting for them, classified by their senders as urgent. In any airport you can see harried executives exiting airplanes and consulting their cell phones to discover that while they traveled the first leg of their business trip, their voice mailbox was filling up with urgent messages, most of them demanding a reply before they board their next flight. Cell phones can be tremendously helpful to leaders as they seek to maintain close contact with their people, but beleaguered executives and pastors are discovering that those phones follow them everywhere, even on their vacations.

Past leaders had certain times in their day when they were inaccessible to people. During such times they could reflect on their situation and make decisions about their next course of action. Technology has made today's leaders constantly and instantly accessible to people. With such access, people often expect immediate responses from their leaders. Such pressure to make rapid decisions and to maintain steady communication can intimidate even the most zealous leader.

The rise of the Information Age has inundated leaders with new information that must be processed as rapidly as possible. Today's leaders are bombarded with books, articles, and seminars on leadership and management theory as well as data pertaining to their particular field of work. An exhausting parade of books claims that if busy executives will simply follow the proposed steps, they will be guaranteed success. Leaders wanting to improve their skills and expand their knowledge base have virtually limitless opportunities to enhance their leadership skills. But where does one begin? Which book does a leader read next? Which seminar is a must? Which management trend vociferously advocated now will be passé by next year? Such a bombardment of information, much of which is contradictory, can cause leaders to become cynical. While it is true the Information Age has given leaders many new tools with which to lead, it has also placed heavy demands on leaders, demands previous generations of leaders never faced. It is no wonder so many leaders express the frustration that they are always hopelessly behind.

Probably the most widespread modern myth is that technology will create more time for leaders. While many modern tools of technology are heralded as time-saving devices, the reality is that these instruments become major information highways bringing an endless stream of data racing toward leaders who feel pressured to respond as quickly as possible. All the while, these leaders are aware that a wrong decision can have disastrous consequences on their organization. Gordon Sullivan and Michael Harper have suggested that the defining characteristic of the Information Age is not speed, but the "compression of time."[1] It is not so much that events are necessarily moving faster but that there is less time for leaders to respond to events than there used to be. This puts enormous pressure upon today's leaders.

Our world craves good leaders. It would seem that effective leadership has become the panacea for every challenge society faces. Whether it's in politics, religion, business, education, or law, the universally expressed need is for leaders who will rise to meet the challenges that seem to overwhelm many of today's organizations. The problem is not a shortage of willing leaders. The problem is an increasingly skeptical view among followers as to whether these people can truly lead. Warren Bennis warned, "At the heart of America is a vacuum into which self-anointed saviors have rushed."[2] People know intuitively that claiming to be a leader or holding a leadership position does not make someone a leader. People are warily looking for leaders they can trust.

LEADERSHIP: IN POLITICS

The political scene is perhaps the most public arena where people have expressed their distrust in those who lead them. These are not easy times in which to be a leader. The world's complexity increases at exponential speed. Political alliances are in constant flux. Threats of nuclear and biological terrorism are a real and frightening possibility. A severe downturn in the global economy can devastate a nation overnight. Violence is epidemic. Nothing shocks us any more. Social norms, previously taken for granted, are publicly ridiculed. Modern society has deteriorated to the point that, like those in the prophet Jeremiah's time, we have "forgotten how to blush" (see Jer. 6:15; 8:12). In the face of such daunting political and social realities, people search frantically for leaders they can trust. Society seeks men and women who will effectively address a multitude of societal and political ills. People are weary of politicians who make promises they are either unwilling or unable to keep. Society longs for statesmen but it gets politicians. Statesmen are leaders who uphold what is right regardless of the popularity of the position. Statesmen speak out to achieve good for their people, not to win votes. Statesmen promote the general good rather than regional or personal self-interest. Harry Truman was a statesman. He left the presidency with a low rating in the public opinion polls, yet history evaluates him as an effective leader during a dangerous and turbulent time. Politicians may win elections; nevertheless, future generations could deride them for their lack of character and their ineffective leadership.

Warren Bennis suggests that the American Revolutionary era produced at least six world-class leaders—Franklin, Jefferson, Washington, Hamilton, Adams and Madison.[3] For a national population of only three million, that was an impressive feat. If the United States enjoyed the same ratio of world-class leaders to its current population, it would boast over five hundred such leaders today. In recent years the term *great* has not been the adjective of choice in describing political leaders. If there was ever a time that called for statesmen rather than politicians, this is it.

LEADERSHIP: IN BUSINESS

The business world cries out for leaders as fervently as the political world. Technology continues to revolutionize the way people do business. The global economy has mushroomed. National economies have become integrated to the point that a financial meltdown in Asia can have instant, stunning repercussions on businesses in North America. Diversity is the pervasive characteristic of the North American work force. Employees represent numerous ethnic groups. More and more people are trading in their desks for laptops so they can work at home or while on the road. Job sharing is common practice. Charles Handy observes, "The challenge for tomorrow's leaders is to manage an organization that is not there in any sense in which we are used to."[4] It requires a Herculean effort to create a corporate culture in which every employee feels a part of the community of the company. Yesterday's workplace was a specific location where employees came together for eight hours a day. The majority of jobs were performed for one reason—a paycheck. Personal fulfillment, though a factor, was secondary. All that has changed. Today's workplace is a forum for people to express themselves and to invest their efforts into something that contributes positively to society. People no longer choose jobs based merely on salary and benefits. They seek companies with corporate values that match their personal values. Daniel Goleman suggests: "Except for the financially desperate, people do not work for money alone. What also fuels their passion for work is a larger sense of purpose or passion. Given the opportunity, people gravitate to what gives them meaning, to what engages to the fullest their commitment, talent, energy, and skill."[5] This has led many people to embark on multiple careers. Robert Greenleaf reflects on this shift in employee focus: "All work exists as much for the enrichment of the life of the worker as it does for the service of the one who pays for it."[6] Consequently, employees expect much more from their leaders than they did in years past.

The complex and critical issues facing today's marketplace only exacerbate the need for effective leaders. Modern business leaders are expected to peer into the turbulent economic future and make the necessary adjustments to avoid disaster for their companies. Today's leaders must mold productive, cohesive teams out of the most diverse workforce in history. Leaders are expected to gain new skills continually and to adjust to dizzying daily changes in the business world. Businesses call on their leaders to understand and lead their industries, though the workplace is filled with specialists who themselves require constant retraining in order to stay current in their fields. Is it any wonder that companies are desperate for someone to lead them into an uncertain future? Is it surprising that the salaries of CEOs have risen astronomically in comparison to the wages of laborers?

In 1996 Apple Computer was sorely in need of leadership. The company was losing hundreds of millions of dollars annually. It needed a

CEO who could quickly turn the company around. In February, Apple Computer hired a new CEO. From February 1996 to July 1996, Apple Computer lost $884 million as sales plummeted 27 percent. What caught the public's attention was not that the CEO was eventually fired, but that he was subsequently paid $9.3 million in salary and severance! The discharged CEO received $6.75 million in severance pay, $997,617 in salary, a $1 million bonus, $509,350 in stock and $471,461 in expense reimbursements.[7] This man was paid $9.3 million for losing $884 million in six months! Labor experts claimed these salary and benefit levels were not out of line for CEOs of major corporations. Companies are willing to spend enormous amounts of money in an effort to enlist effective leadership!

LEADERSHIP: IN THE CHURCH

Sadly, Pastor Edwards is not the only Christian minister who is frustrated at leading his church. Like every other segment of society, the religious community has not escaped the leadership drought. Jesus Christ warned his followers about false prophets who would rise up to lead many astray (Matt. 24:11), but who could have anticipated the plethora of would-be spiritual leaders who have flooded the airwaves and descended upon churches with their books and their theories, clamoring for followers? It boggles the mind that destructive and delusional gurus such as Jim Jones and David Koresh could gain so many devoted followers. It is incomprehensible that well-educated people with lucrative jobs, upscale houses, and comfortable lifestyles have sold everything and abandoned their families, friends, and reputations to follow a self-declared messiah who assured them they would one day be taken away by UFOs! It is even more amazing that sincere people would follow such delusional prophets to violent deaths for the sake of oblique causes. What motivates people to blindly follow these would-be messiahs? People are desperate for leaders who can make positive changes in their lives!

Society at large is displaying widespread and growing interest in spiritual issues. Amazingly, at a time of renewed societal interest in spiritual things, many churches and denominations are declining. According to George Barna, "the American church is dying due to a lack of strong leadership. In this time of unprecedented opportunity and plentiful resources, the church is actually losing influence. The primary reason is the lack of leadership. Nothing is more important than leadership."[8] Immorality is an epidemic in the church. Pastors face issues today far more complex and divisive than ministers faced only a generation ago. In order to survive, churches are seeking leaders who can not only overcome the voluminous challenges churches are facing, but also attract new members and resources in order to finance an increasingly expensive organization. One thing seems certain: while many theological seminaries are enjoying healthy enrollments, denominational leaders are bemoaning the fact that their schools are graduating so few leaders. Although the leadership shortage is universally acknowledged, there is little consensus on how to discover and develop leaders. Seminary professors are bewildered that so few successful leaders are emerging from their graduating classes.

LEADERSHIP: SECULAR OR SPIRITUAL?

This issue of leadership holds a deeper dimension for Christians: Is Christian leadership the same thing as secular leadership? Modern bookstores have capitalized on the chronic thirst for leadership. They stock shelves and shelves with books on leadership and management. Leaders who have been successful in business, sports, politics, or any other field have written autobiographies detailing their success. The myriad of such books testifies to the large number of people eagerly scouring the pages hoping to find the secret to their own effectiveness as leaders in their respective fields. The question many Christian leaders face is whether the principles that make people successful leaders in sports or business are equally valid when applied to leadership issues in the kingdom of God. The pastor examines the leadership style of a successful football coach and wonders: Will these same principles work for me as I lead my church?

This raises a significant issue for Christian leaders: Do leadership principles found in secular writing and seminars apply to work done in God's kingdom? Many Christian leaders think so. The current generation of Christian leaders has immersed itself in the popular leadership writings of its day. This acceptance of secular approaches by Christian leaders can be observed in numerous places. The shift in the traditional nomenclature from the pastor's study to the pastor's office is one consequence. In times past, churches focused on the Great Commission. Today's churches adopt mission statements. In earlier times, churches spoke of building fellowship. Contemporary Christian leaders build teams and lead their people through team-building exercises. Churches used to put church signs in front of their buildings in the hopes of attracting people to their services. Today's churches use state-of-the-art marketing principles to reach their communities. Pastors of large churches (and some not so large) are beginning to act more like CEOs than shepherds. The pastor's office is located in the Executive Suite, next to the boardroom where the leadership team meets. Is this adoption of secular leadership methodology a sorely needed improvement for churches? Or is it woefully inadequate? Is it a violation of biblical principles? Many church leaders claim these innovations have resulted in dramatic growth in their congregations, including a significant proportion of converts. Other Christian leaders decry such approaches as blatant theological and biblical compromise.

The trend toward a CEO model of ministry has changed the churches' evaluations of effective leadership. The pastor's ability is measured in terms of numbers of people, dollars, and buildings. The more of each, the more successful the pastor. As Pastor Edwards discovered, the godliness of a minister may not be enough to satisfy a congregation looking to keep up with the church down the street. Likewise, Christian organizations seem willing to overlook significant character flaws, and even moral lapses, as long as their leader continues to *produce*.

The trend among many Christian leaders has been for an almost indiscriminate and uncritical acceptance of secular leadership theory without measuring it against the timeless precepts of Scripture. This book will look at contemporary leadership principles in light of scriptural truth. It will become clear that many of the "modern" leadership principles currently being espoused are, in fact, biblical principles that have been commanded by God throughout history. For example, secular writers on leadership are insisting on integrity as an essential characteristic for modern leaders. This is nothing new for Christians. The Bible has maintained that as a leadership standard for over two millennia.

Paradoxically, concurrent with the churches' discovery of popular leadership axioms, secular writers have been discovering the timeless truths of Christianity. A partial explanation for this juxtaposition may be that many secular writers on leadership are Christians, or at least religious people. More fundamentally, this shift to Christian principles is because leadership experts are discovering that doing business in a Christian manner, regardless of whether one is a practicing Christian, is, quite simply, good for business. Earlier leadership theories assumed the best CEOs were larger-than-life, charismatic people who stood aloof from those they led, giving orders to be followed unquestioningly. In contrast, today's leadership gurus are writing books that appear almost Christian. Book titles such as *Jesus CEO, Management Lessons of Jesus, Servant Leadership, Love and Profit, Leading with Soul,* and *Encouraging the Heart* sound like they ought to be shelved in a Christian college, not in the office of a corporate CEO.

The Christian tenor of these books goes beyond their titles. It is common to read in secular leadership books that companies should make covenants with their people, that business leaders should love their people, that managers should be servant leaders, that leaders should show their feelings to their employees, that business leaders must have integrity, that leaders must tell the truth, and interestingly, that leaders must strive for a higher purpose than merely making a profit. These principles appear to be more in keeping with the Sermon on the Mount than with the Harvard Business School. Incredibly, as secular writers are embracing Christian teachings with the fervency of first-century Christians, Christian leaders are inadvertently jettisoning many of those same truths in an effort to become more contemporary!

GOD OR KING?

The willingness of God's people to barter their spiritual birthright for the benefit of contemporary secular thinking is not unique to this generation. During Samuel's time, the Israelites were a small, insignificant nation in the midst of international superpowers. They were content to have Samuel as their spiritual guide and God as their king. But as Samuel grew old, his ungodly sons abused their leadership positions. The Israelites compared themselves to neighboring nations and envied their powerful armies, their magnificent cities and the glory of their monarchies. Rather than trusting in God to win their battles, to direct their economy and to establish laws for their land, the Israelites wanted to be just like all the other nations with a king who would do this for them. They took their request to Samuel. In response, Samuel gave them God's appraisal of where this pursuit for a king would lead them.

Samuel told all the words of the Lord to the people who were asking him for a king. He said, "This is what the king who will reign over you will do: He will take your sons and make them serve with his chariots and horses, and they will run in front of his chariots. Some he will assign to be commanders of thousands and commanders of fifties, and others to plow his ground and reap his harvest, and still others to make weapons of war and equipment for his chariots. He will take your daughters to be perfumers and cooks and bakers. He will take the best of your fields and vineyards and olive groves and give them to his attendants. He will take a tenth of your grain and of your vintage and give it to his officials and attendants. Your menservants and maidservants and the best of your cattle and donkeys he will take for his own use. He will take a tenth of your flocks, and you yourselves will become his slaves. When that day comes, you will cry out for relief from the king you have chosen, and the LORD will not answer you in that day." But the people refused to listen to Samuel. "No!" they said. "We want a king over us. Then we will be like all the other nations, with a king to lead us and to go out before us and fight our battles." When Samuel heard all that the people said, he repeated it before the Lord. The LORD answered, "Listen to them and give them a king" (1 Sam. 8:10–22 NIV).

The world measured a kingdom's success by its grand palaces and magnificent armies. The glittering trappings of such monarchies dazzled the Israelites. But citizenship in such a kingdom came with a stiff price. Sustaining a monarchy required oppressive taxes from its citizens. The Israelites wanted a mighty army, but a royal army would require even heavier taxation as well as a draft of young Israelite men for the king's purposes. A monarchy could not function without a legion of servants; this would require the people's children to be conscripted to serve the king. God could not have been more clear about the consequences of choosing worldly leadership over divine leadership. Yet the Israelites stubbornly persisted in their pleas, so God granted them a perfect specimen of a worldly leader. Saul was handsome and physically impressive—yet he was insecure and incredibly vain. He was decisive, sometimes making on-the-spot pronouncements—but many of these had to be rescinded later because they were foolhardy. He was a passionate man—but he was also prone to violent temper tantrums. Saul was a hands-on general—who spent the bulk of his time chasing after his own citizens. The Israelites clamored for a leader who would lead them by worldly principles. God gave them one, and the results were disastrous.

What went wrong? The problem was the Israelite's assumption that spiritual concerns, such as righteous living and obedience to God, belonged in the religious realm while the practical issues of doing battle with enemies, strengthening the economy, and unifying the country were secular matters. They forgot that God himself had won their military victories, brought them prosperity, and created their nation. He was as active on the battlefield as he was in the worship service. When the Israelites separated spiritual concerns from political and economic issues, their nation was brought to its knees. Scripture indicates that it is a mistake to separate the spiritual world from the secular world.

Applying spiritual principles to business and political issues doesn't call for Baptist pastors to serve as military generals, nor does it require seminary professors to run the economy. God created people to be spiritual beings. Every person, Christian and non-Christian alike, is a spiritual person with spiritual needs. Employees, customers, and governing boards all have spiritual needs that God wants to meet through his servants in the workplace. God is also the author of human relationships. He has established laws in relationships that have not changed with the passing of time. To violate God-ordained relationship principles in the workplace is to invite disaster. Jesus Christ is the Lord of all believers whether they are at church or at work. The kingdom of God is, in fact, the rule of God in every area of life, including the church, home, workplace, and neighborhood. To ignore these truths when entering the business world or political arena is to do so at one's peril.

Society's problem is more than just a lack of leaders. Society's great deficit is that it does not have enough leaders who understand and practice Christian principles of leadership. Effective leaders are not enough. Hitler was an effective leader. The world needs people in business who know how to apply their faith in the boardroom as well as in the Bible study room. Jesus summed up this truth for every executive, politician, schoolteacher, lawyer, doctor, and parent, when he said: "'But seek first his kingdom and his righteousness, and all these things will be given to you as well'" (Matt. 6:33 NIV).

Mike, the young CEO, struggled to understand how he could remain true to his Christian beliefs and still be effective in the business world. The truth, as Mike was discovering, is that one's calling as a Christian not only takes precedence over his or her career; it actually gives direction to that career. Moreover, a Christian's calling will give meaning to every area of life. Is it possible to seek God's kingdom first, while striving in business or politics? A growing number of Christian leaders are proving that it is. Books such as *Loving Monday* by John Beckett, *It Is Easier to Succeed Than to Fail* by Truett Cathy of Chick-fil-A, and *Character Is the Issue: How People with Integrity Can Revolutionize America* by Governor Mike Huckabee of Arkansas provide examples of Christians who have successfully incorporated their Christianity into their business and politics. The business world has recognized these leaders and rewarded them for their leadership efforts. The world needs political leaders who seek their guidance from the Holy Spirit and not from the latest public opinion poll. The world needs religious leaders who are on God's agenda and not on their own. The world needs husbands and wives, mothers and fathers who know how to apply biblical promises in their homes rather than merely implementing advice from the latest self-help books.

CONCLUSION

Christian leaders who know God and who know how to lead in a Christian manner will be phenomenally more effective in their world than even the most skilled and qualified leaders who lead without God. Spiritual leadership is not restricted to pastors and missionaries. It is the responsibility of all Christians whom God wants to use to make a difference in their world. The challenge for today's leaders is to discern the difference between the latest leadership fads and timeless truths established by God. It is to this end that this book has been written. We hope it will encourage you to be the Christian God is calling you to be. It is our sincere belief that the following passage applies to every Christian: "The eyes of the LORD move to and fro throughout the earth that He may strongly support those whose heart is completely His" (2 Chron. 16:9a).

CONCEPTS AND SCRIPTURES FOR CONSIDERATION

- People know intuitively that claiming to be a leader or holding a leadership position does not make someone a leader.
- Society longs for statesmen, but it gets politicians.
- People no longer choose jobs based merely on salary and benefits. They seek companies with corporate values that match their personal values.
- At a time of renewed societal interest in spiritual things, many churches and denominations are declining.
- Is Christian leadership the same thing as secular leadership?
- Paradoxically, concurrent with the churches' discovery of popular leadership axioms, secular writers have been discovering the timeless truths of Christianity.
- The Israelites clamored for a leader who would lead them by worldly principles. God gave them one, and the results were disastrous.
- Christian leaders who know God and who know how to lead in a Christian manner will be phenomenally more effective in their world than even the most skilled and qualified leaders who lead without God.

Jeremiah 6:15; 8:12
Matthew 24:11
1 Samuel 8:10–22a
Matthew 6:33
2 Chronicles 16:9a

CHAPTER TWO

The Leader's Role
What Leaders Do

"LEADERSHIP IS ONE OF THE MOST observed and least understood phenomena on earth" asserts James MacGregor Burns.[1] Voluminous material is currently being published on the subject of leadership, yet there seems to be no simple, universally accepted understanding of what leaders do. Without clearly understanding their role, leaders are destined for failure. Perhaps that is why so many modern leaders are voraciously reading leadership materials and attending leadership seminars. There is the feeling among many leaders that despite their heroic efforts and tedious labor, they are still missing the mark somehow. It is to those leaders who feel that somehow God wants there to be more to their leadership than there currently is that this book is written. We will seek to guide the reader through the modern literature on the subject as well as to evaluate current leadership theories in light of scriptural truth. Our hope is that, in reading our material, people will gain a clear sense of their role as spiritual leaders and will be able to focus their energies on that which God is calling them to do.

WHAT IS LEADERSHIP?

Warren Bennis and Burt Nanus in their book, *Leaders: Strategies for Taking Charge*, report that they discovered over 850 different definitions of leadership.[2] No wonder today's leaders are unsure how they measure up. There are too many standards to meet! Each definition offered seeks to contribute a new insight to the understanding of leadership, and many of them do. The following is a small sampling of the diversity of helpful definitions that have been offered:

- "Leadership is the process of persuasion or example by which an individual (or leadership team) induces a group to pursue objectives held by a leader or shared by the leader and his or her followers." John W. Gardner, *On Leadership.*[3]

- "Leadership over human beings is exercised when persons with certain motives and purposes mobilize, in competition or conflict with others, institutional, political, psychological, and other resources so as to arouse, engage, and satisfy the motives of followers." James MacGregor Burns, *Leadership.*[4]

- "Leadership is influence, the ability of one person to influence others." Oswald Sanders, *Spiritual Leadership.*[5]

- "A Christian leader is someone who is called by God to lead; leads with and through Christlike character; and demonstrates the functional competencies that permit effective leadership to take place." George Barna, *Leaders on Leadership.*[6]

- "The central task of leadership is influencing God's people toward God's purposes." Robert Clinton, *The Making of a Leader.*[7]

Each of these definitions helps bring focus upon the role of leaders. Some are secular definitions and, therefore, although they address general leadership principles, they do not take God and his purposes into account. In this chapter and following we will use the term "spiritual leadership." This is not to distinguish between leaders of religious organizations and business leaders guiding secular companies. It is to identify leaders who seek to lead God's way. To be a spiritual leader is just as essential in the marketplace as in the church.

John Gardner's definition employs the terms "persuasion" and "example" to indicate the means leaders should use to move people toward their objectives. According to Gardner, leaders' persuasion is never enough unless accompanied by personal example. Spiritual leaders would do well to heed Gardner's emphasis on persuasion and example as leadership tools as opposed to bullying and dictatorial methodology.

However, this secular definition fails to take into account God's will and the guidance he gives to leaders. Secular leaders may lead people to achieve their goals, even goals held by their followers. But this is not the focus of spiritual leaders. Spiritual leadership involves more than merely achieving goals. People can accomplish all of their goals and still not be successful in God's kingdom.

Burns, a respected scholar in leadership theory, makes it clear that leaders are motive-driven. He also identifies the institutional, political, and psychological fields as arenas in which leaders work. Furthermore, Burns notes that leaders may have to first arouse motives within their followers before they can engage and satisfy those motives. This brings to mind Harry Truman's maxim: "A leader is a man who has the ability to get other people to do what they don't want to do and like it." Nevertheless, while Burns's definition is beneficial to leaders, it also falls short of describing the role of spiritual leaders. While it is true that leaders have motives, spiritual leaders are directed by the Holy Spirit, not by their own agendas. Their leadership is not always in the face of conflict or competition but sometimes simply in the midst of the powers of spiritual inertia. At times, embracing the status quo is the greatest enemy to advancing in Christian maturity, and it is the leader's task to keep people from becoming complacent. Finally, spiritual leaders do not try to satisfy the goals and ambitions of the people they lead but those of the God they serve. Spiritual leaders must be spiritual statesmen and not merely spiritual politicians.

Sanders, in his classic work *Spiritual Leadership*, suggests that leadership is influence. The term "influence" pervades current discussions of a leader's role.[8] Sanders is exactly right in asserting that leaders who make no difference in their followers' lives are not actually leaders. We heartily agree that leaders must exert influence if they are to lead. Influence, however, may be too broad a term to describe adequately the act of leadership. A prankster can call the local post office and claim to have placed a bomb on the premises. That is exerting an influence. Yet, forcing terrified employees to flee a building while the bomb squad vainly searches for explosives is certainly not leadership. There are well-meaning people in leadership positions who believe that creating a stir or making things happen is exercising leadership. In reality, however, all they are doing is exerting a negative influence. Robert Greenleaf observed that, rather than choosing to become true leaders, "Too many settle for being critics and experts."[9] While benefiting from the contribution of Sanders, today's leaders need help in knowing how to exert an influence that is according to God's will.

Barna presents a thorough definition of leadership. Everything in his definition is technically correct. Barna's three *c*'s of call, character, and competencies are crucial to effective leadership. If anything were to be added to this definition, it might be the aspect of consequences, or results. Leadership is ultimately measured not according to the leader's skills but on the leader's results. As Peter Drucker points out, "Popularity is not leadership. Results are."[10] While people may hold a position of leadership, one wonders if a person has truly led until someone has followed, and more importantly, until God's purposes are advanced. All the "functional competencies" may be for naught if the people who are to follow remain where they are. It is also hazardous to try to quantify and qualify specific abilities of leaders. Although there are obviously certain skills common to most leaders, the biblical record suggests that God used people who didn't look or act like leaders in the traditional sense. Certain biblical characters greatly impacted their society but demonstrated few of the commonly recognized leadership competencies. Rather, God chose to use the weak of this world to demonstrate his strength (1 Cor. 1:26–27; 2 Cor. 12:9–10).

Robert Clinton's definition encompasses the spiritual nature of leadership in that God's people are led toward God's purposes. Clinton wisely observes that God's purposes are the key to spiritual leadership—the dreams and visions of leaders are not. While we find this to be a helpful definition, we would like to add at least two dimensions to it. First, spiritual leaders can lead those who are not God's people as well as those who are. Christian leadership is not restricted to within church walls but is equally effective in the marketplace. Second, Clinton notes that leaders lead their people toward God's purposes. However, simply leading people toward an objective may not be adequate for a spiritual leader. Many pastors have left their churches after serving less than two years. They may argue that they moved their church forward, yet nothing of lasting significance was accomplished. They are like the

pastor whose church was continually losing members. Every time
someone asked him how his church was doing he would reply grimly, "I
think we have turned a corner." The pastor said this so often people
wondered if he was the pastor of a maze or a church! Just as Moses was
not released from his followers when they disobeyed God and began a
forty-year hiatus in the wilderness, so true leaders stay with their people
until they have successfully achieved God's purposes. Moses himself had
remained faithful to God, yet God would not release him from his rebellious people. To abandon followers because they refuse to follow is to
forsake the sacred calling of a leader. Spiritual leaders know they must
give an account of their leadership to God; therefore, they are not satisfied merely moving toward the destination God has for them; they want
to see God actually achieve his purposes through them for their generation (2 Cor. 5:10–11).

A New Definition

There are a number of helpful definitions of leadership available,
but we believe true spiritual leadership can be defined in one concise
statement:

Spiritual leadership is moving people on to God's agenda.

This is a brief definition, perhaps not as technically precise as some, but
we believe it describes what is at the heart of being a spiritual leader. At
least five truths are inherent in this definition.

The Spiritual Leader's Task

Spiritual leadership is not identical to leadership in general. While
spiritual leadership involves many of the same principles as general
leadership, spiritual leadership has certain distinctive qualities that must
be understood and practiced if spiritual leaders are to be successful. The
following are the distinctive elements of spiritual leadership implied in
our definition.

1. *The spiritual leader's task is to move people from where they are to where
God wants them to be.* This is influence. Once spiritual leaders understand God's will, they make every effort to move their followers from

following their own agendas to pursuing God's purposes. People who fail to move people on to God's agenda have not led. They may have exhorted, cajoled, pleaded, or bullied, but they will not have led unless their people have adjusted their lives to God's will. There are many ways to move people; subsequent chapters will examine methodology more closely. Gardner used the verb *induce*. Burns's term was *mobilize*. Moving people is not the same thing as driving or forcing people to do something. It is, as Gardner noted, a process of "persuasion and example" by which leaders cause their people to change their attitudes and behaviors and to move forward to achieve God's purposes. Our definition assumes that spiritual leaders use spiritual means to move or influence people as opposed to methods devoid of God. When spiritual leaders have done their jobs, the people around them have encountered God and obeyed his will.

2. *Spiritual leaders depend on the Holy Spirit.* Spiritual leaders work within a paradox, for God calls them to do something that, in fact, only God can do. Ultimately, spiritual leaders cannot produce spiritual change in people; only the Holy Spirit can accomplish this. Yet the Spirit often uses people to bring about spiritual growth in others. Moses dealt with this paradox when God commissioned him to go to Egypt to free the Israelites. God said, "'I have surely seen the affliction of My people who are in Egypt, and have given heed to their cry because of their taskmasters, for I am aware of their sufferings. So I have come down to deliver them from the power of the Egyptians, and to bring them up from that land to a good and spacious land . . .'" (Exod. 3:7–8). So far, this sounded fine to Moses. God was going to do something that only God could do. Then God added an unsettling instruction, "'Therefore, come now, and I will send you to Pharaoh, so that you may bring My people, the sons of Israel, out of Egypt'" (Exod. 3:10). That is the crux of spiritual leadership. Leaders seek to move people on to God's agenda, all the while being aware that only the Holy Spirit can ultimately accomplish the task.

3. *Spiritual leaders are accountable to God.* Spiritual leadership necessitates an acute sense of accountability. Just as a teacher has not taught until students have learned, leaders don't blame their followers when they don't do what they should do. Leaders don't make excuses. They

assume their responsibility is to move people to do God's will. Until they do this, they have not yet fulfilled their role as leaders. True spiritual leadership is taking people from where they are to where God wants them to be.

4. Spiritual leaders can influence all people, not just God's people. An important reality that must not be overlooked is that spiritual leaders can influence all people, not just God's people. God is on mission at the local factory as well as at the local church. His agenda applies in the marketplace as well as the meeting place. Although spiritual leaders will generally move God's people to achieve God's purposes, God can also use them to exert significant godly influence upon unbelievers. The biblical account of Joseph is a case in point. God's plan was to spare the Egyptians from a devastating seven-year famine and, through the Egyptians, to provide food for other Middle Eastern people as well. Pharaoh was an unspiritual leader. He did not understand the message God was giving, so God sent Joseph to advise him. It was Joseph, a man of God, who was able to interpret God's warning and to mobilize the pagan nation to respond to God's activity. There may not be anything overtly spiritual about building grain storage bins or developing a food distribution system, but these activities were on God's agenda. God did not choose to use the religious experts of the day. Instead, he chose to make himself known to an unbelieving society through a God-fearing government official.

History is replete with examples of Christian men and women exerting spiritual leadership upon secular society. Christians in business ought not to assume that spiritual leadership is purely the local minister's domain. Spiritual leadership occurs down the middle of everyday life. Henry Blackaby maintains regularly scheduled conference calls with a group of more than sixty CEOs, many from Fortune 500 companies. These are all Christians who want their faith to make a difference in the way they lead their companies. These are influential people: they play golf with world leaders; they serve on prestigious boards; they supervise billions of dollars and thousands of employees. They make time to dialogue regularly with one another about how Christ helps them lead their companies. They are spiritual leaders as well as business leaders. Is this possible? Absolutely!

5. Spiritual leaders work from God's agenda. The greatest obstacle to effective spiritual leadership is people pursuing their own agendas rather than seeking God's will. God is working throughout the world to achieve his purposes and to advance his kingdom. God's concern is not to advance leaders' dreams and goals or to build their kingdoms. His purpose is to turn his people away from their self-centeredness and their sinful desires and to draw them into a relationship with himself. For example, when Jesus took Peter, James, and John with him to the Mount of Transfiguration, God the Father had a specific will for his Son. The Father brought Moses and Elijah to encourage Jesus for the great work of redemption he was about to accomplish. So glorious and sacred was that moment that Jesus was transfigured and the glory of God radiated about him. Peter and his companions, however, had been asleep. When they awoke and saw the magnificent scene unfolding, Peter spoke up: "'Master, it is good for us to be here; let us make three tabernacles: one for You, and one for Moses, and one for Elijah . . .'" (Luke 9:33). The moment Peter began talking, the vision was removed, and only Jesus remained visible. It's not clear what Peter's intention was, beyond simply breaking the holy silence, but it is obvious that Peter's agenda was not God's agenda. The heavenly Father immediately rebuked Peter, saying, "'This is My Son, My Chosen One; listen to Him!'" (v. 35). Incredibly, Peter attempted to get Jesus, Moses, Elijah, James, and John to adjust their lives to his plan, instead of seeking to understand God's agenda and adjusting his own life accordingly.

Peter's mistake is all too prevalent among spiritual leaders. Too often, people assume that along with the role of leader comes the responsibility of determining what should be done. They develop aggressive goals. They dream grandiose dreams. They cast grand visions. Then they pray and ask God to join them in their agenda and to bless their efforts. That's not what spiritual leaders do. Spiritual leaders seek God's will, whether it is for their church or for their corporation, and then they marshal their people to pursue God's plan.

The key to spiritual leadership, then, is for spiritual leaders to understand God's will for them and for their organizations. Leaders then move people away from their own agendas and on to God's. It sounds simple enough, but the truth is that many Christian leaders fail to put this basic truth into practice. Too often leaders allow secular models of leadership to corrupt the straightforward model set forth by Jesus.

Spiritual Leadership: Jesus as the Model

Even secular writers recognize Jesus as a compelling model of good leadership. Numerous scholars have attempted to explain Jesus' leadership style. Scholars have developed complete leadership systems and leadership training models based on what they discovered as they examined Jesus' methods of leadership. Jesus' life is so profound and so beyond our common experience that we must continually reexamine it, lest we assume Jesus operated merely by leadership theory that we value today.

Jesus did not develop a plan nor did he cast a vision. He sought his Father's will. Jesus had a vision for himself and for his disciples, but the vision came from his Father. Some portray Jesus as a leader who first accepted the enormous assignment of redeeming a lost and corrupt world, and then was sent to figure out how to do it. At times, leadership experts present Jesus as though he stood on a mountaintop overlooking Jerusalem musing to himself, "How am I going to gain a following and spread the gospel worldwide? Should I seek to convince the religious establishment? Should I preach to the masses? Should I perform an impressive array of miracles? No, I'll invest myself in the lives of twelve men. I'll train them so thoroughly that after I am gone they will be able to carry out my mission for me. As they invest in other leaders they will multiply themselves and hence they will multiply my ministry until they have extended my kingdom throughout the world." This is clearly a misunderstanding of Jesus' ministry.

Some leadership development proponents observe that Jesus concentrated primarily on training twelve followers; they conclude this model of leadership must be the pattern for all spiritual leaders. While not depreciating the value of leadership development or the significance of small group dynamics, leaders would be remiss to infer that the methodology Jesus adopted is the key to spiritual leadership. It is not. The key to Jesus' leadership was the relationship he had with his Father.

Scripture indicates "when the fulness of the time came, God sent forth His Son, born of a woman, born under the Law" (Gal. 4:4). The salvation plan had always belonged to the Father. Even as he expelled Adam and Eve from the Garden of Eden after they fell into sin, the Father knew how he would ultimately redeem humanity. His plan involved developing a people for himself out of Abraham's descendants. It called for the Law, introduced under Moses, to reveal sin's nature and its consequences. The Father's plan culminated in his Son's lowly birth, his excruciating crucifixion for sins he did not commit, his resurrection, and ultimately his ascension to the right hand of the Father. This plan was not the Son's. It was the Father's (John 3:16).

Scripture indicates that as a young man, Jesus "grew in wisdom and stature, and in favor with God and men" (Luke 2:52 NIV). In other words, Jesus developed his relationship with God the Father as well as with people. Since he knew the Father, Jesus recognized his voice and understood his will. Because he knew the Father's will, Jesus did not allow people's opinions to sidetrack him from his mission (Mark 1:37–38). The temptations in the wilderness were Satan's attempts to prevent Jesus from obeying the Father (Matt. 4; Luke 4:1–13). Satan approached Jesus with a proposition: "So, your assignment is to bring salvation to the people of the earth. That's a big job. Let me help you. Turn these stones into bread, because if you feed the people they will follow you." Jesus refused, so Satan offered another suggestion: "Cast yourself from the top of the temple. When the angels save you, everyone will see the miracle and they'll know you are God's Son. Then they will follow you." Again, Jesus refused. Satan offered a final alternative: "Jesus, there's no point in fighting over the dominion of this earth. Bow down and worship me, and I will hand over all the people to you. Then you won't have to do battle with me and you can avoid the cross. Crucifixion is despicable and is totally unnecessary in order for you to accomplish your goals." Once again, Jesus refused to take any shortcuts in carrying out his Father's will. This would not be the last time Jesus would have to resist such temptations (John 6:15; Matt. 12:38; Matt. 27:40).

Satan's overt temptations during this time in Jesus' life are obvious. First, there's an easier way, with a lower personal cost. Second, God's way is not necessarily the only option in achieving the desired goals. But there was also a more subtle temptation at work here. Satan sought to persuade Jesus that saving the world was *his* job, so he should develop his own plan to get the job done. Satan was offering what appeared to be shortcuts to God's will, but shortcuts that carried with them devastating consequences. Jesus, however, was never required to develop ministry goals or action plans. He was sent to follow the *Father's* plan, to the letter. Jesus had no freedom to negotiate with Satan over various approaches to redeeming mankind. The Father had already developed the plan and Jesus' responsibility was to carefully obey his Father's will. Jesus' own words say it best: "I tell you the truth, the Son can do nothing by himself; he can do only what he sees his Father doing, because whatever the Father does the Son also does. For the Father loves the Son and shows him all he does. Yes, to your amazement he will show him even greater things than these. . . . By myself I can do nothing; I judge only as I hear, and my judgment is just, for I seek not to please myself but him who sent me" (John 5:19–20, 30 NIV).

The setting was Bethesda, a healing pool in Jerusalem. There, Jesus encountered a multitude of invalids, all vainly surrounding the pool and hoping an angel might come and stir up the waters. Tradition suggested the first person entering the pool when this happened would be cured. Among the crowd that day was a man who had been lame for thirty-eight years. Of all the people there that day, it appears Jesus chose to heal only this one man. When the religious leaders challenged Jesus' actions, he explained that he was doing exactly what the Father showed him to do. Jesus had cultivated such a close relationship with his Father that he could recognize his Father's activity even in the midst of a large crowd. Whenever and wherever he saw his Father at work, Jesus immediately joined him.

Significantly, even choosing the twelve disciples was not Jesus' idea but his Father's. Scripture says Jesus spent an entire night praying before he chose his disciples. "One of those days Jesus went out to a mountainside to pray, and spent the night praying to God. When morning came, he called his disciples to him and chose twelve of them, whom he also designated apostles" (Luke 6:12–13 NIV).

This was a critical juncture in Jesus' ministry; perhaps it took most of the night to understand clearly the Father's plan for the Twelve.

Perhaps the Father spent time explaining the role of Judas to his Son during those intimate hours of prayer.

On the night of his crucifixion, Jesus once again indicated that the Father had chosen his disciples. In what is commonly referred to as Jesus' High Priestly Prayer, he gave an account to his Father for all that the Father had given him. "I have revealed you to those whom you gave me out of the world. They were yours; you gave them to me and they have obeyed your word. Now they know that everything you have given me comes from you" (John 17:6–7 NIV).

This passage indicates clearly that Jesus did not choose twelve disciples as a matter of strategy. Nor was there any formula in the number twelve. Jesus did not calculate that twelve was the optimum number for his ministry. Jesus had twelve disciples because that is how many his Father gave him. Would Jesus have chosen Judas if he were simply implementing a discipleship strategy to multiply his efforts? Judas was included because he was given to Jesus as a part of God the Father's redemptive plan.

According to Jesus, even the teaching he gave his disciples came from the Father (John 6:49–50; 14:10; 15:15; 17:8). If these twelve men were to develop into the leaders God wanted them to be, the disciples would need the Father's teaching. Jesus understood that he was to facilitate the relationship between his disciples and his Father. His task was to bring his disciples face to face with the Father so they could develop the same intimate relationship with him that Jesus enjoyed (John 14:8–11). When the twelve began to mature in their understanding of spiritual things, they recognized Jesus as the Christ. Jesus knew this was not the result of his teaching methods, but it was due to the Father's work in their lives. This truth is evident in Jesus' response when Peter confessed him as the Christ: "Blessed are you, Simon son of Jonah, for this was not revealed to you by man, but by my Father in heaven" (Matt. 16:17 NIV).

Jesus made it clear that when his disciples developed spiritual understanding, it was not due to his efforts, but to his Father's teaching. It is incredible that Jesus, the wisest teacher of all time, would recognize his Father's strategy and not his own as the impetus behind any breakthrough in his disciples' spiritual understanding! Even in that sacred moment when he fell on his face and pled with his Father to let the terrible cup of crucifixion pass from him, Jesus yielded himself entirely to his Father's will (Matt. 26:39). Never was there any question about replacing or modifying the Father's plan with the Son's plan.

Further evidence of Christ's complete dependence on his Father is the fact that Jesus did not know when his own Second Coming would be: "No one knows about that day or hour, not even the angels in heaven, nor the Son, but only the Father" (Matt. 24:36 NIV).

Jesus came to fulfill his Father's plan of salvation. He spent each day looking to see what the Father would reveal about his will. When he observed the Father at work, Jesus adjusted his life to join him. When Jesus entered the large city of Jericho, with masses of people crowding along the streets trying to catch a glimpse of him, Jesus did not set the agenda for that day. He did not strategize: "This is the last time I will pass through this great city. What can I do to make the greatest impact on the crowd and see the most people accept the gospel?" Instead, Jesus spotted the diminutive Zaccheus in a tree. Out of the intimate relationship Jesus had with his Father, he recognized the Father's activity in the despised tax collector's life, and he invited Zaccheus to spend time with him (Luke 19:1–10). Had Jesus entered the city planning to have lunch with the most notorious sinner of that region? No. He had simply watched for the first sign of the Father's activity. Once he saw where the Father was working, Jesus immediately knew the agenda for his ministry. Likewise, he trained his disciples to watch for God's activity rather than to set their own agendas.

Even in the most difficult assignments, including the cross, Jesus accepted his Father's will unwaveringly. Jesus left his future, as well as his Second Coming, for the Father to determine. Jesus characterized his entire ministry with these words: "By myself I can do nothing" (John 5:30 NIV).

CONCLUSION

Jesus has established the model for Christian leaders. It is not found in his "methodology." Rather, it is seen in his absolute obedience to the Father's will. Current leadership theory suggests good leaders are also good followers, and this is particularly true of spiritual leaders. Spiritual leaders understand that God is their leader. If Jesus provides the model for spiritual leadership, then the key is not for leaders to develop visions and to set the direction for their organizations. The key is to obey and to preserve everything the Father reveals to them of his will. Ultimately, the Father is the leader. God has the vision of what He wants to do. God does not ask leaders to dream big dreams for him or to solve the problems that confront them. He asks leaders to walk with him so intimately that, when he reveals what is on his agenda, they will immediately adjust their lives to his will and the results will bring glory to God. This is not the model many religious leaders, let alone business leaders, follow today, but it encompasses what biblical leadership is all about.

Is it possible for God to guide leaders so that their actions, and even their words, are not theirs, but his? Yes. Does God have an agenda for what he wants to see happen in the workplace? He does. Our prayer should be that which Jesus instructed his disciples to pray: "Your kingdom come, your will be done, on earth as it is in heaven" (Matt. 6:10 NIV). If Christians around the world were to suddenly renounce their personal agendas, their life goals and their aspirations, and begin responding in radical obedience to everything God showed them, the world would be turned upside down. How do we know? Because that's what first century Christians did, and the world is still talking about it.

CONCEPTS AND SCRIPTURES FOR CONSIDERATION

- People can accomplish all of their goals and still not be successful in God's kingdom.
- Spiritual leaders do not try to satisfy the goals and ambitions of the people they lead but those of the God they serve.
- Christian leadership is not restricted to within church walls but is equally effective in the marketplace.
- Spiritual leaders know they must give an account of their leadership to God; therefore, they are not satisfied merely moving toward the destination God has for them; they want to see God actually achieve his purposes through them for their generation.
- Spiritual leadership is moving people on to God's agenda.

- People who fail to move people on to God's agenda have not led.
- Leaders don't blame their followers when they don't do what they should do.
- God's concern is not to advance leaders' dreams and goals or to build their kingdoms.
- Spiritual leaders seek God's will, whether it is for their church or for their corporation, and then they marshal their people to pursue God's plan.
- Jesus did not develop a plan nor did he cast a vision. He sought his Father's will.

---

1 Corinthians 1:26–27; 2 Corinthians 12:9–10
2 Corinthians 5:10–11
Luke 2:52
John 5:19–20, 30
Luke 6:12–13
John 17:6–7
Mark 1:37–38
Matthew 6:10

CHAPTER THREE

The Leader's Preparation
How God Develops Leaders

THE GREATNESS OF AN ORGANIZATION will be directly proportional to the greatness of its leader. It is rare for organizations to rise above their leaders. Giant organizations do not emerge under pygmy leaders; therefore, the key to growing an organization is to grow its leaders. Certainly leadership involves some specific skills, but ultimately leadership is more about "being" than about "doing." Leadership development is synonymous with personal development. As leaders grow personally, they increase their capacity to lead. As they increase their capacity to lead, they enlarge the capacity of their organization to grow. Therefore, the best thing leaders can do for their organization is to grow personally.

The question is: how do people become leaders? Are certain people endowed with natural leadership ability? Are some people born to lead, or is leadership a set of skills that anyone can learn? Religious leaders are seeking the answers to these questions. George Barna conducted a survey of senior pastors from across various denominations. When asked if they believed they had the spiritual gift of leadership, only 6 percent responded yes.[1] The fact that 94 percent of the senior pastors surveyed did not believe they were gifted to be leaders may explain the sense of desperation many church leaders express as they examine their ministry and its current effectiveness.

The Making of a Leader

Innate Qualities

There is little doubt that some people display an early aptitude for leadership. Observe the dynamics on any playground and it soon becomes apparent which children have innate leadership ability. For some, the influence comes with their size and strength. Others have keen imaginations that enable them to conceive new games and gather a following. Some children are naturally charismatic and easily attract a crowd.

Many world leaders demonstrated precipitant signs of leadership ability. As a young boy, Napoleon Bonaparte organized intricate battles with his classmates. When Winston Churchill was a child, he staged elaborate battlefield maneuvers with fifteen hundred toy soldiers and became engrossed in politics at an unusually young age. Benito Mussolini, Italy's fascist dictator, gave early evidence of the negative orientation of his future leadership. He was expelled from school on two occasions for stabbing fellow students.

An examination of the early lives of famous leaders usually reveals telltale signs that they were oriented to be leaders. Indeed, the next generation of great leaders is already evolving, but today's adults may be too preoccupied to notice. If churches are concerned about future leaders, they would do well to nurture their children, for any strategy for developing spiritual leaders must take into account those emerging leaders currently in their preteens. It is a church's folly to consign its young people to a youth building across the parking lot so their loud music doesn't disturb the adults' worship. Wise churches will explore leadership opportunities for their teenagers rather than waiting until they are adults to begin finding avenues for them to lead.

Jacob's son, Joseph, was obviously destined to be a leader. God gave him dreams indicating he would one day be a great man. More specifically, his dreams revealed that he would lead his ten older brothers (Gen. 37:5–11). Even though this vision for a great future was not enthusiastically shared by his older siblings, years later they would stand trembling before Joseph, the highest ranking official in Egypt, depending on him for their very survival. Then they probably wished they had taken Joseph's leadership potential more seriously while he was a youth.

Contemporary leadership writing reveals that most scholars believe leaders are both born *and* made. Although certain factors outside their control come to bear on people, predisposing them to lead, there are other factors, within people's control that, if developed, can significantly enhance their leadership ability. The media often portray leaders to the public as unusually gifted, charismatic, physically imposing and attractive people. Based on this distorted representation, society might assume all great leaders have the eloquence of Martin Luther King Jr., the physical presence of George Washington, and the charisma of Charles de Gaulle. This skewed image of leadership can lead to self-doubt on the part of many would-be leaders. Reality, however, suggests that most people can exercise leadership in some arena of life if they are willing to grow as people and to develop certain leadership skills.

In truth, most of history's famous leaders have been decidedly ordinary people. Many of them were neither physically impressive nor academically gifted. Napoleon Bonaparte, though a giant military figure of the eighteenth century, stood only five-feet-six-inches tall. Likewise, Joseph Stalin, terrorist dictator of the Soviet Union, was a man of diminutive size. When Harry Truman first met the five-foot-five-inch Stalin, Truman noted with surprise that Stalin was "a little bit of a squirt."

Lincoln, America's first modern president, was subjected to abundant ridicule because of his irregular features. His homely face and gangly physique caused him extreme self-consciousness. At one point, Lincoln rejoined, "Someone accused me of being two-faced. If I were two-faced, would I wear the one I have?" Harry Truman, describing himself as a child, said he was "blind as a mole" and "something of a sissy." Winston Churchill's biographer concluded: "Sickly, an uncoordinated weakling with the pale fragile hands of a girl, speaking with a lisp and a slight stutter, he had been at the mercy of bullies. They beat him, ridiculed him, and pelted him with cricket balls. Trembling and humiliated, he hid in a nearby woods. This was hardly the stuff of which gladiators are made."[2] George Marshall, the top American military commander of World War II, was an average student who did not even bother to apply to West Point. Eleanor Roosevelt has been described as "an unattractive, almost ugly duckling child who felt chronically inferior to other members of her family, was always fearful, and craved praise."[3]

Peter Senge, in his book *The Fifth Discipline* observed: "Most of the outstanding leaders I have worked with are neither tall nor especially handsome; they are often mediocre public speakers; they do not stand out in a crowd; they do not mesmerize an attending audience with their brilliance or eloquence. Rather, what distinguishes them is their clarity and persuasiveness of their ideas, the depth of their commitment, and their openness to continually learning more."[4] Peter Drucker observed: "There seems to be little correlation between a man's effectiveness and his intelligence, his imagination or his knowledge."[5]

Life Experiences

Clearly, people's life experiences can greatly affect the kind of leaders they become. Something as basic as birth order can have a profound impact on one's development as a leader. Oldest children are more likely to lead because they are generally given more responsibility by their parents and they often have a greater sense of affiliation with their parents than their younger siblings. Their superiority in size, strength, and knowledge compared to their younger siblings gives them confidence and enables them to begin exercising leadership in their homes at an early age.

Home Life. The influence of a leader's childhood home cannot be underrated as a major factor in leadership development. While some great leaders grew up in wholesome, supportive environments, many did not. Numerous famous leaders lost a parent to death, usually their father, while they were still young. When Martin Luther King Jr. lost his grandmother, to whom he was very close, he became so distraught he threw himself out a second-story window in an apparent suicide attempt. Eleanor Roosevelt had lost both parents by the age of ten, whereupon her grandmother raised her. Her extended family suffered alcoholism, adultery, child molestation, rape, and other vices, which left an indelible impression on the future first lady. James MacGregor Burns noted that many famous leaders grew up in dysfunctional homes. Burns observed that often these leaders had a distant relationship with their fathers and an unusually close relationship with their mothers. Adolph

Hitler was close to his mother but hated his father. Joseph Stalin and George Marshall were dearly loved by their mothers but beaten by their fathers. Winston Churchill was sent to a boarding school at age seven and, despite his pitiful pleading, was not visited by his preoccupied parents even when his father was attending meetings near Winston's school. Churchill's biographer later observed, "The neglect and lack of interest in him shown by his parents was remarkable, even by the standards of late Victorian and Edwardian days."[6] Gandhi loved his mother, but felt he was partially responsible for his father's death. Martin Luther King Jr.'s father disciplined him with severe beatings. Abraham Lincoln was so estranged from his father that he did not invite his family to his wedding. He refused to visit his dying father or to attend his funeral. Woodrow Wilson's father constantly criticized him, never giving him his approval. Queen Elizabeth I's father, Henry VIII, had her mother, Anne Boleyn, beheaded on charges of adultery. Alexander the Great's father was assassinated while Alexander was a young man. Some historians speculate it was Alexander's mother who may have orchestrated the murder. John F. Kennedy had to compete with his brothers to win the approval of his highly ambitious father. Bill Clinton lost his father as an infant and then lived the next three years with his grandparents. Clinton's mother eventually married a man known for his alcoholism, gambling, and unfaithfulness. When his parents' marriage ended in divorce, Clinton had to testify in court concerning the abuse his mother suffered at the hands of his stepfather. It was in such a home that Bill Clinton was prepared for the presidency of the United States.

It seems that growing up with an aloof, abusive, or absent father figure often inspired people to strive for greatness as a means of enhancing their battered sense of self-esteem. Having failed to win the approval of their fathers, these people attempted to compensate by winning the devotion of large followings. The young Churchill idolized his parents even though he often was painfully neglected. Of his mother, Churchill confessed: "She shone for me like the Evening Star. I loved her dearly—but at a distance. My nurse was my confidante."[7] Churchill's father, Lord Randolph, rarely had time for his son since he was a prominent member of parliament. Churchill later surmised from his father's encouragement for him to enter the military: "For years I thought my father with his experience and flair had discerned in me the qualities of military genius. But I was told later that he had only come to the conclusion that I was not clever enough to go to the Bar."[8] When Churchill's father died, he resigned himself to the fact that "all my dreams of comradeship with him, of entering Parliament at his side and in his support, were ended. There remained for me only to pursue his aims and vindicate his memory."[9]

Some of the world's famous leaders were raised in homes where fear for their own safety was a constant reality. This motivated them to gain power as a way to control their environment and escape their feelings of insecurity. Some leaders developed such bitterness as children that their anger drove them to positions of influence as adults.

It would be wrong to assume only secular leaders have been influenced by difficult childhoods. Religious leaders have not been exempt from growing up in dysfunctional homes, or from suffering the effects of turbulent upbringings. J. Frank Norris, the infamous Fundamentalist pastor of First Baptist Church, Fort Worth, provides a classic example. Not only was Norris the pastor of First Baptist Church in Fort Worth, from 1909 until 1952; he also simultaneously served as pastor of Temple Baptist Church in Detroit for fourteen years beginning in 1935. During that time, over 25,000 people joined the two churches. Norris was a leading figure among Fundamentalists of his day. He published his own widely distributed paper, *The Fundamentalist*, and he was considered a spellbinding preacher. Yet many people wondered why Norris had such a stormy ministry. His house, as well as his church, burned down, and in both cases Norris himself was accused of arson. He was embroiled in constant controversy, haranguing everyone with whom he disagreed. He sued his own church. Norris even shot a man to death in his church office. To comprehend Norris's flamboyant and vindictive leadership style, one must consider his childhood. When Norris was a young boy, his father, an alcoholic, beat him mercilessly. Two gang members once came to the Norris home and began shooting at his father. The young boy charged at the two ruffians with a knife. He was shot three times. Norris was raised in poverty and turmoil. He later recalled the shame of his childhood:

I was about eight years old, one day I was standing on the porch of the public school in Columbiana, two boys came up, one was 12 and one 14, each one of them had on a nice suit of clothes, a nice overcoat. I had on a little cotton suit, no overcoat, and the coat was tight around me—these boys, sons of a banker—they came up, looked at me, and they said, "Your coat is too little"—well I knew it. Then one of them pointed his finger at me while all the boys gathered around and said, "Your daddy is a drunkard and mine is a banker." I turned and went into the school room, buried my face in my hands . . . Mother said, as she put her tender arms around me, and brushed away my tears, "Son, it is all right, some day you are going to wear good clothes—some day you will make a man—some day God will use you."[10]

Norris's turbulent past compelled him to strive for success, yet it also drove him into destructive, egocentric patterns of behavior that marred much of what might have been a productive ministry.

Whether for good or for bad, there's no escaping the influence of the childhood home in the shaping of a leader. Nurturing, supportive families provide an environment conducive to the healthy personal growth of leaders. A wholesome background can build a strong sense of self-esteem and effective people skills that enable people to become healthy leaders. Leaders born into dysfunctional homes may also rise to prominence, as Norris did, but their past can sometimes hinder their ongoing growth and success as leaders.

A significant number of well-known Christian leaders grew up in dysfunctional homes. Many of these leaders have experienced God's healing grace, which has transformed them into healthy, successful leaders. Others, for whatever reason, are unwilling or feel unable to allow God's grace to free them from their troublesome pasts. These people emerge as adults with feelings of inferiority, inadequacy, and anger, all despite their outward success. Gary McIntosh and Samuel Rima in their book *Overcoming the Dark Side of Leadership* concluded that many of today's Christian leaders continue to be motivated, albeit subconsciously, by their dysfunctional pasts. Interestingly, McIntosh and Rima observe: "In almost every case, the factors that eventually undermine us are shadows of the ones that contribute to our success."[11]

One of the greatest limitations for today's spiritual leaders is their inability to understand and acknowledge how their past cripples their current effectiveness. They are blind to their emotional and spiritual need, so they do not seek the healing that is available to them in Christ. Instead, they press on, never really examining what lies behind their desire to be a leader. Some Christian leaders are motivated more by anger than by love. Others are so insecure they cannot tolerate disagreement from anyone. Still others, desperate for approval, lead by surrounding themselves with people who love and admire them. It is not only possible, but sadly common, for people to seek positions of spiritual authority as a means of personal edification rather than as an avenue to serve God and build his kingdom. This is a negative and destructive motivation; yet many leaders today are driven, far more than they realize, by the scars of their past.

Failures. Failure is a powerful force in the making of a leader. The failure itself is not the issue; it's what failure leads to that is so determinative in leadership development. For true leaders, failure will not destroy them but will, instead, further develop their character. A high percentage of famous leaders suffered dramatic hardships and failures during their early years. George Washington lost five out of the first seven major battles he fought as he led the hopelessly outnumbered and untrained revolutionary army against the British. Winston Churchill suffered financial ruin more than once while his political career was seemingly aborted on several occasions. Perhaps it was Churchill's numerous failures that led him to define success as "going from failure to failure without loss of enthusiasm." Abraham Lincoln's failures are well documented. He, too, suffered bankruptcy. In his first attempt at elected office Lincoln placed eighth in a field of thirteen candidates. When he ran for president, ten states did not even carry his name on the ballot, and he was burned in effigy in several of the Southern states. Ulysses S. Grant could not find a successful career until the Civil War began. Harry Truman's life was full of setbacks. He and his father both suffered bankruptcy. West Point rejected his application. In fact, Truman experienced so many failures as a young man that he once wrote to his sweetheart, Bess, "I can't possibly lose forever." Truman was his party's fourth choice for senator. He was the underdog in every election he fought. He was so poor that even after he was elected senator, he was forced to use a public health dentist and to sleep occasionally in his car while on the campaign trail. Bob Jones, president of Bob Jones University, pronounced the young Billy Graham a failure to his face, telling him he would never amount to anything.

Crises. Events beyond a person's control can have the same effect as failures. They can either crush an aspiring leader or they can develop the character and resolve within the emerging leader that enables him to reach greater heights in the future. Teddy Roosevelt suffered severe asthma as a child and was considered too frail and sickly to attend school. As a young man, he lost both his beloved mother Mittie to typhoid fever and his loving wife, Alice, to childbirth, on the same day, February 14, 1884. So stunned and disoriented did this leave the future president that he wrote in his diary, "The light has gone out of my life."[12] Robert E. Lee endured the loss of everything he owned, as well as numerous loved ones and friends during the Civil War. Franklin Roosevelt, considered by some to be one of America's most successful twentieth-century presidents, suffered from debilitating polio that left him in a wheelchair. (In a survey of historians released in 2000, the five most successful U.S. presidents in American history based on ten leadership qualities were: Abraham Lincoln, Franklin Roosevelt, George Washington, Theodore Roosevelt, and Harry Truman).[13] Mahatma Ghandi was imprisoned numerous times and survived several attempts on his life before he was assassinated. Martin Luther King Jr., an ardent admirer and disciple of Gandhi, had multiple threats against his life and was frequently imprisoned. According to one study cited by Howard Gardner, 60 percent of major British political leaders lost a parent in childhood.[14]

Personal Struggles. Surprisingly, perhaps, many of history's famous leaders experienced difficulty in public speaking as children. Winston Churchill, famous for his eloquence, had a speech impediment as a boy. Theodore Roosevelt spoke with difficulty. Mahatma Ghandi was so fearful of public speaking that in his first attempt to represent a client as her lawyer he became tongue-tied when it was time for him to speak in court. The embarrassed lawyer was forced to refund his fee and locate another lawyer for his client.[15] D. L. Moody showed no early signs of developing into the forceful speaker he would become later in life. So poor was Moody's grammar and so sparse his knowledge of the Bible that when he applied for membership in the Mount Vernon Congregational Church he was turned down upon his first application. When the young Moody attempted to speak in public during his church's prayer meeting, he noted that it made adults "squirm their shoulders when I got up." Some of the adults complained that Moody did not know enough grammar to address the congregation, and he was eventually asked to abstain from commenting in public.[16]

It is intriguing that so many great leaders suffered severe romantic heartache as young people. Harry Truman was so painfully shy that it took him five years to muster the courage to speak his first words to his future wife. Because of his family's misfortunes, it was not until Truman was thirty-five that he finally felt able to marry the girl of his dreams. Reading Truman's correspondence to Bess during those years reveals a young man desperate to win the affection of a young lady for whom he felt completely unworthy. Lincoln was also woefully inept around women and suffered painful rejection before eventually marrying. Winston Churchill had the first woman he had ever truly cared for marry another man while two other women rejected his marriage proposal before he finally married Clementine at age thirty-seven. John Wesley, the famous English preacher, endured great frustration regarding a young woman while he was a missionary in America. As a result, he returned to England a brokenhearted, disillusioned, and unsuccessful missionary. Roger Williams, the first Baptist pastor in America, fell into severe depression when his low social status prevented him from marrying the young lady he loved. A young Billy Graham was devastated when Emily, the girl of his dreams, rejected his marriage proposal for another suitor who showed more promise of making something of himself. Graham remembered: "That woeful night in the spring of 1938 when she called it quits between us was Paradise Lost for me. In my despondency, I looked up Dr. Minder . . . I wept out my misery to his understanding ears."[17] Eleanor Roosevelt suffered the agonizing discovery that her husband Franklin was unfaithful. Historians have suggested that much of the energy and passion she later invested in social causes stemmed from an absence of fulfillment in her relationship with her husband. In each of these cases, it seems, early disappointment gave the aspiring leaders both a sense of humble reality and a renewed zeal to achieve something significant in their lives.

Success Through Hardship. So many of history's great leaders suffered major failures, crises, and disappointments in their development as leaders that these traumas almost seem prerequisite to leadership success. If any conclusion can be drawn from the biographies of great leaders, it is that none enjoyed easy paths to greatness. It could, in fact, be argued that, had they avoided hardship, greatness would also have eluded them. This painful process of leadership development may be seen in the lives of biblical leaders as well. Moses, arguably the greatest figure in the Old Testament, had a life filled with adversity and failure. As a newborn, his life was threatened, so his mother gave him away to a foreigner. Although Moses was raised among Egyptian royalty, he was regularly reminded that his ancestry was, in fact, slavery. His bungled attempt to rescue a fellow Hebrew meant he had to flee for his life into the desert. Moses spent forty years herding sheep in the wilderness for his father-in-law because of a mistake he made in his youth. He spent another forty years wandering in the wilderness because of a mistake made by those he was leading. He would ultimately die outside the land he had dreamed of entering because of a mistake he made while wandering in the wilderness. Yet, despite his significant failures, even secular historians recognize Moses as one of the most influential leaders of all time. The apostle Paul, perhaps the greatest figure in the New Testament after Christ, was a murderer, as was King David in the Old Testament. In fact, several of the most influential people mentioned in the Old and New Testaments were murderers.

It would be a mistake to conclude that hardship and failure *always* produce successful leaders, just as it would be simplistic to assume that good leaders emerge only out of adversity. Everyone experiences some form of hardship, as well as some degree of prosperity. Everyone experiences both failure and success in life. The key to leadership development lies not in the experiences, whether good or bad, but in peoples' responses to those experiences. When some people face hardship, they become bitter or fearful and they quit trying. Others suffer similar setbacks, but choose instead to learn from their crises and to become stronger for the experience. The distinguishing characteristic of leaders is that they use their experiences as learning tools and they gain renewed motivation from their failures. Regarding Abraham Lincoln, Donald Phillips concluded: "Everything—failures as well as successes—became stepping stones to the presidency. In this sense, Lincoln's entire life prepared him for his future executive leadership role."[18] Leaders are not people who escape failure, but people who overcome adversity. Their lives confirm the axiom: "A mistake is an event, the full benefit of which has not yet been turned to your advantage."[19] Failure and personal crises do not disqualify people from becoming leaders. Rather, God can use adversity to build certain qualities deep within one's character that could not be fully developed in any other way.

GOD'S WORK IN LEADERS' LIVES

God Gives His Holy Spirit

Although childhood experiences, physical strength, failures, successes, and even birth order can impact general leadership abilities, there is an added dimension to the growth of a spiritual leader that is not found in secular leadership development. That dimension is the active work of the Holy Spirit in leaders' lives. Oswald Sanders notes: "There is no such thing as a self-made spiritual leader."[20] Spiritual ends require spiritual means, and spiritual means come only by the Holy Spirit. The apostle Paul identifies leadership as something the Holy Spirit enables people to do (Rom. 12:8). This truth is evident in God's message to Zerubbabel, the governor over Jerusalem, who oversaw the rebuilding of the temple after the Jewish exiles' return from Babylon. Zerubbabel was confronted with the doubly daunting task of governing a region decimated by war and exile, as well as rebuilding a massive temple that lay in ruins. At this critical juncture, he received this message from God: "'Not by might nor by power, but by My Spirit,' says the Lord of hosts." (Zech. 4:6). Zerubbabel may have thought his primary concerns were brick and mortar, finances, taxation, and the enemies surrounding him. But the deluged governor learned an invaluable lesson—spiritual leaders require the Spirit to work in their lives even when they are performing what appear to be unspiritual tasks. Erecting buildings, administering people, and raising money are all spiritual jobs when the Spirit is involved. Without the Spirit's presence, people may be leaders, but they are not spiritual leaders.

God Sets the Leader's Agenda

The fact that God can bring character development and personal growth out of any situation is conditional on people's willingness to submit to God's will. God is sovereign over every life, but those who yield their will to him will be shaped according to his purposes. When God directs a life for his purposes, all of life is a school. No experience, good or bad, is ever wasted (Rom. 8:28). God doesn't squander people's time. He doesn't ignore their pain. He brings not only healing but growth out of even the worst experiences. Every relationship can be God's instrument to mature a person's character. The world can offer its best theories on leadership and provide the most extensive training possible, but unless God sets the agenda for a leader's life, that person, though thoroughly educated, will not be an effective spiritual leader.

Robert Clinton, a professor at Fuller Seminary, wrote *The Making of a Leader*, in which he puts forth a six-stage model of how God develops leaders. Clinton believes God matures leaders over a lifetime. God uses relationships and events in leaders' lives as two primary means for growing people into leaders. The six stages of leadership development in Clinton's model are:

- Phase One: Sovereign Foundations
- Phase Two: Inner Life Growth
- Phase Three: Ministry Maturing
- Phase Four: Life Maturing
- Phase Five: Convergence
- Phase Six: Afterglow or Celebration

Clinton provides a helpful model that speaks directly to the development of spiritual leaders, but which also has applications to leadership development in general. *Sovereign Foundations* involves God's activity during life's formative years. Parental love, birth order, childhood illness, prosperity or poverty, loss of loved ones, stability versus constant upheaval—these are all factors over which children have no control. History demonstrates that the way emerging leaders respond to these factors determines much of their leadership potential.

Inner Life Growth is the period in which people develop their character as well as their spiritual life. It is during this stage that people experience conversion. Once people have the indwelling presence of the Holy Spirit, they are no longer subject to the whims of fate but are in a position where they can be systematically transformed into people who think and act like Christ. Leaders without the Holy Spirit are much more subject to their pasts than those whose characters are shaped by the Holy Spirit working within them. Thus, people without the Holy Spirit will often have major areas of their character that remain underdeveloped.

During the *Ministry Maturing* phase people make their earliest attempts at spiritual leadership. They may volunteer to lead a church program, or they may venture to share their faith with someone. Through such experiences God teaches them more specifically what it means to be spiritual leaders. When people first attempt to exercise leadership, they often fail or experience great frustration. It is as they develop leadership skills, as well as a résumé of experiences, that people begin to understand their strengths and weakness. At this stage the focus is more on who leaders are rather than on what they do. What leaders learn from these early experiences will largely determine how they advance in leadership ability.

The *Life Maturing* period is when spiritual leaders begin to focus on their strengths and to find leadership opportunities in which they can be most effective. Whereas until this time, God was working primarily *in* the leader, now God begins to work increasingly *through* the leader. An experiential understanding of God matures at this time. Through significant life experiences God teaches people about life and relationships. It is through the normal experiences of failure and success, criticism and praise, loyalty and betrayal, illness and loss that God matures people. Again, much depends upon the leader's reaction to the life circumstances through which God brings them. Positive responses to these circumstances will guide the person into a more mature level of leadership.

During the *Convergence* phase, people's ministry experiences and their life experiences converge into a specific job or responsibility wherein they draw on all they have learned in order to enjoy maximum effectiveness. This will be the job or role for which leaders are best known and in which they experience their greatest success.

Clinton's focus is on the development of spiritual leaders, but the general principles can apply to secular leaders as well. Both can experience the merging of their life and work experiences into a leadership role that successfully integrates all they have learned with who they have become. Many of history's most famous leaders did not assume their most influential roles until late in life. Winston Churchill did not become prime minister until he was a senior adult. He considered all his life experiences a preface to his time as British prime minister during World War II. Although Churchill failed many times, and was severely criticized throughout his life, it appears his earlier years were a training ground to prepare him for his great moment on the world stage as Hitler's chief antagonist. General George Marshall, the celebrated American military commander of World War II, was not promoted to general until the age of fifty-nine. He was sixty-seven when he developed the famous Marshall Plan that rebuilt postwar Europe. Harry Truman was sixty-seven when he became president. Pope John XXIII was seventy-seven when he was chosen to lead the Roman Catholic Church. Unfortunately, many people never reach convergence. Some leaders never find jobs or challenges that bring to fruition all that has gone before in their lives. The full benefit of their past is never brought to bear on society's needs. The Holy Spirit will work to pull together all the experiences in Christians' lives in order to bring them to a deeper maturity. When leaders neglect the Holy Spirit's role in their lives they never reach their full potential as spiritual leaders.

Afterglow or *Celebration*, is a level of leadership Clinton says few people achieve. It comes after one has successfully led others for a significant period of time. For spiritual leaders this phase occurs after they have faithfully allowed God to accomplish his will for their lives as well as for their organizations. Successful spiritual leaders spend this final period of their lives celebrating and building upon the work God did in and through them. This is also a time for teaching the next generation. Leaders in this sixth phase have nothing to prove. Others respect them not because of their position of influence, or even because they are continuing to lead, but because of who they are and what they represent. It is not uncommon for great leaders to spend their final years associated with a school. Jonathan Edwards, renowned spiritual leader during the First Great Awakening, spent his final days as president of Princeton University. Charles Finney, the outstanding evangelist of the Second Great Awakening, became president of Oberlin College. Charles Spurgeon invested much time in developing the young pastors training in his college. Robert E. Lee spent his final years as president of Washington College developing a new generation of southern leaders. A true leader can expect to be sought out by people one day for the singular reason of what the leader represents. Just as the face of Moses used to glow after having been in the presence of God, so there will be unmistakable evidence that leaders in this leadership stage have walked intimately and powerfully with God for many years. When people recognize that someone has walked with God in this manner, they will seek to be around them and to learn from their spiritual pilgrimage.

GOD GIVES THE ASSIGNMENT

People may become leaders by responding in a healthy manner to all they encounter in life, but they will not become spiritual leaders unless God calls them to this role and equips them for it. Secular leadership is something to which people can aspire. It can be achieved through sheer force of will. Spiritual leadership, on the other hand, is not a role for which one applies. Rather, it is assigned by God. God determines each person's assignment. Historically, God has chosen ordinary people, most of whom were not looking for a divine assignment. Nevertheless, God saw something in their hearts that led him to assign particular tasks. While there is nothing wrong with wanting to experience God working powerfully in one's life, those wishing for God to use them mightily should not pursue leadership positions in God's kingdom (1 Tim. 3:1). They should seek God with all their hearts and wait upon his will. The greatest area of concern for spiritual leaders is their hearts. When God sees people with righteous lives, he may exercise his prerogative to show himself strong in their lives in order to accomplish his divine will.

BIBLICAL EXAMPLE: ABRAHAM

Numerous examples could be taken from the Bible of how God develops leaders for his purposes. Few people receive the extensive treatment of Abraham. Abraham's life provides a thorough example of how God chooses ordinary people and turns them into effective spiritual leaders.

Abraham Was an Ordinary Person

Abraham was born in Ur, among the moon-worshiping Chaldeans. Abraham's agenda for his life was probably not complicated. He likely planned to live out his days raising his herds and flocks. His wife Sarah was unable to bear children, so parenthood would not factor into Abraham and Sarah's plans. God's agenda was radically different from Abraham's. God's plan for Abraham was not that he live a settled life without children, but that he become a nomadic patriarch. Abraham would become father to a holy nation. His life would be a spiritual example to God's people for thousands of years. The Messiah would be Abraham's descendant. Abraham's life would prove to be a pivotal point in history. Generations of believers would find inspiration and eternal salvation because of Abraham's life. To say that God's plans dwarfed Abraham's plans would be an understatement! The key was not for God to bless Abraham's plans but for Abraham to discard his agenda in favor of God's will.

It is not surprising that, since God had so much in store for Abraham, he took time to prepare him thoroughly. Spiritual leadership does not happen by accident. It develops as God matures people in their character as well as in their relationship with him. Character includes wisdom, integrity, honesty, and moral purity. Relationship involves trust in God, obedience to him, and love for him. Although God often used people who appeared to be the least likely candidates for true leadership, the common denominator was that these people were all upright in character and they walked closely with him (1 Sam. 16:7). The greater God's assignment, the greater the character and the closer the relationship with God that is required (Matt. 25:23).

The Bible gives numerous examples showing how God chose and developed people to serve him. These men and women were as diverse as people can be from one another, and God's call on each person's life was unique. Abraham's life is just one example of how God develops leaders, but its extensive biblical coverage clearly identifies the key aspects to God's leadership-development process.

Abraham Built on His Heritage

When God first spoke to Abraham and told him to leave his homeland in Ur, God had already used Abraham's father, Terah, to begin the process (Acts 7:2–4; Gen. 11:31–32). What God began with Abraham's father, he continued through Abraham's life and eventually completed through Abraham's descendants. Terah would only get as far as Haran. It would be his son Abraham who would complete the family's journey to Canaan. Heritage can be a powerful factor in leadership. As in Abraham's case, God may begin a work in one generation that is brought to fruition in succeeding generations. God wanted Abraham to go to Canaan, so he also gave that desire to Abraham's father. God called a son to be a nomad, so he initiated a restlessness in the father.

Abraham Grew Through Failure

Every event in Abraham's life contributed to his character development. Abraham did not begin his life as a paragon of faith, but gradually, over many years, he developed a mature and deep relationship with God. God used Abraham's failures to prepare him for leadership. For example, God specifically instructed Abraham to leave his family behind but instead Abraham took Lot with him to Canaan (Gen. 12:1, 4). This meant Abraham would have to separate from Lot later, taking the land Lot rejected (Gen. 13). Still later, Abraham would find himself interceding with God on Lot's behalf, pleading for the wicked city of Sodom when God was about to destroy it (Gen. 18:16–33). Lot's descendents, the Moabites and the Ammonites, would cause tremendous grief to Abraham's descendants (Gen. 36–38). With one act of seemingly minor disobedience, Abraham inadvertently endangered the inheritance God wanted to give him and his descendants. Through this failure, Abraham learned a valuable lesson regarding his modification of God's will. Abraham's mistake makes it clear that adding to God's will is as devastating as rejecting God's will.

Why is it so important to follow God's will exactly as it is and not try to add to it so it makes more sense? God's ways are not man's ways. It seems ridiculous for God to call a seventy-five-year-old man to have a child and then to spend twenty-five years preparing him for the child-rearing task. Yet God had plans for Isaac far beyond what Abraham could ever have imagined. God intended for Isaac to be a patriarch for the people of God. For such an assignment, Isaac required a godly, faithful father.

Abraham Built Spiritual Landmarks

Abraham's spiritual pilgrimage can be traced by examining the altars he built. Every time Abraham came to a milestone in his life, or whenever he learned something new about God, he built an altar. "The LORD appeared to Abram and said, 'To your descendants I will give this land.' So he built an altar there to the LORD who had appeared to him. Then he proceeded from there to the mountain on the east of Bethel, and pitched his tent, with Bethel on the west and Ai on the east; and there he built an altar to the LORD and called upon the name of the LORD" (Gen. 12:7–9).

Each altar provided a testimonial to Abraham's growth in understanding God's ways and to his trust in God. For today's leaders, spiritual markers provide a backdrop by which they can see where God has helped them mature in their relationship with him. God's current instructions are always best understood in light of the knowledge of all he has done in a leader's life so far.

When a severe famine swept across Canaan, Abraham took matters into his own hands and moved to Egypt. Unfortunately, he did not consult the Lord, either when he left for Egypt or when he arrived. No mention is made of an altar being built while Abraham was in Egypt (Gen. 12:10–20). Whenever Abraham made decisions without consulting God, the results were disastrous.

Abraham Experienced God's Redemption

It is significant to note from biblical examples that God seldom intervened when people were about to make mistakes. Rather, he allowed them to fail, but stood ready to redeem them. Many individuals, through the process of failure and redemption, saw God's character revealed in a deeper dimension than if God had simply stepped in to help them avoid failure. If there is anything leaders must carefully evaluate and process, it is their mistakes. By systematically reviewing mistakes and making the necessary adjustments to ensure that the same errors are not repeated, leaders can derive great benefit.

Abraham, fearing Pharaoh would kill him in order to marry his wife, had Sarah lie about their marriage. This lie would cost Abraham and his descendants dearly. It was one event that happened in the fear of the moment. However, the lie indicated a flaw in Abraham's faith and character. Abraham's lie revealed that he had not yet learned to trust God fully. There was more work to be done in his life before he could be entrusted with raising another patriarch. This flaw in Abraham's character would manifest itself again (Gen. 29). Interestingly, his son Isaac would also lie about his wife when faced with a similar situation (Gen. 26:7) and Isaac's son Jacob would become a notorious deceiver. Character flaws, left unchecked in people's lives, can tenaciously reappear in subsequent generations (Exod. 34:7; Deut. 5:9). Nevertheless, God continued to forgive Abraham and to work in his life until Abraham became the model of faith for generations of God's people.

Abraham Learned by Experience

Abraham's understanding of God was not theoretical. He didn't learn it from books. He learned it through encounters with God. Each time God revealed a new facet of his character to Abraham; it was through experience. For example, God gave Abraham a brilliant victory over a superior army (Gen. 15:1). Thereafter, Abraham knew he could trust God as his shield. This was not just because God said he could protect Abraham, but because Abraham had experienced God's protection firsthand. Spiritual leaders must make the connection between God's activity in their lives and God's character.

Abraham Was Not Allowed to Take Shortcuts

Abraham's life shows that attaining spiritual maturity is a lifelong process. Spiritual leaders don't take shortcuts. Genesis 16 details a low point in Abraham's life. Despite the incredible covenant God made with him to make him the father of countless descendents, the fact was that he remained childless. At this crucial time of testing, Abraham listened to the counsel of people instead of listening to God. His wife, Sarah, advised him to produce a child through her servant Hagar. This was a commonly accepted practice in Abraham's day. It was worldly reasoning at its best, but it was not God's way. After ten years of waiting on God, Abraham's faith wavered and he opted for Sarah's plan. Hagar did produce a son, Ishmael, who would become the founder of the Arab nations. These nations would eventually become Israel's fierce enemies. Thousands of years later, people continue to suffer and die because Abraham chose to take a shortcut rather than to trust God's word.

Abraham was one hundred years old when Isaac was born. He had waited twenty-five years for God to carry out his promise. Abraham learned a lesson about the difference between God's timing and people's timing. God sees things from an eternal perspective. People see things from a temporal view. Spiritual leaders court disaster when they panic and assume they must take matters in their own hands. When spiritual leaders wait patiently on the Lord, regardless of how long it takes, God always proves himself absolutely true to his word. Sometimes the time it takes God's promise to be realized can seem eternally long, but a promise fulfilled by God is always worth the wait. Many more leaders would see major accomplishments occur in their lives and in their organizations if only they were willing to wait as long as necessary to see God accomplish his will.

Abraham Demonstrated His Faith

By the time Abraham was a senior citizen, God had developed him into a godly husband and father. Still, God had even greater plans for him. God intended for Abraham to be more than a father to Isaac; he wanted him to be the father of the faithful, a model of faithfulness for the rest of time. For this, Abraham had to advance farther in his relationship with God than anyone had gone before. In order to develop a great faith in God, Abraham was asked to make the most difficult decision of his life. "Now it came about after these things, that God tested Abraham, and said to him, 'Abraham!' And he said, 'Here I am.' And He said, 'Take now your son, your only son, whom you love, Isaac, and go to the land

of Moriah; and offer him there as a burnt offering on one of the mountains of which I will tell you.' So Abraham arose early in the morning and
saddled his donkey, and took two of his young men with him and Isaac
his son; and he split wood for the burnt offering, and arose and went to
the place of which God had told him" (Gen. 22:1–3).

There was no mistaking what God was asking. The question was:
would Abraham obey? Most of the time, the problem with Christian
leaders is not that they don't know what God wants them to do. The
problem is that they know only too well, but they are unwilling to do it.

To modern readers, God's command seems unusually cruel. But to
Abraham, it would not have seemed peculiar. Abraham lived in a land of
fanatical idol worship. Idolaters, desperate to gain their god's favor,
would sacrifice their first-born children on altars. In essence, God's
command would prove whether or not Abraham was as committed to
his God as the people around him were to theirs. If Abraham was to be
father of the faithful, it would require of him a deeper faith in God than
the average man had. For Abraham to do extraordinary things, he
would need an extraordinary relationship with God.

Abraham Obeyed God

Through obedience, people experience God working through their
lives and they come to know more about God's character. In response
to Abraham's obedience, God spared Isaac's life. Abraham named that
place "The Lord will provide," for he learned that when people are willing to give everything they have to God, God will provide all they need.
Abraham's response reveals the kind of man he had become. Scripture
testifies: "So Abraham rose early . . ." Abraham received the single most
difficult assignment God had ever given to any man, and he obeyed
without hesitation. In passing this test, Abraham not only went deeper
in his relationship with God; he also demonstrated his readiness to be a
great leader of God's people. "By Myself I have sworn, declares the
Lord, because you have done this thing, and have not withheld your
son, your only son, indeed I will greatly bless you, and I will greatly
multiply your seed as the stars of the heavens, and as the sand which is
on the seashore; and your seed shall possess the gate of their enemies.

And in your seed all the nations of the earth shall be blessed, because you have obeyed My voice" (Gen. 22:16–18).

Far more hinged on Abraham's obedience than he first realized. Abraham came to understand that his actions did not affect him alone, but his obedience to God would impact generations to follow.

Abraham Became a Friend of God

What was the result of God's work in Abraham's life over the years? He became a godly man; he became the patriarch of a nation; he became father of the faithful. But God's activity in Abraham's life helped him to become something even more important than all of these things. Abraham became a friend of God (2 Chron. 20:7; Isa. 41:8). It is one thing to call God your friend. It is quite another for God to call you his friend. Abraham is the only person to whom Scripture gives this distinction. "And the Scripture was fulfilled which says, 'And Abraham believed God, and it was reckoned to him as righteousness,' and he was called the friend of God" (James 2:23).

Abraham was far from perfect. He made many mistakes. Yet his heart was open before God, and God chose to develop him into a man of faith. God didn't choose Abraham because of his leadership ability. He chose Abraham because of his heart. The key was not that Abraham attended all the best leadership seminars. The key was that he came to know God and he allowed God to transform him into a leader through his obedience. When people strive to have their hearts right before God, then God promises to "show himself strong" (2 Chron. 16:9).

God appoints leaders. People may apply for various leadership positions, but God is the one who ultimately determines which leadership roles they will have. Leadership development comes through character development, because leadership is a character issue. Therefore, the first truth in leadership development is this: God's assignments are always based on character—the greater the character, the greater the assignment (Luke 16:10). Before God will give leaders larger assignments, he will build in them greater characters. No role is more important than that of a spiritual leader; therefore, God will first build a character that is capable of handling such a meaningful assignment.

Character building can be a slow, sometimes painful process. But the person willing to allow God to complete the process will know the joy of being used by God. Even better, those who submit their lives to God's refining process will experience the profound joy that comes with knowing God in a deeply personal way.

Character building takes time. There are no shortcuts. Two factors determine the length of time required for God to develop character worthy of spiritual leadership—trust in God and obedience to God.

God builds character through the ordinary experiences and crises of life. Most character building does not occur while one is attending a seminar or taking a course. Rather, God uses everyday events, both good and bad, to shape leaders. Often these events are situations that are beyond peoples' control—events that require people to place their trust in God.

Significant character development occurs as God redeems leaders from their mistakes. God does not always intervene when people are determined to go in a harmful direction, but he is always available to redeem people. Through the redemption process, they learn more about themselves and more about God. The best leaders know themselves well. God uses life's experiences to teach leaders what they are really like. Wise leaders allow God to make the most of their mistakes. Those willing to submit themselves to the leadership development track of the Lord have the potential of growing into the leaders God wants them to become.

CONCEPTS AND SCRIPTURES FOR CONSIDERATION

- The greatness of an organization will be directly proportional to the greatness of its leader.
- Ultimately, leadership is more about "being" than about "doing."
- Any strategy for developing spiritual leaders must take into account those emerging leaders currently in their preteens.

- Most of history's famous leaders have been decidedly ordinary people.
- So many of history's great leaders suffered major failures, crises, and disappointments in their development as leaders that these traumas almost seem prerequisite to leadership success.
- God can use adversity to build certain qualities deep within one's character that could not be fully developed in any other way.
- God seldom intervened when people were about to make mistakes. Rather, he allowed them to fail, but stood ready to redeem them.
- No experience, good or bad, is ever wasted.
- People may apply for various leadership positions, but God is the one who ultimately determines which leadership roles they will have.
- God's assignments are always based on character—the greater the character, the greater the assignment.

Zechariah 4:6
Romans 8:28
2 Chronicles 16:9
1 Samuel 16:7
Matthew 25:23
Exodus 34:7; Deuteronomy 5:9; James 2:23
Genesis 22:1–3
Luke 16:10

CHAPTER FOUR

The Leader's Vision
Where Do Leaders Get It and How Do They Communicate It?

WHEN IT COMES TO VISION, NO statement is more frequently quoted (or misquoted) by Christians and non-Christians alike than King Solomon's observation: "Where there is no vision, the people perish" (Prov. 29:18 KJV). Scripture's timeless wisdom once again proves relevant to modern life. Leadership pundits claim vision is crucial for an obvious reason: if you can't see where you are going, you are unlikely to get there. Vision can serve as the North Star for organizations, helping leaders keep their bearings as they move their people forward. Hence, any organization that does not have a clear vision of where it is going is in danger of becoming sidetracked and failing to accomplish its purpose.

How do contemporary leaders respond to this need for vision? Many inundate their organizations with discussions, memos, meetings, seminars, retreats, and slogans, all about vision. Vision statements are in vogue. They are everywhere—on letterheads, on business cards, posted in offices and in advertisements. Leaders spend extensive energy encouraging their people to buy in to their vision. Those who don't embrace the corporate vision are often eventually forced out of the organization.

Vision is critical for organizations, so it stands to reason that leaders must be visionaries. Visionary leaders understand at least three fundamental issues: Where does vision come from? How does vision inspire people? How do leaders communicate vision?

WHERE DO LEADERS OBTAIN THEIR VISION?

If it is true that great visions inspire great people and great organizations, the crucial task for leaders is to develop the loftiest vision possible for their organizations. Walt Disney had a broad vision—to make people happy—and he redefined the entertainment industry. Henry Ford sought to democratize the automobile, and the result was a prodigiously successful automotive empire. George Marshall's vision was to develop the mightiest army in the world; he began with an army of 200,000 men in 1939 and by 1945 had created a force of 8.3 million. Bill Gates had a vision that every computer in the world would use Microsoft software; his success is legendary. When people consider the examples of great business leaders, they feel pressured to develop grandiose visions that will likewise propel their organization to greatness. But where do leaders find visions that inspire people and unite them to great accomplishments? There are many sources from which leaders draw their vision.

"Because It's There"

In 1924, George Leigh Mallory, a British schoolmaster and socialite, determined he would ascend the as-yet unconquered peak of Mount Everest. When a reporter asked why he intended to climb the formidable mountain, he replied: "Because it's there." On June 8, the thirty-eight-year-old father of three young children was last sighted trudging up the mountain with his companion Andrew Irvine. Seventy-five years later, in 1999, an American climbing team discovered Mallory's perfectly preserved body on the slopes of the mountain. Mallory had sacrificed his life in an attempt to accomplish an unnecessary goal.

While it is one thing for people to risk their lives in pursuit of a dream, it is quite another for leaders to take their organizations on a misguided and unnecessary quest just because the opportunity lies before them. The only vision some leaders have is for their organizations to conquer the obstacles immediately in front of them. They do not reflect on why they are doing what they are doing. They do not consider the long-term ramifications to them personally or to the organizations they lead. They hardly consider their alternatives. They value action over reflection—or more precisely, reaction over reflection. They assume that moving forward is always better than standing still. Hence, when a challenge suddenly presents itself, they impulsively charge forward. Many of these leaders eventually collapse on the slopes of their mountains, never realizing that their labors and the sacrifices of their followers have been for naught.

How can you identify leaders who subscribe to this reactionary approach to vision? A leader may launch into a new building program without considering its long-term cost or effect. Once the expense of the building project escalates and the people begin to grumble, these leaders find themselves halfway up a mountain without resources to complete the climb. They may also begin new programs or hire more staff simply because opportunities arise. Christians often call these opportunities "open doors." Because an opportunity presents itself, the leader assumes it must be God's will to move forward. This is an undiscerning approach to leadership. There is much more to determining God's will than merely assuming that every "open door" is an invitation from God.

Duplicating Success

Some leaders borrow their visions. A bountiful source of vision for some is the past. They do things the way they do because that's the way they've always done it. The easiest course of action is often the one taken previously, especially if it was successful. But sometimes success becomes the leader's greatest enemy. Max Dupree warns: "Success can close a mind faster than prejudice."[1] A leader may be reluctant to reject previously successful methods in order to lead in a new direction. It's too risky. Peter Drucker observed: "No one has much difficulty getting rid of the total failures. They liquidate themselves. Yesterday's successes, however, always linger on long beyond their productive life."[2] Christian organizations should take careful note that, throughout Scripture, God rarely worked in the same way twice. God's activity was always unique to the people with whom he was dealing and the time in which he was working. God's activity cannot be reduced to a formula because God is always more concerned with peoples' obedient response to his will than with the means of communicating his will. Churches are remiss if they assume that because God worked mightily in a particular way in the past, he will choose to work in exactly the same way in the present. Many organizations today are locked into doing things a certain way, not because it is still effective, but because it was effective yesterday. This is the curse of success.

Just as depending on past successes can be futile, adopting the current methods of others can be equally impotent. Businesses often imitate others' successful marketing techniques or acquire similar technology in order to keep up with their competition. If one church develops an innovative way to enlist new members, other pastors jump on board and lead their people to do the same thing. Mimicking the successful strategies of others is enticing to some leaders because it eliminates the need to think reflectively. They merely react to whatever opportunities lie before them. Martin Luther King Jr. lamented the shortage of leaders willing to pay the price of prolonged, creative, problem-solving thinking. He concluded: "There is an almost universal quest for easy answers and half-baked solutions. Nothing pains some people more than having to think."[3]

In the case of churches emulating the success of other churches, it seemingly eliminates the need for Christian leaders to cultivate an intimate relationship with God. While there is nothing wrong with churches making use of successful programs and methods developed by others when they sense God has led them to use them, church leaders can be seduced into thinking all they need to lead their church is the latest seminar or popular book. They spend their energy chasing after whatever new program or fad gains their attention. Such leaders spend too little time examining and evaluating the effectiveness of their own organizations and cultivating their relationship with the Head of the church while spending an inordinate amount of time focusing on the activities of others. Pity the people who follow such thoughtless leadership.

Vanity

Although it is not always readily apparent, vanity is a source of vision that motivates many leaders. Some leaders set the goals for their organization based on what will bring them the most personal success or praise. Business leaders may choose a course of action more out of a desire to expand their reputations and advance their careers than from concern for what will benefit their companies. Religious leaders may lead their churches to build larger auditoriums or to televise their services, not because they genuinely sense God's leadership to do these things but in order to enhance their reputation as preachers. Such egocentric leadership is generally cloaked in statements of loyalty to the organization or in pious proclamations about the kingdom of God. But in truth, the growth of the organization merely feeds the leader's pride. Countless businesses have crumbled under leaders who were motivated by vanity rather than by vision. Churches have been saddled with crippling debts as they sought to repay bills incurred by former pastors looking to make a name for themselves.

Napoleon Bonaparte was constantly involved in warfare as he led the French Empire in its attempt to conquer Europe. In defeat, Napoleon surmised, "If I had succeeded, I should have been the greatest man known to history."[4] There is no doubt that Napoleon made a name for himself in history, but it's questionable whether his soldiers would have willingly sacrificed their lives on the battlefields of Europe had they known the primary cause was to secure their emperor's fame. Today, many are called upon to make sacrifices and to give their best efforts on behalf of their organizations, but they do so with nagging doubts that their personal sacrifices are for no more noble purpose than furthering their leader's career.

Need

A popular basis for setting vision is perceived needs. Need-based visions are established by surveying target groups to determine their desires. Businesses find out what people are seeking, then they develop a product to meet the expressed need. While this has long been a profitable practice for secular businesses, Christian organizations are increasingly favoring the need-based approach in determining their vision. Churches survey their communities to discover the needs of the people, then compile, categorize, and prioritize the data. Then they set the church's agenda in response to the survey's results.

The advantage of the need-based approach is obvious. In the marketplace, producers are assured that consumers consider their product necessary. Organizations gain a sense of relevance when they are equipped to meet the expressed desires of the general public. Churches reap a similar benefit—those churches most in touch with their community's expressed needs will be viewed as a more relevant, viable option by those whose needs they address.

Using the expressed needs of a target audience to establish an organization's vision is not a foolproof approach, however. Successful companies are not entirely market-driven. Rather, successful businesses sometimes drive the market. Many of the popular inventions and products of history came, not from the expressed need of the public but from the creative innovation of an enterprising company. Companies that simply respond to society's expressed needs find themselves in a large pool of similar companies, all competing for the same consumers. Innovative companies, however, look to the future to anticipate eventual needs, or they create a sense of need in the public. Then they position themselves to lead the industry in meeting the resulting demand.

Need-inspired visions, while relevant to a point in the marketplace, are only one aspect of successful businesses. Religious organizations should be cautioned about basing their ministries solely on meeting the needs being expressed by people. While churches must be sensitive to the needs in their communities, a need expressed is not the same thing as a call by God.

Moreover, when churches survey their neighborhoods, they are generally talking with unregenerate people. People who are not born again cannot fully understand their own spiritual needs. One church, surveying its community, found the greatest need expressed was for a bridge to be built across a river to provide easier neighborhood access to the downtown. The church asked, and the people responded. But the church was left in an awkward position because it could not possibly meet the need expressed. As a result, some in the community continued to view the church as irrelevant.

Non-Christians may recognize the symptoms of evil in society, but they probably do not understand the root cause. For example, when parents run their families by worldly standards, their children may experiment with the temptations of the world. The parents may believe what they need is a community center to keep their teenagers off the streets. In reality, what they need is to have Christ as the head of their home and to raise their children using God's standard instead of the world's. Need-based visions not only allow unregenerate people to set the agenda for churches, but they also tempt churches to focus on symptoms rather than causes.

God's assignment for a church may not include meeting every need being expressed in that church's community. God equips each church for particular assignments (1 Cor. 12:12–31). The church must discover its vision not by seeking the opinions of people but by seeking God's will. Often, need-based church visions cause Christians to neglect their relationship with the Head of the church as they focus their energies on meeting people's needs. Jesus addressed this problem when Mary took a pound of costly perfume and freely poured it on his feet. She then humbly wiped Jesus' feet with her own hair. Judas was indignant. "Why was this perfume not sold for three hundred denarii, and given to poor people?" he asked. Jesus' response was pointed: "For the poor you always have with you, but you do not always have Me" (John 12:5, 7). A relationship with Jesus is always a higher priority than meeting people's physical needs. Jesus did not conduct his ministry based on what people wanted, but on where he saw his Father at work (Mark 1:23–39; Luke 19:1–10; John 5:17, 19–20). If his Father was working with the multitude, that is where the Son invested himself. If the Father was working in the life of a lone sinner, that is where Jesus directed his efforts. If determining vision is nothing more than the result of tabulating a door-to-door survey, a relationship with the heavenly Father is unnecessary to growing a church.

Business leaders need to understand that their companies' needs are not the sole determining motivator for their leadership. Certainly, making a profit and increasing productivity are desirable and necessary. But even secular writers on leadership have conceded that profit cannot be the only determining factor in business. Warren Bennis observed, "Too many Americans believe that the bottom line isn't everything, it's the only thing, and America is strangling on that lack of vision."[5] Bennis also noted, "It isn't either a bull or a bear market anymore, it's a pig market."[6]

Spiritual leaders should be motivated by the Holy Spirit. As Henry regularly consults with Christian CEOs, it is startling what they share God is revealing to them about his purposes. Corporate CEOs are finding that when they meet with world leaders, they are not only able to transact multimillion-dollar business deals, but also to give their witness for Christ. For example, some Christian business leaders have found that God's agenda was for them to give Bibles to foreign business and political leaders, or to invest company funds in providing community centers for underprivileged children. Some privately owned businesses are using a substantial portion of their profits to support orphanages or to provide food internationally, or to translate the Bible into foreign languages, or to sponsor missionaries. These CEOs have found that profits are merely a means to the end rather than an end in itself and that their need to make a profit to satisfy investors is not the only driving force for their leadership.

Available Resources

The availability of resources sometimes induces vision. That is, organizations gravitate toward certain activities or priorities simply because resources such as manpower, or finances, or equipment are available to them. Church programs are often motivated in this manner.

- A church is informed that its denomination is making copies of evangelistic videos available for distribution in the community. The church decides this opportunity is too good to pass up, and it orders one thousand videos. For the next four Saturdays, church members are enlisted to go door to door in their community handing them out.
- A church hosts several young missionaries each summer for the simple reason that Christian college students are made available to them for the summer by a local campus ministry.

- A foreign missions agency offers free literature if the church will conduct a mission fair, so the church schedules one.
- The denomination alerts the church that funds are available for starting a new church in the area, so the missions committee begins surveying neighborhoods, seeking interest in a new church plant.
- When an elderly member donates a piano to the church in memory of her deceased husband, the auditorium is rearranged and the worship program is adjusted to accommodate the new equipment.

Churches are eager to take advantage of every opportunity that presents itself, but in time find themselves burdened by the weight of trying to use available resources. Rather than the resources serving the churches, the churches become enslaved to the resources.

Such a reactionary response to available resources can also occur in the business world.

- The head office makes certain sales incentives available, so the branch manager decides to promote a competition among her salespeople, though this method goes against her personal views of team building.
- A business experiences a profitable quarter, so it purchases new equipment and hires additional personnel, simply because the money is currently available.

Incredibly, military commanders have engaged in battles simply because troops were available to fight!

Wise leaders do not allow the availability of resources to determine the direction of their organization. For one thing, such resources often come with strings attached. Accepting equipment, volunteers, or program funds may mean committing one's organization to a philosophy of operations that runs counter to the leader's personal values. Moreover, such "gifts" might directly contradict a company's corporate values.

As a general rule, resources should follow vision, not determine it. Leaders must first decide the vision for their organization and then marshal the necessary resources to achieve it. Foolish leaders will thoughtlessly accept resources and then try to piece together a vision that uses the resources they have accumulated.

Leader-Driven

Many people assume that being a visionary leader involves personally developing a vision for one's organization. The imagery is that of a solitary figure ascending a mountain seeking a vision with the combustibility to spark a significant movement among the people below. Such leaders take on the responsibility of creating a vision apart from those they lead, assuming that vision casting is one job they cannot delegate or share. Many well-known writers support leader-based vision development. Warren Bennis notes: "Just as no great painting has ever been created by a committee, no great vision has ever emerged from the herd."[7] While Barna believes God gives vision to leaders, he notes: "God never gave a vision to a committee."[8] While most leaders know that vision is important, understanding how to achieve that vision is not a simple endeavor. Burt Nanus asks, "So where does a leader's vision come from? Vision is composed of one part foresight, one part insight, plenty of imagination and judgment, and often, a healthy dose of chutzpah."[9] Kouzes and Posner claim that visions "flow from the reservoir of our knowledge and experience."[10]

How do leaders generate vision? They envision a desirable future for their organization and then develop a plan to achieve the results. This venture can put enormous pressure on leaders as they assume responsibility for interpreting the rapid, global changes around them and for peering into the future to determine the best approach for their organizations.

What kind of person is qualified for such a demanding task? Leaders who have had a broad range of experiences, who have traveled extensively, have read broadly, who know a wide variety of people, and who have stretched their thinking through education and a mosaic of life experiences are thought to have a good chance of developing compelling and innovative visions. But the job doesn't end there. Once leaders develop a vision, they have the onerous task of selling it to their constituents.

Often, leaders put their reputations and credibility on the line as they seek to win support for their vision. When people reject leaders' visions they are expressing a lack of trust in their leaders. Leaders feel pressured to develop visions that are grand enough and compelling enough that people want to "sign up." If people still refuse to follow, leaders may attempt to develop a still more impressive and attractive vision that will enlist people's commitment. James C. Collins and Jerry I. Porras in their book, *Built to Last*, talk about "Big Hairy Audacious Goals," or BHAGs.[11] These are organizational goals that are so large and so challenging they compel people to unite together to achieve the seemingly impossible. Companies have embraced such goals and the results have, on occasion, been impressive.

Many Christian leaders have adopted BHAGs with gusto. Yet, at times, there seems to be a hollowness to their rhetoric. They say, "We need to dream big dreams for God," or "We must set goals that are worthy of the mighty God we serve." This all sounds exciting and can generally elicit a chorus of amens from the audience, but is it biblical? Isaiah 55:8–9 cautions: "'For My thoughts are not your thoughts, neither are your ways My ways,' declares the LORD. 'For as the heavens are higher than the earth, so are My ways higher than your ways and My thoughts than your thoughts.'"

The message is clear. Leaders' best thinking will not build the kingdom of God. Why? Because people do not naturally think the way God does. The apostle Paul observed, "Where is the wise man? Where is the scribe? Where is the debater of this age? Has not God made foolish the wisdom of the world?" (1 Cor. 1:20). God's ways are completely different from man's ways. He has different priorities, different values. When people "think great thoughts *for* God" and "dream great dreams *for* God," the emphasis is on dreams and goals that originate from people rather than from God. The danger is in believing that human reasoning can build God's kingdom. It cannot.

Jesus demonstrated this truth throughout his ministry. In the wilderness Satan tried to entice Jesus into using the world's methods to accomplish God's will (Matt. 4:1–11). Satan said in effect, "Provide food, and you'll attract a large following. Use dramatic miracles, and you'll win followers. Worship me, and you'll provide Christianity without a cross." Of course Jesus saw through Satan's guise and recognized his reasoning as unscriptural. In fact, Jesus identified many of the world's commonly accepted principles as being contrary to God's ways. The world says being first is preferable. Jesus said the last shall be first. The world idolizes strength. Jesus said God demonstrates his strength through people's weakness. The world values large numbers. Jesus chose a small group to be his disciples and often ignored the crowds to focus on individuals. The world seeks happiness. Jesus said blessed are they that mourn. The world is attracted to large, spectacular performances. Jesus said his kingdom would be like a mustard seed. The world does good deeds in order to win people's praise. Jesus said, do your good deeds in secret, because the Father will see them and give a reward. The world uses slick marketing campaigns to attract people. Jesus said no one can come to him unless the Father draws them. Over and over again Jesus rejected human reasoning in favor of God's wisdom. What is the difference between human reasoning and God's wisdom? Ephesians 3:20 says: "Now to him who is able to do immeasurably more than all we ask or imagine, according to his power that is at work within us" (NIV).

This Scripture ought to motivate Christian leaders as they seek God's will for their organizations. How significant are our Big Hairy Audacious Goals when viewed in light of this verse? Can leaders impress God with their grandiose visions? Is it possible for a leader to dream any dream that is worthy of God? Can even the most perceptive leader look into the future and determine what would be the most desirable outcome for their organization to achieve? The apostle Paul's words put vision into its proper perspective. God remains unimpressed with leaders' grandiose schemes and dreams because he is able to do immeasurably more than mortals can comprehend. Spiritual leaders who develop their own visions, no matter how extensive, rather than understanding God's will, are settling for their best thinking instead of God's plans. It's a sure way to shortchange their followers.

A poignant account of vision casting is found in Luke 9:51–56:

And it came about, when the days were approaching for His ascension, that He resolutely set His face to go to Jerusalem; and He sent messengers on ahead of Him. And they went, and entered a village of the Samaritans, to make arrangements for Him. And they did not receive Him, because He was journeying with His face toward Jerusalem. And when His disciples James and John saw this, they said, "Lord, do you want us to command fire to come down from heaven and consume them?"

But He turned and rebuked them, and said, "You do not know what kind of spirit you are of; for the Son of Man did not come to destroy men's lives, but to save them." And they went on to another village.

When Jesus and his disciples encountered a rude reception from the Samaritan villagers, how did James and John respond? Call down fire! Incinerate them all! What were these overzealous "Sons of Thunder" thinking? The Bible doesn't say. Perhaps this account reveals racism on the brothers' part, for Jewish people and Samaritans had a mutually contemptuous relationship. Here was an opportunity to destroy an entire community of Samaritans! It is interesting that James and John never suggested such a drastic action against the Pharisees, even after Jesus called them a brood of snakes.

James and John may have had good motives. Perhaps they saw this as an opportunity for Jesus to demonstrate his power so that, in sacrificing one village, many others would come to believe. It could be they were acting out of misguided protectiveness toward Jesus. They would not stand for their Lord to be mistreated. Whatever their reasoning was, Jesus rebuked the brothers. Their best thinking was completely out of line with the Father's plan.

Acts 8:14–17 provides an interesting epilogue to this event. The gospel message began to spread rapidly out from Jerusalem. Word came back to the apostles that the Samaritans were receiving the gospel, so the Jerusalem church sent Peter and John to investigate. One can only imagine what was going through John's mind as he entered the same Samaritan villages he had passed through with Jesus. Perhaps he came upon the village he and James had sought to destroy. This time, rather than fire coming down, the Holy Spirit came down and filled the Samaritan believers. What a contrast! Man's vision for that place would have wreaked total destruction. God's plan produced joyful deliverance. Man's vision would have brought death. God's agenda brought eternal life. There is perhaps no more graphic depiction of the difference between man's best thinking and God's way than in this account. Every time leaders choose to develop their own vision for their people instead of seeking God's will, they are giving their people their best thinking instead of God's. That is a poor exchange indeed.

God's Revelation

The previous six sources of vision have one thing in common—they are all generated by worldly thinking. This is not surprising; *the world functions by vision.* But God does not ask his followers to operate by vision. *God's people live by revelation.* Proverbs 29:18, although widely used, is also widely misapplied. The popular translation is, "Where there is no vision, the people perish" (KJV). A more accurate translation of the Hebrew is: "Where there is no revelation, the people cast off restraint" (NIV). There is a significant difference between revelation and vision. Vision is something people produce; revelation is something people receive. Leaders can dream up a vision, but they cannot discover God's will. God must reveal it. The secular world ignores God's will, so nonbelievers are left with one alternative—to project their own vision. Christians are called to a totally different approach. For Christians, God alone sets the agenda. Throughout the remainder of this book, the term *vision* will continue to be used, but it will not connote the popular idea of a leader-generated goal or dream. Instead, vision will be used to refer to what God has revealed and promised about the future. The visions that drive spiritual leaders must be derived from God.

Wise leaders recognize that life is far too complex to comprehend apart from God's revelation and guidance. Arkansas governor Mike Huckabee has faced this reality many times. Huckabee was a prominent pastor of a twenty-five-hundred-member church in Texarkana. By all accounts he was a successful spiritual leader, yet there was an uneasiness in his soul. In talking with Henry Blackaby, Huckabee acknowledged that God clearly led him to resign his church and enter Arkansas politics. Later, while governor of Arkansas, Huckabee regularly faced situations that were beyond his wisdom to know what to do. Huckabee notes: "Being governor has led me to depend on faith with a new sense of urgency. I face situations every day that would be insurmountable without using the faith God has given me to make decisions."[12] Huckabee's career and leadership of his state was dependent in large part on God's revelation of his will to Huckabee and Huckabee's subsequent response of obedience to what he believed God was revealing. Is it possible for a governor to be led by God's revelation? Certainly!

John Beckett, CEO of R. W. Beckett Corporation, faced a crisis. An Arab oil embargo had caused oil prices to double, dramatically affecting his company's sales of oil heating products. Beckett's competitors followed a predictable course, curtailing sales initiatives, laying off staff, and adopting a siege mentality. Beckett, however, was a part of a men's prayer group that regularly prayed for God's guidance for the company. As they sought God's will for the present situation, they all felt impressed that God was revealing to them that the embargo would be short-lived and that the company should continue with its operations and even increase sales efforts. The group sensed God saying, "Take one day at a time and let me lead." God's guidance, though completely contrary to generally accepted business logic, proved brilliant. The company emerged from the crisis stronger than ever and ready to assume the position as the undisputed leader in their industry. Vision was born out of the revelation of God, not a textbook approach to crisis management.[13]

Yet many Christian leaders adopt the world's approach to vision and miss out on God's way. In seeking to serve God, they inadvertently try to take on the responsibility of God. The truth is, God is on mission to redeem humanity. He is the only one who knows how to do it. Leaders must understand, as Christ did, that their role is to seek the Father's will and to adjust their lives to him. Too often Christian leaders operate under a false sense of assurance that they *are* seeking God's will. Being proactive by nature, leaders want to rush into action. As a result, they don't spend enough time seeking to hear clearly from God. Instead, they simply have a cursory moment of prayer and then begin making their plans. They seek out a few relevant Scriptures and hurry into the goal-setting phase, falsely confident that because they incorporated prayer and Scripture into their goal-setting process, their plans are "of God."

Asking God to set one's goals and to bless one's dreams does not ensure that they are from God. Only God can reveal his plans and he does so in his way, on his time schedule, and to whom he wills. How often do Christian leaders claim to have received their vision from God when in fact they have simply dreamed up the most desirable future they could imagine and then prayed for God to bless their efforts as they set out to achieve it? It is critical for leaders to walk closely with the Father, so they are keenly aware of his revelation and are ready to respond in obedience to his initiatives. The role of spiritual leaders is not to dream up dreams for God but to be the vanguard for their people in understanding God's revelation. The Christian leader is far better described as a servant of God.

The manner in which God leads his people is best understood by examining the Scriptures. When God revealed his plans, he frequently did so in the form of a promise accompanied by vivid imagery. Thus, when God spoke, his people clearly knew what he planned to accomplish and could often describe God's coming activity in rich symbolism. For example, when God revealed to Noah his plans for the earth, God made a promise—he would destroy all the peoples of the earth. He also gave Noah a clear picture of how this promise would be fulfilled—a terrible flood would consume and cover the earth (Gen. 6:17). Noah's ministry of preaching and constructing the ark was not driven by his vision of how he could best serve his community; neither was it his imagining the best possible future for his society. Noah's vision came from God's promise of an imminent flood. After the flood subsided, God made another promise to Noah. This time the symbol of God's promise was a rainbow (Gen. 9:12–13).

God also approached Abraham with a promise. Not only would Abraham have a son in his old age, but God also promised to produce through Abraham a multitude of descendants who would bless all nations of the earth (Gen. 12:1–3). God provided several images to help Abraham grasp the enormity of the promise. Abraham's descendents would be as countless as dust particles (Gen. 13:16), as numerous as the stars (Gen. 15:5), as innumerable as the grains of sand on the seashore (Gen. 22:17). God's revelation to Abraham came as a promise, clothed in vivid imagery.

When God promised to deliver the Israelites from their bondage in Egypt, he referred to a land flowing with milk and honey, giving the downtrodden slaves an inspiring vision of comfort and prosperity (Exod. 3:8). When the risen Christ promised his followers an eternal home in heaven, he used the imagery of a groom coming for his bride and of a spectacular celebration feast (Rev. 19:7–9). God often presents his promises in images that captivate people's imaginations.

An examination of God's promises, as seen through the Scriptures, makes two things obvious: (1) God's promises are impossible to achieve apart from him, and (2) God's promises are absolute. They are not open for discussion or amendment. Apart from a miracle, Abraham could not even become the father of one, let alone the father of a multitude. God supplied the miracle—Isaac, in fulfillment of his promise to Abraham and in accordance with his desire to use Abraham's life for his divine purposes. On the surface, God's promise to Abraham and Sarah was laughable (Gen. 17:17; 18:12). Perhaps that is why they named their child Isaac, meaning "laughter." Then, incredibly, after giving Abraham a son, God commanded him to sacrifice Isaac on an altar. God was telling Abraham to give up what appeared to be the one key ingredient to God's promise. Why? Because the real key to God's promises is not people or physical resources, but God. Abraham needed to understand that, as long as he had an intimate relationship with God, God's promises were assured, no matter how impossible his situation appeared.

Abraham learned that God's promises are perfect. God does not need man's wisdom to help get the job done. On at least two occasions Abraham attempted to modify God's promise in order to make it more attainable. First, Abraham suggested using his adopted son, Eliezer of Damascus, as his heir (Gen. 15:2–3). This was an accepted custom in Abraham's day. But God refused. God's promise was for Abraham's descendent to come through Abraham and Sarah. After living in Canaan for ten years without a child, Abraham then attempted to produce an heir through his servant Hagar (Gen. 16:1–4). Hagar did bear a son, Ishmael, but using him as Abraham's heir was not in accordance with God's promise. Even when Abraham pleaded, "Oh that Ishmael might live before Thee!" God stood firm to his original promise (Gen. 17:18).

Spiritual leaders must resist the temptation to insert their own best thinking where God has promised a miracle. Attempting to hurry the process or to adjust God's plan to make it more achievable are both signs of immature spiritual leadership. Spiritual leaders must continually remind themselves that what God has promised, God will accomplish completely in his time and in his way (Phil. 1:6). The leader's job is to communicate God's promise to the people, not to create the vision and then strive to enlist people to buy in to it.

> ## Sources of Vision
> 1. Because it's there
> 2. Duplicating success
> 3. Vanity
> 4. Need-based
> 5. Available Resources
> 6. Leader-driven
> 7. God's revelation

HOW DOES VISION INSPIRE AND MOVE PEOPLE?

It is undeniable that great visions move people. John F. Kennedy's vision to place a man on the moon by the end of the decade mobilized a nation to accomplish the seemingly impossible. Martin Luther King Jr's "I have a dream" speech on the steps of the Lincoln Memorial before 250,000 people electrified his listeners and shook his nation. Burt Nanus claims, "There is no more powerful engine driving an organization toward excellence and long-range success than an attractive, worthwhile, and achievable vision of the future, widely shared."[14]

The challenge for leaders is to understand how vision can motivate followers to do things they would never attempt otherwise. Vision statements are not enough. Many an office cubicle has an aging poster tacked to the wall, with the company vision statement printed on it. Such statements, generally decreed from the top down, have little effect on those who work for the organization each day. Even when the organizations' members are allowed to give input into the development of vision statements, often this is little more than an exercise wherein the administration merely guides people to a preestablished conclusion.

Many lofty vision statements carry no innate appeal to the people lower down in the organization. Companies can generate goals such as "Five percent gain in market share next year" or "10 percent less waste next year." These goals may be worthwhile, but they do not carry with them any obvious personal benefit to those being asked to do the work.

Churches do the same thing: "10 percent increase in membership" or "reach the second phase of our capital campaign." In reality, visions consisting of numbers rarely have the same impact as a vision involving vivid imagery. As James Champy said, "Numbers by themselves never mobilize anyone but an accountant."[15] Just as God used memorable images to symbolize his promises, so wise spiritual leaders will attempt to put into pictures the promise they believe God has given their organization. Vision must be clear, compelling, and common to all the people.

The problem with many organizations is that they ask their people to make great sacrifices on behalf of puny visions. They encourage their people to give their best but fail to spell out any clear benefit. Moreover, it can appear to those laboring in support of the vision that those benefiting the most from their efforts are the ones promoting the vision. Leaders often fail to appeal to people's innate need to believe they have made a valuable contribution to society. People want their lives to make a difference. George Bernard Shaw's poignant message rings true: "This is true joy in life, the being used up for a purpose recognized by yourself as a mighty one; the being a force of nature instead of a feverish, selfish little clod of ailments and grievances complaining that the world will not devote itself to making you happy. And also the only real tragedy in life is the being used by personally minded men for purposes which you recognize to be base."[16]

To the world, a good vision is an image of something that is both desirable and attainable. The difference between worldly visions and God-given visions is that God-given visions are always impossible to achieve apart from God. In this regard, Christian leaders have a tremendous advantage over secular leaders. People want to be a part of something significant. People want their lives to make a difference in their world. People want to be a part of something God is doing. If it is clear that God has made a promise to a group of people, there should be little difficulty in enlisting the support of group members.

HOW DO LEADERS COMMUNICATE VISION?

Sometimes spiritual leaders spend a lot of energy trying to get their people to "buy in" to their vision because their vision is not from God. In the Christian context, the process of selling a vision is flawed. If a vision must be sold to others, it is not a compelling vision and is probably not from God. Spiritual leaders don't sell vision; they share what God has revealed to them and trust that the Holy Spirit will confirm that same vision in the hearts of their people. Today, Christian leaders often develop a vision for their organizations and then demand the members either get on board or find another organization. This approach could not be further from the New Testament pattern. Spiritual leaders know they cannot change people; only the Holy Spirit can do this. If the Holy Spirit is not convincing people to follow in a new direction, it may be that God is not the author of the new direction. Secular writers agree that selling vision is difficult. Peter Senge observes that "90 percent of the time, what passes for commitment is compliance."[17]

People may change their behavior in response to a leader's encouragement, but that doesn't mean they have changed their core values and beliefs. Values go deep—they will not be altered by a memo or sales pitch—people either believe something or they don't. God's people either hear from God or they don't. Either people have moved on to God's agenda or they haven't.

Establishing that the leader's role is not to set the vision or to sell the vision begs the question: "What *is* the spiritual leader's role?" It is to bear witness to what God says. Spiritual leaders must bring followers into a face-to-face encounter with God so they hear from God directly, not indirectly through their leader. Jesus shared the Father's revelation with his disciples corporately (John 15:15). Spiritual leaders may never convince their people they have heard from God personally, but once their people hear from God themselves, there will be no stopping them from participating in the work God is doing. That is because the Holy Spirit will take the truth, as shared by the leader, and confirm it in the hearts of the people. The leader cannot convince people that a particular direction is from God. This is the Holy Spirit's task.

As people grow in their relationship with God, they will hear from God themselves and want to follow him. No one will have to cajole them or entice them into following. It will be a natural heart response. The key to spiritual leadership, then, is to encourage followers to grow in their relationship with their Lord. This cannot be done by talking about God. It cannot be accomplished by exhorting people to love God. It can only be achieved when leaders bring their people face to face with God and God convinces them that he is a God of love who can be trusted.

We met with an extremely frustrated pastor. Let's call him Jim. Jim believed he knew what God wanted his church to do, but the people refused to follow his leadership. He asked whether we thought he should resign his church and find a group of people who were willing to follow God. We sensed that, in his heart, Jim truly wanted to be involved in God's activity. We empathized with his frustration as his people resisted his efforts to lead them forward. Nevertheless, we had to ask, "Jim, what is it about your leadership that your people are unwilling to follow?" The question caught him by surprise. He had assumed the problem lay with his church members, not with his leadership. What became evident as we talked, however, was that this eager young pastor was not taking the time to help his people grow in their relationship with God. Jim had been asking his church to follow a God they did not know very well.

We advised him to worry less about the people's activity in the church and to concentrate instead on encouraging their walk with God. If their relationship with God grew strong, their obedience would follow. We further encouraged Jim to present his church's activities in terms of what God was doing in their midst, rather than in terms of programs to support or activities to attend. This enthusiastic pastor had been urging his congregation to participate in church outreach events and mission activities, but he had made no connection between what he was asking them to do and the activity of God. Jim was asking his busy people to give up their valuable time to support church programs. Then he wondered why they were not enthusiastically complying. Jim was neglecting an important truth: a church program never changed a life. Only God does that. Church activities are nothing more than busywork unless God initiates them. As people see God at work around them and as they are encouraged to join him, they will demonstrate much more than compliance. They will enthusiastically participate in the things they sense God is doing.

As Jim discovered, people are willing to adjust their lives when they are helped to see God at work. We have observed people make enormous sacrifices in direct response to the activity of God. Doctors have relinquished successful practices for the mission field because they sensed God leading them to do so. We have seen successful businessmen give up lucrative jobs rather than transfer to another city with their companies. Why? Because they would not leave their church at a time when they sensed God was mightily at work. If people are not following a vision, the problem may not lie with the people. For a vision to move people, the people must be convinced the vision is a promise from almighty God and is not merely the dream of an ambitious leader. When people sense they are a part of something God is doing, there is no limit to what they will be willing to do in response.

Communicating Vision Through Symbols

Although leaders should not sell their vision to their people, and although they cannot prove their vision is from God, leaders can relate what they have seen and experienced from God to their people. There are at least two ways leaders communicate vision: by using symbols and telling stories. As the saying goes, "A picture is worth a thousand words." Good symbols can be powerful vehicles for communicating the values and the vision of organizations. For example, we are aware of a new church that is currently renting a public school each week in order to hold services. Their vision is to eventually construct a multipurpose recreation facility. They intend to be a unique kind of church. They will conduct weekly worship services, but they will do much more. They will also provide a wide variety of recreational and educational opportunities to their community each week. There will be an indoor track and an indoor soccer field in their future facility. There will be exercise equipment as well as various seminars on practical subjects offered. The conceptual drawing of their future facility is an important symbol. It is not simply a drawing of a future building. It is a symbol of an entire philosophy of ministry that sets them apart from other churches in their city.

Mahatma Ghandi used symbols for powerful effect to mobilize his followers in their quest to liberate India from British domination. Ghandi adopted the spinning wheel as a symbol of how people in India could pull themselves out of dire poverty. By making homespun products on their spinning wheels, the Indian people could become more economically self-sufficient, and they could boycott British-made products at the same time. Ghandi chose to use salt as a symbol of his people's desire for freedom in their own country. The British had a monopoly on salt in India and made it illegal for Indians to produce it for themselves. In response, Ghandi led the "salt march" beginning March 12, 1930. Hundreds of people marched with him to the sea, where he symbolically picked up some dried salt on the beach. Salt became an electrifying symbol of freedom to the people of India.

Winston Churchill also knew how to use symbols. During England's bleakest moments during World War II, Churchill's upraised hand making the sign for victory became a rallying symbol for his demoralized nation. One of the most memorable images of World War II is that of the determined Churchill holding out his hand in the sign of victory.

When Duncan Campbell, the great revivalist of the Hebrides in Scotland, was visiting Saskatoon, Canada, in 1969, he shared the vision God had given him. He described flames spreading across western Canada. He did not know when this would occur, but the imagery of a great fire sweeping across the Canadian prairies was graphically vivid. Within five years a revival swept across western Canada, and when it came, people recognized that the image God had given Campbell was beginning to be fulfilled.

A helpful exercise for leaders is to attempt to draw a picture of the promise they believe God has given them of the future. It is one thing to describe in words what leaders believe God has promised; it is another to portray it in a symbol. One church's symbol may be a multipurpose church facility. Another church might symbolize their efforts to set people in their community free from sin. Another church might portray their church as a lighthouse in a sin-darkened community. Leaders discover symbols that summarize what the organization believes about itself and its future and use them to communicate their vision to others.

Communicating Vision Through Stories

One of the most effective ways for leaders to relate what God is doing is through the telling of stories. Often when leaders see God at work around their organization, they neglect to relate what has happened to their people. This robs the people of an exciting opportunity to experience the powerful activity of God. It also prevents them from making the connection between what God is doing and their own involvement in the organization. The power of stories is that they appeal both to the mind and the heart. A PowerPoint presentation with a series of graphs appeals to the mind. An impassioned story appeals to both mind and heart. When the people of God are making decisions, it is not enough to simply know in their minds they are making the logical decision. They also need to know in their hearts that God is the author of their activity.

Wise leaders continually help their people see how God is working in their midst. Leaders can do this by telling stories—true stories of how God has worked in the past and how God is working at present. Leaders also link what God has done and is doing with what he has promised to do in the future. Moses did this for his followers. The Book of Deuteronomy is essentially a series of sermons in which Moses recounted to the Israelites all God had done for them up to that point. Joshua, Moses' successor, continued the tradition. In Joshua 24:1–13, the old warrior recalled all that God had done for his people over the years. God spoke through Joshua saying, "I took your father Abraham . . . led him through all the land of Canaan . . . multiplied his descendents . . . I gave Jacob and Esau . . . to Esau I gave Mount Seir . . . I sent Moses and Aaron . . . I plagued Egypt by what I did . . . I brought you out . . . I brought your fathers out . . . I brought you in to the land of the Amorites . . . I gave them into your hand . . . I destroyed them . . . I delivered you . . . I gave them into your hand . . . I sent the hornet . . . I gave you a land." Incredible! Joshua recounted the entire history of the Israelites in a story in which God was the central character. After hearing all that God had done, the people were motivated to move forward to see what God would do next!

When Stephen gave a defense of his faith shortly before his martyrdom, he recited the account of God's activity through the ages (Acts 7:1–53). When the apostle Paul defended his mission work among the Gentiles, he would always recount the story of God's call and commissioning of his life. The Bible is essentially the story of how God has related to mankind throughout history. The telling of stories has always been an essential component to leading God's people.

Howard Gardner claims that leaders are essentially storytellers. But, Gardner notes, "It is important that a leader be a good storyteller, but equally crucial that the leader embody that story in his or her life."[18] The leader is a symbol as well as a "keeper of the stories" concerning what God has been doing in that organization. It is said that revival is spread on the wings of the testimonies of those whose lives have been changed in revival. The leader is both the messenger and the message.

A story is a compelling method of communicating vision. Graphs and charts can convey data and engage people's minds, but a story detailing God's activity in the midst of a secular world can engage people's hearts and gain their commitment. There are at least three kinds of stories leaders need to regularly share with their people.

1. *Stories from the past.* Leaders should relate stories from the past as Moses and Joshua did. What has God done for that organization throughout its history? (Ps. 111:3-4). God's activity is never haphazard. He always builds on what he has done before. Winston Churchill claimed the farther one looked back in history, the farther into the future one could see. Based on that truth, Churchill said he wished Adolph Hitler would read British history so he would know what his fate would be!

2. *Stories for the present.* Leaders should also share stories relating to the present. What is God doing right now? Leaders should never assume their people will automatically make the connection between what is happening in their midst and God's activity. The leader's role is to help people make the connection.

3. *Stories that light the future.* Third, leaders should hold before the people images of the future. God himself did this, using such imagery

as the "land flowing with milk and honey" to help his people grasp the essence of what he was promising. The difference between secular story-telling and God-centered stories is their source. When Coca-Cola envisioned people all over the world drinking a Coca-Cola product, or when Bill Gates envisioned personal computers worldwide using Microsoft products, the images were people-generated for the purpose of making a greater profit and defeating the competition. When spiritual leaders relate stories of the future, they are not simply describing a desirable future. Rather, they are relating what God has indicated he intends to do. For spiritual leaders, all past, present, and future stories should come from God and be God-centered.

A School in Canada

In 1993, Richard became president of a small seminary in Canada. At that time, the school was in critical condition. There were few students. Resources were scarce. Facilities were limited. Some of the school's constituents and donors were becoming hesitant in their support, wondering whether the school would have a legitimate role to play. Richard sensed that God did want to use the school to impact Canada and the world for Christ. Nevertheless, he realized that if people were going to support the work of the seminary, they needed to see that God was actively at work in that place. Richard began to collect a repertoire of stories that demonstrated God's continuing involvement in the school.

During Richard's second year as president, events began to unfold that gave him a compelling story to tell of God's activity in the past year. While Richard was praying for God to show him what he should do as the school president, he received a call from Wilton, a man in Texas, who indicated that his organization felt led by God to construct a new academic building for the seminary. Richard met with Wilton and told him that the building, with volunteer help, would cost $1.4 million. He informed Wilton that the seminary did not have a dime to put into such a project. Wilton smiled and said, "I still believe God is in this." He then told Richard about a godly woman who, if she were willing, could give some significant funds to get the project started. "But," Wilton exclaimed, "I have been trying to talk with her for over three years to see if she would help our organization, but I have never been able to meet with her." The two men prayed and then opened the door to leave the conference room. As the door swung open, it almost knocked over a woman walking down the hall. It was the woman Wilton had just mentioned. She did give generous support, which enabled the project to be completed. During the construction project, Richard would often relate this story to the trustees and seminary staff to reaffirm with them that God had been the author of the project from the very beginning.

During the construction of the facility, several events arose that could have discouraged the many volunteers working at the seminary. These men and women were mostly retirees who could have been enjoying a restful summer. When difficulties arose, it was crucial that everyone connected with the project be reminded that God had not only initiated the project but that he was also sustaining it. One incident that demonstrated this truth occurred while the volunteers were attempting to hang trusses. On the day the trusses were to be hung, a violent wind was blowing. Even for the foothills of the Rocky Mountains, it was unusually strong. Its force was so powerful that the men had to hold on to their hats to keep them from blowing off and disappearing across the field. As the volunteers gathered to pray that morning, they knew their situation was serious. An expensive crane had been rented that was quickly consuming what little building funds there were. To delay hanging the trusses would throw the entire schedule of volunteers into disarray. Everyone knew it would be too dangerous to hang the trusses with the wind blowing as violently as it was. At the close of the prayer time, the men stepped outside. There was an eerie calm. Not a trace of wind. For the next three days, while the trusses were hammered into place, not even a breeze was felt. As the last two trusses were hung, the wind returned and, as the last nail was hammered, the wind was back to full strength.

Richard told that story over and over again. It was more than just a story; it was a dramatic symbol, confirming that the work of the seminary was not something people were doing, but something God was authoring and sustaining. That made all the difference.

As the seminary was completing the academic building, God gave Richard a promise for the future. This promise came in the form of a vivid picture. In the future, as people walked down the hallway of the academic building, they would pass by one classroom where students were studying at the college level, another classroom where students were studying Religious Education at a Master's level, another classroom filled with students in the Master of Divinity program, and still another room where students were doing doctoral work. Richard could have simply concluded, "The seminary needs to expand and diversify its academic programs," but what God gave him was an image that symbolized a promise. Richard repeated this image of the future many times, and it became apparent that others, too, were convinced of God's promise. Richard often heard his professors and staff sharing this vision with visitors to the seminary. In November 1999, this image became a reality.

Leadership Is Communication

You cannot be a poor communicator and a good leader. Max Depree observed: "I learned that if you are a leader and you're not sick and tired of communicating, you probably aren't doing a good enough job."[19] Spiritual leaders don't just tell stories for the sake of telling stories. They rehearse what God has done, they relate what God is doing, and they share what God has promised to do. If the story is about God's activity and promises, the Holy Spirit will affirm its authenticity in people's hearts. People don't have to buy into a vision; they simply have to see that God is making a promise. Leaders cannot grow weary of bearing witness to God's activity. Some stories need to be repeated over and over again so that each member of the organization is familiar with them. Churches ought to have stories that all the members know and recite that remind the people of God's ongoing activity in their midst. As the stories of God's activity are recounted, the people will see that God is the one who has led them thus far, and that God is currently leading them and he has a plan for their future.

CONCLUSION

Vision is crucial for an organization. Its source is God's revelation of his activity. God's revelation can usually be stated as a promise and can be expressed through an image. When leaders successfully communicate vision to their people, it will be God who sets the agenda for the organization, not the leader, and the people will know it is God.

CONCEPTS AND SCRIPTURES FOR CONSIDERATION

- The danger is in believing that human reasoning can build the kingdom of God. It cannot.
- Is it possible to dream any dream that is worthy of God?
- Every time leaders choose to develop their own vision for their people, instead of seeking God's will, they are giving their people their best thinking instead of God's.
- The world functions by vision; God's people live by revelation.
- Vision is something people produce; revelation is something people receive.
- Leaders can dream up a vision, but they cannot discover God's will. God must reveal it.
- The role of spiritual leaders is not to dream up dreams for God, but to be the vanguard for their people in understanding God's revelation.
- When God revealed his plans, he frequently did so in the form of a promise accompanied by vivid imagery.
- God's promises are impossible to achieve apart from him.
- The real key to God's promises is not people or physical resources, but God.
- The problem with many organizations is that they ask their people to make great sacrifices on behalf of puny visions.
- People want to be a part of something God is doing.
- Spiritual leaders cannot prove that God has spoken to them. They can only bear witness to what God said. The key to spiritual leadership is bringing your people into a face-to-face encounter with God so that they hear from God directly and not indirectly through you.
- If you have to "sell" your vision and are having to encourage people to "buy in" to it, then perhaps the vision is not from God.

Proverbs 29:18
Isaiah 55:8–9
Ephesians 3:20
Luke 9:51–56
Joshua 24:1–13
Genesis 12:1–3; 13:16; 15:5; 17:17; 18:12; 22:17
Psalm 111:3–4
Mark 1:23-39; John 5:17; 19–20
John 15:15

CHAPTER FIVE

The Leader's Character
A Life That Moves Others to Follow

"I HAVE MET MANY OF THE GREAT MEN of my time, but Lee alone impressed me with the feeling that I was in the presence of a man who was cast in a grander mold, and made of different and finer metal than all other men."[1] This was the observation of Field Marshall Viscount Wolseley after he met Robert E. Lee. Lee's leadership is fascinating because even though he was grossly underequipped in both manpower and supplies, he rarely lost a battle. Even more impressive is that, though they were overwhelmingly outnumbered and though they received few benefits, his soldiers were fiercely loyal to him throughout the Civil War. Even when the war was lost and it was futile to resist the vastly larger and better-equipped Union army, Lee's soldiers were prepared to continue fighting if he would only give the orders.

What inspired such loyalty among Lee's followers? One thing is certain: it was not his rank as general. Other generals did not enjoy such loyalty from their troops. Nor was it Lee's ability to court-martial traitors; he was generally loath to do it. It is best concluded the key was Lee *himself.* Lee's soldiers followed him because of who he was.

Certainly all leaders would desire such loyalty from their followers. The predominant challenge for leaders is how to get people to follow them. Leaders without followers are not leaders. Yet many would-be leaders fail because they cannot inspire people to follow them. We have encountered many frustrated would-be leaders who had noble aspirations and grandiose dreams but who could not enlist anyone to support them or their vision. For some people, the greatest challenge is becoming the kind of person that others want to follow.

The issue of influence is critical, especially in Christian leadership. In people's attempts to enlist a following, some have resorted to developing the appearance of a leader rather than developing the character of a leader. It has never been easier to create the image of a leader than it is today. In contemporary society, someone who writes a book or earns a doctorate is immediately labeled as an expert. Professional consultants provide "reputation management" for aspiring leaders to create the perception that they are genuinely qualified to lead. With the right kind of help, people can generate a lot of hype, but they are really only pseudo leaders. They have image but no substance.

Illegitimate Sources of Influence

The catchword for leadership today is *influence*. But how do people achieve influence over others? Personal influence can come from several sources, some legitimate, others questionable. Influence in itself is not evidence of true leadership if that influence is gained improperly. Following are three illegitimate ways people gain influence over others.

Position

Previous generations generally associated authority and influence with position. Bosses were automatically respected by virtue of their position. In spiritual matters, people trusted their ministers implicitly and offered them reverence as a matter of course. As a result, would-be leaders pursued positions and offices of prominence in order to gain the respect they desired. Each promotion up the corporate ladder rewarded ambitious executives with greater accolades from those a rung or two below them. Each call to a larger, more prestigious church brought greater dignity to the aspiring minister.

This manner of gaining influence through one's station has inherent flaws. For one, this approach lends itself to flagrant abuses. People can achieve influential positions without developing a character to match their assignment. People who use political or unethical means to acquire positions lack the integrity they need to maintain the respect of those they lead. Moreover, those yearning for recognition and approval from others rarely find that positions of authority fill the void in their lives that drove them to achieve their status in the first place. They inadvertently sought a worldly remedy for a spiritual problem. Both the secular and the spiritual realms see countless men and women erroneously trying to satisfy their empty souls by amassing a following. Why are we shocked to hear about successful CEOs who commit suicide? Why are we scandalized to discover the pastor of a megachurch has committed adultery? We have accepted the false assumption that those in high positions have achieved their status based on sound character. Clearly this is not always a safe assumption.

The sad truth is that many Christian organizations and churches are led by people who sought an office for all the wrong reasons. These people directly associated the size of their ministry with their own self-worth. Oswald Sanders asked, "Should it not be the office that seeks the man, rather than the man the office?"[2] Much of the writing on contemporary society argues that the age of automatic respect for hierarchy is gone. This is the age of the "knowledge worker." Knowledge is the currency of today's workplace. To gain knowledge, one must have an education. Today, people are not so impressed with titles and positions as were their less-educated predecessors. In previous generations, the local minister was often the most educated person in the community. Today, average church members often have as much or more training and experience in their fields as pastors have in theirs. These educated church members have access to Bibles in numerous translations, as well as software that holds more scriptural information than traditional ministers have typically possessed in their entire libraries. The Christian community is inundated with information. No longer do congregations meekly accept the minister's word unchallenged. Church members now have the knowledge with which to critique their minister's views. In both the secular and the religious domains, the assumption that position guarantees respect is no longer valid.

If there are any leaders who should not rely upon their position for their influence, it is spiritual leaders. Spiritual leadership is based on the work of the Holy Spirit and on spiritual character. Without the guiding, empowering presence of the Spirit, leaders may hold positions but they will not be spiritual leaders. The Holy Spirit will not confirm their authority with their people. For example, gaining a position as the pastor of a church does not make one Spirit-filled. Graduating from seminary does not make one a spiritual leader. Holding a leadership position in a Christian organization does not automatically come with God's anointing. Many a misguided minister started out with the mistaken assumption that people would follow his leadership merely because he was their pastor. Then, when the congregation refused to follow, the disgruntled pastor assumed the people were unspiritual and left to find a more "spiritually responsive" church. Some leaders, realizing that position alone doesn't automatically bring them authority, will pursue influence over their people by using force and manipulation. Such insidious bullying carries with it even more disastrous consequences.

Power

When Margaret Thatcher won a monumental third victory as prime minister of Great Britain during the 1980s, she seemed an invincible political force. But members of her party chafed under a leader with such strong convictions. Ultimately her own party, not the opposition, forced her to resign. Once people chose not to follow, the most successful British leader of her era could no longer lead.

Mao Tse-tung claimed power came from a gun. He was unapologetic about using force to achieve his goals. However, even totalitarian rulers ultimately govern on the basis of their people's willingness to submit to them. People give authority to leaders when they choose to follow them. This phenomenon was clearly evident in the downfall of communism in Eastern Europe. Communism was one of the most effective systems of totalitarian government in history, yet it could not withstand the popular will of the people once they refused to follow.

The business world has realized that it cannot operate with a totalitarian mind-set. There was a time when dominant business leaders such as Henry Ford could bully labor movements and make arrogant statements such as, "Customers can have a car in any color they want, as long as it's black." That time is past. Max Depree goes so far as to argue that business leaders must treat their top employees as volunteers.[3] The current state of the economy gives valuable employees clout because they can usually find another job. These employees are not forced to stay with the company; they *choose* to stay where they are as long as the company is in harmony with their personal values. To impose authority and submission on such people is to risk losing valuable personnel to the competition.

Christian leaders also invite rebellion when they use force to achieve their organizational goals. The my-way-or-the-highway approach fares no better in the church than in business. Pastors have used numerous strong-arm tactics to get their way. Some have volatile tempers. They are charming and cordial as long as church members submit to their leadership. But when challenged, they become angry and lambaste anyone who dares oppose them. Others use the pulpit as a soapbox from which to castigate those who disagree with them. Some church leaders lobby for support from influential church members as if they were seeking to get a bill passed through Congress. Some are so misguided that they ostracize their detractors, treating them as wolves rather than as sheep in need of a shepherd. Pastors who bully their people into submission will eventually find themselves in one of two positions: preaching to empty seats or searching the want ads. Incredibly, when this happens, many pastors will still stubbornly blame the people for refusing to follow their God-appointed leader.

Spiritual dictatorships can be the most oppressive form of tyranny. It is one thing to dominate people because you have an organizational chart on your side, but it is quite another to manipulate people because you claim to have God on your side. Some Christian leaders believe that God delegates his authority to leaders and that followers are obligated to submit to them unquestioningly as if they were obeying God.

Watchman Nee, the great Chinese Christian leader and writer, set forth this view in his book *Spiritual Authority*. Nee maintained that God delegates his authority to human leaders. Thus he claimed: "We do not obey man but God's authority in that man."[4] Nee alleged that the key responsibility of followers was unquestioning obedience to their spiritual leaders. He concluded, "Henceforth authority alone is factual to me; reason and right and wrong no longer control my life"[5] Nee explained his position this way: "People will perhaps argue, 'What if the authority is wrong?' The answer is, If God dares to entrust His authority to men, then we can dare to obey. Whether the one in authority is right or wrong does not concern us, since he has to be responsible directly to God. The obedient needs only to obey; the Lord will not hold us responsible for any mistaken obedience, rather He will hold the delegated authority responsible for his erroneous act. Insubordination, however, is rebellion, and for this the one under authority must answer to God."[6]

It is easy to see how dictatorial leaders could abuse this teaching in order to justify their tyrannical leadership style. Cult groups demand absolute obedience to their leaders. They denounce independent thought by their followers. Nothing could be more unbiblical! Christians are commanded to voluntarily submit to those in positions of authority because God has, out of his sovereignty, allowed those leaders to hold office (Rom. 13:1–2). But people are not to obey leaders blindly and unquestioningly, simply because of the position they hold. Scripture is clear that all people must give an account to Christ for everything they have done, regardless of who told them to do it (2 Cor. 5:10). Christ does not need a mediator to exercise his lordship over people. The Holy Spirit dwells within every believer, leaders and followers alike, guiding, teaching, and convicting every Christian. When leaders claim that God bypasses their followers and speaks directly to them, they greatly diminish all God does through the lives of believers. God does appoint leaders into secular as well as religious leadership positions. To rebel against such leadership is to reject what God has done in appointing that leader. Nevertheless, while God may choose to work through leaders to accomplish his purposes, obeying a leader is not necessarily equal to obeying God. God will tolerate no substitutes for a personal relationship with him. He exercises his lordship directly over his followers. People who obey leaders as though they were responding to God are in danger of committing idolatry.

As mentioned in chapter 3, insecurity and a need for affirmation drive some people to seek leadership positions. A telling sign of such leaders is their intolerance toward anyone who challenges them. Insecure leaders find it much simpler to label their opponents as unspiritual or rebellious than to actually examine the truth of their critics' words. Sometimes people refuse to follow a leader's vision because they want to hear from God directly, and not second hand. Leaders who begrudge people the opportunity to seek God themselves and who do not actively teach their people how to hear God's voice have disqualified themselves as spiritual leaders.

Personality

As every child learns, there is usually more than one way to get what you want. If it doesn't come automatically (position) and if bullying doesn't work (power), you can always turn on the charm! (personality). People often follow leaders strictly because of their charisma and winsome personalities. The popularity of a leader is not in itself a bad thing, but it cannot be the only thing. Leaders must offer more to their people than charm. Followers need competence and a sense of direction from their leaders. Countless businesses have been led to ruin by silver-tongued CEOs who were impressive, but incompetent. Churches have blindly voted to follow their pastors into disastrous projects because they loved their leader, not because they heard from God. Numerous churches have ultimately dismissed their pastors with this sad commentary: "We loved our pastor. He was a wonderful Christian. He just couldn't lead!" By itself, an engaging personality is not enough to constitute spiritual leadership.

Collins and Porras, in their book *Built to Last*, concluded that the contention that "visionary companies require great and charismatic visionary leaders" is a myth. On the contrary, they determined that "a charismatic visionary leader is absolutely *not required* for a visionary company and, in fact, can be detrimental to a company's long-term prospects."[7] Great leaders, they discovered, built great organizations, not necessarily great reputations. When organizations are built around the personality of a leader, not only is the organization susceptible to the weaknesses and whims of its leader, but it also faces an inevitable crisis when the leader leaves the organization. When a church plummets in attendance after its pastor leaves or a company's profits significantly decline after the CEO resigns, this may indicate the organization was built more on personality than on a healthy process or product.

This important principle is relevant for churches seeking new pastors. Christ said *he* would build his church (Matt. 16:18). In order to thrive, churches do not need leaders who exude charm. In fact, choosing a pastor based solely on personality is choosing to build a church on a person rather than on Christ. Often pastor search committees erroneously look for a striking and charismatic personality whose allure will attract new members. They value charisma over consecration as the preeminent quality in a potential candidate. But personality without purpose and charm without competence are recipes for ruin. Pastors who function more on personality than on true leadership qualities rarely stay in one place for long. They typically breeze into a church, preach through their small repertoire of sermons and then, as their charm begins to wear thin, move on. They seldom accomplish anything of substance. They make a great first impression but rarely leave lasting results.

Position, power, and personality are all misconceived sources of influence for leaders. What then are the standards by which true spiritual leaders can be measured? Christian leaders should demonstrate specific characteristics that confirm their legitimacy as spiritual leaders.

Illegitimate Sources of Influence

1. Position
2. Power
3. Personality

LEGITIMATE SOURCES OF INFLUENCE

God's Authentication

There are several ways leaders can exert influence on others through their life, but none is as powerful as when God chooses to affirm leaders before the eyes of their people. The first and most important test of legitimacy for spiritual leaders is God's authentication. There are numerous biblical and secular examples of men and women whom God affirmed as genuine spiritual leaders.

Moses. Arguably the greatest leader in Old Testament history was Moses. However, he could not attribute his success to his own leadership abilities, for he was not naturally gifted as a leader. By his own admission, he was a poor public speaker (Exod. 4:10); he was inept at delegating (Exod. 18:13–27); he had a temper problem (Exod. 32:19; Num. 20:9–13). Worst of all, he was a murderer. Nevertheless, Moses' accomplishments as a spiritual leader came from the depth of his relationship with God, not from the strength of his personality. Scripture indicates that "the Lord used to speak to Moses face to face, just as a man speaks to his friend" (Exod. 33:11). The Israelites recognized Moses' close walk with God. Whenever Moses would descend from the mountain after meeting with God, his face would glow with the glory of God (Exod. 34:29–35). God's presence in Moses' life was unmistakable!

Significantly, despite his close relationship with the Lord, Moses was not a proud or arrogant leader. In fact, Scripture indicates: "Moses was very humble, more than any man who was on the face of the earth" (Num. 12:3). Moses was so demure that when Aaron and Miriam criticized him, it was the Lord who came to his defense, rebuking his companions for their insolence: "Hear now My words: If there is a prophet among you, I, the Lord, shall make Myself known to him in a vision. I shall speak with him in a dream. Not so, with My servant Moses, He is faithful in all My household; With him I speak mouth to mouth, Even openly, and not in dark sayings, And he beholds the form of the LORD. Why then were you not afraid to speak against My servant, Moses?" (Num. 12:6–8).

Moses was not defensive. He didn't need to be. He did not demand respect or act with a heavy hand. This could be why God chose to honor him before the people. Moses could have appealed to his position of authority to gain peoples' respect. He could have lost his temper or attacked his detractors. Moses did neither. God's methods of authenticating his leaders are far more convincing. Leaders who become preoccupied with defending themselves and their reputations display an acute lack of faith, for they do not trust God to authenticate them as spiritual leaders. Some people are constantly seeking to have their friends and associates promote them before others. True leaders don't need to do this. They know that God's approval surpasses any honor that people could bestow on them. Likewise, true leaders do not despair when people conspire against them. Those who are secure in their relationship with God know that the antagonism of their fiercest foe cannot prevent them from achieving God's purposes for their lives (Rom. 8:31).

Joshua. Stepping into the shoes of a popular and successful leader can be a disconcerting experience. Most people would feel somewhat inadequate when asked to assume a position vacated by a celebrated and revered leader. Joshua had plenty of reasons to feel insecure when God called him to lead the Israelites into Canaan. He faced powerful, hostile armies. His enemies were well equipped with iron chariots and fortified cities. And his predecessor had been Moses, the most famous and respected figure in Israelite history. No wonder God gave Joshua the following assurances:

> "No man will be able to stand before you all the days of your life. Just as I have been with Moses, I will be with you; I will not fail you or forsake you. Be strong and courageous, for you shall give this people possession of the land which I swore to their fathers to give them. Only be strong and very courageous; be careful to do according to all the law which Moses My servant commanded you; do not turn from it to the right or to the left, so that you may have success wherever you go. This book of the law shall not depart from your mouth, but you shall meditate on it day and night, so that you may be careful to do according to all that is written in it; for then you will make your way prosperous, and then you will have success. Have I not commanded you? Be strong and courageous! Do not tremble or be dismayed, for the LORD your God is with you wherever you go" (Josh. 1:5–9).

God did not flatter Joshua, nor did he encourage Joshua to draw confidence from his own strengths and abilities. Rather, God made it abundantly clear to Joshua that he need not fear his own inadequacies because God would be in control. Joshua could lead the Hebrew nation with absolute confidence, not in his own leadership skills, but in the assurance of the Lord's presence.

Even the Israelites understood who their true leader was. They did not ask Joshua to lead like Moses. They did not compare the two leaders according to their strengths and weaknesses. Instead they pledged:

"Just as we obeyed Moses in all things, so we will obey you; only may the LORD Your God be with you as he was with Moses" (Josh. 1:17). By this time the people had seen enough miracles to know whom they were following—not a man but God himself. More than anything else, people are looking for spiritual leaders who are clearly experiencing God's presence. There is no greater source of influence for spiritual leaders than the manifest presence of God in their lives.

True to his word, God did work mightily through Joshua. As the Israelites prepared to cross the Jordan River, God reaffirmed his promise to Joshua: "This day I will begin to exalt you in the sight of all Israel, that they may know that just as I have been with Moses, I will be with you" (Josh. 3:7). Leaders do not have to prove God is guiding them. God's presence will be unmistakable. Joshua had no need to prove himself continually to the people. God did that. Whenever Joshua led the people into battle, God placed a crippling fear in the hearts of Israel's enemies (Josh. 2:11). When the Israelites fought, God caused the enemy soldiers to be routed (Josh. 23:10). God miraculously intervened so Joshua's army was victorious (Josh. 6:20; 10:13). Everyone could see that God supported Joshua and his army. There was no question that Joshua's army was victorious because of God's mighty presence. As Joshua came to the end of his life, he recounted God's faithfulness: "Now behold, today I am going the way of all the earth, and you know in all your hearts and in all your souls that not one word of all the good words which the LORD your God spoke concerning you has failed; all have been fulfilled for you, not one of them has failed" (Josh. 23:14).

Joshua had not embarked on a quest for military glory and fame. God gave it to him. Joshua owed every achievement and victory to God. Joshua's success as a leader clearly came from God. God was the one with the ability. Joshua's part was to live in obedience to God. The lesson for leaders is obvious: spiritual success is not defined in terms of ability—it is a matter of obedience.

Samuel. The entire Bible reveals a consistent pattern in the way God relates to his people: "Those who honor Me I will honor, and those who despise Me will be lightly esteemed" (1 Sam. 2:30). Eli the priest dishonored the Lord by the way he led his family, and God rejected him in favor of Samuel. Scripture indicates: "Samuel was growing in stature and in favor both with the LORD and with men" (1 Sam. 2:26).

In turn, God honored Samuel as long as Samuel honored him. Scripture reveals an interesting thing about the way God worked through Samuel. We are told "the LORD was with him and let none of his words fail" (1 Sam. 3:19). Whenever Samuel spoke to people, God guaranteed that the words Samuel spoke came to pass. What an awesome confirmation from God! Whenever Samuel declared what God promised, it always happened. That gave Samuel unmistakable authority every time he spoke. Ultimately, when the Israelites refused to heed Samuel's instructions, God vindicated Samuel and fulfilled all Samuel predicted. Like Joshua, Samuel refused to demand respect from the people, and, like Joshua, he was greatly venerated.

Deborah. Deborah served as a judge of God's people during a dangerous and turbulent period in Israel's history. God bestowed such wisdom on Deborah that people would come from far away to the hill country of Ephraim to seek her judgment. When Israel's enemies oppressed them, Deborah counseled Balak, the commander of Israel's army, on how God would give his forces victory over their oppressors. Despite this assurance, Balak responded to Deborah that he would go to battle only on one condition: "If you will go with me, then I will go; but if you will not go with me, I will not go" (Judg. 4:8). Deborah was not trained in military tactics, nor was she a valiant warrior, but Balak recognized God's dynamic presence in her life. He concluded that Deborah's presence in his army meant God's presence. Balak realized his army would not be successful without God's involvement on its side.

Jesus. Jesus Christ exemplified the unpretentious life the heavenly Father honors in his servants. The only person in history with justifiable reason to exalt himself was the Lord Jesus, God's only Son. Yet he chose to live and die in extreme humility. It was the Father who continually affirmed his Son, as at Jesus' baptism, when God proclaimed in an audible voice: "This is My beloved Son, in whom I am well-pleased" (Matt. 3:17). Likewise, on the Mount of Transfiguration when Peter attempted to step in and take charge of that sacred moment, the Father, not the Son, intervened: "This is My Son, My Chosen One; listen to Him!" (Luke 9:35).

Throughout Jesus' life, at his death, and finally through the resurrection, God the Father exalted his Son—Jesus never promoted himself, even when Satan tried to entice him to do so. This is the pattern of true spiritual leadership. When spiritual leaders pursue the praise and respect of others, they may achieve their goal, but they also have their reward in full. Some people solicit awards, positions, and honors from others. If they succeed, they will be esteemed but their honor will come from people, not God. Those who seek God's affirmation receive a true and lasting honor. There is no comparison between the fleeting praise of people and the esteem of God.

Charles Finney. When God is pleased with a leader's life, his divine presence is unmistakable. Charles G. Finney was a nineteenth-century evangelist whose life demonstrated the obvious presence of God. During a visit to New York Mills in 1826, he visited a cotton manufacturing plant where his brother-in-law was superintendent. As Finney passed through a spacious room in which many women were working at looms and spinning jennies, he noticed several young women watching him and speaking among themselves. As Finney approached them, they became more agitated. When Finney was about ten feet away, one woman sank to the ground and burst into tears. Soon others were sobbing, overcome with conviction of their sin. This outpouring of the Spirit spread rapidly throughout the building until the entire factory was singularly aware of God's presence. The owner, an unbeliever, realized God was at work and temporarily closed the plant. He asked Finney to preach to his employees and tell them how they might find peace for their souls. Finney had not spoken to any of the laborers. He had simply entered the factory. God's powerful presence in Finney's life had been too overwhelming to ignore.[8]

When God chooses to exalt one of his servants, the world sits up and takes notice. The secular leader Abimilech and his military commander Phicol conceded to Abraham: "God is with you in all that you do" (Gen. 21:22). When King Solomon ruled over Israel, the wisdom God gave him was so famous that the queen of Sheba traveled to Jerusalem to meet him and to pay him homage (1 Kings 10:1–10). World leaders long recognized Billy Graham as possessing divine wisdom. Graham's ministry to political and economic leaders has spanned over half a century as numerous powerful secular figures have sought him out for spiritual counsel. When President George Bush ordered the commencement of the Persian Gulf War on January 16, 1991, he asked Graham to sit with him at the White House to receive the initial reports of the battle. The army was the most well-equipped and modern army the world had seen. Bush had some of the most brilliant military and diplomatic minds at his disposal, yet the commander in chief chose a recognized spiritual leader as his companion during the tense moments of the outbreak of war.[9]

God's authentication. It is imperative for spiritual leaders to evaluate their lives to determine whether God is confirming their leadership. There should be ample evidence of God's affirmation. For one thing, God will fulfill his promises to the leader and the leader's organization. Leaders who continually present new ideas and visions for the future but who never see those dreams come to fruition are clearly presenting their own visions and not God's.

Second, when God affirms a leader, God will vindicate that person's reputation over time. All leaders suffer criticism during the course of their work. Criticism is not necessarily a sign of poor leadership. It may stem from people resisting God rather than rejecting the leader. The way to tell the difference is that God will ultimately exculpate those who are led by the Spirit.

A third sign of God's presence in a leader is changed lives. When someone leads in the Spirit's power, lives are changed. People are moved to experience God in a new dimension. Leaders may entertain people, or impress people, or even motivate people, but if there is no spiritual advancement in the people they lead, their leadership originates from the leader's talent, but not necessarily from God.

A fourth characteristic of God-inspired leadership is that others recognize God as the driving force behind the leader's agenda. When God chooses a leader who is willing to submit to his will and to trust him to do what he promises, God is pleased to work powerfully through that leader. If nothing unusual or divine is happening under a person's leadership, the leader may be operating in his own strength rather than by the power of the Holy Spirit. Leaders who are led by God will be willing to lead their people to accept God-sized assignments. Leaders who walk by sight, however, will never see God perform miracles as leaders will who walk by faith.

Finally, the unmistakable mark of leaders who are authenticated by God is that they are like Christ. They function in a Christlike manner and those who follow them become more like Christ. The success of a spiritual leader is not measured in dollars, percentages, numbers, or attendance. A person is truly a spiritual leader when others are moved to be more like Christ.

How does one attain God's authentication? The key lies not in the leader, but in God. There is nothing a leader can do that will guarantee God's affirmation. All a leader can do is submit. Some spiritual leaders try to be more committed. What they need is to be more submitted. There is a significant difference between a personal determination to try harder and a complete abandonment of one's self to God's purposes. The former rests on people and their commitment; the latter relies on God and his sufficiency. The biographies of history's greatest spiritual leaders reveal specific divine encounters wherein these men and women yielded themselves to God at the deepest levels of their lives. All spiritual leaders have a point in their lives when they yield to Christ as their Lord and Savior, but the greatest leaders also have subsequent encounters with Christ in which they fervently, unconditionally yield every aspect of their lives to him. The more these people come to know God, the more they recognize their own limitations and the more compelled they are to yield to God.

Encounters with God

People do not choose to become spiritual leaders. Spiritual leadership flows out of a person's vibrant, intimate relationship with God. You cannot be a spiritual leader if you are not meeting God in profound, life-changing ways.

Charles Finney had a unique encounter with Christ that propelled him to become one of the greatest evangelists in American history. As a young lawyer, Finney entered the woods near his home and experienced conversion. That same week, in his law office, he had a further encounter with Christ that, while not a conversion experience, forever changed his life:

All my feelings seemed to rise and flow out and the thought of my heart was, "I want to pour my whole soul out to God." The rising of my soul was so great that I rushed into the room back of the front office to pray. . . . As I went in and shut the door after me, it seemed as if I met the Lord Jesus Christ face to face. . . . He said nothing, but looked at me in such a manner as to break me right down at his feet. It seemed to me a reality that he stood before me, and I fell down at his feet and poured out my soul to him. I wept aloud like a child and made such confessions as I could with my choked words. It seemed to me that I bathed his feet with my tears . . . I received a mighty baptism of the Holy Spirit. Without any expectation of it, without ever having the thought in my mind that there was any such thing for me, without any memory of ever hearing the thing mentioned by any person in the world, the Holy Spirit descended upon me in a manner that seemed to go through me, body and soul. I could feel the impression like a wave of electricity, going through and through me. Indeed it seemed to come in waves of liquid love, for I could not express it in any other way. It seemed like the very breath of God. I can remember distinctly that it seemed to fan me, like immense wings.

No words can express the wonderful love that was spread abroad in my heart. I wept aloud with joy and love. I literally bellowed out the unspeakable overflow of my heart. These waves came over me, and over me, one after another, until I remember crying out, "I shall die if these waves continue to pass over me." I said, "Lord, I cannot bear any more," yet I had no fear of death.[10]

So profound was Finney's encounter with God that his life was forever changed. Finney went on to become the greatest evangelist of his day.

Dwight L. Moody was experiencing great success as the director of the YMCA in Chicago. Moreover, he was pastor of a thriving church. Moody had gathered a team of committed Christian leaders around him, including the gifted singer, Ira Sankey. By all appearances Moody was a successful minister of the gospel. Then in June 1871, Mrs. Sarah Anne Cooke and Mrs. Hawxhurst sat in the front row of the church and diligently prayed during the service. Moody approached them to ask the reason for such fervent prayer. They told him they were praying for him because they sensed he needed the power of the Spirit in his life and ministry. A change began to take place in Moody. He confessed, "There came a great hunger into my soul. I did not know what it was. I began to cry out as I never did before. I really felt that I did not want to live if I could not have this power for service." Moody asked the two women to pray with him every Friday afternoon until he had received the powerful anointing of the Holy Spirit.

Moody finally yielded every part of his life and will to his Lord. Suddenly, he felt the overwhelming presence of God in an unprecedented manner. Moody quickly found a room in which he could be alone with God. "The room seemed ablaze with God. He dropped to the floor and lay bathing in the Divine. Of this Communion, this mount of transfiguration," Moody said, "'I can say that God revealed Himself to me, and I had such an experience of His love that I had to ask Him to stay his hand.'"11

It was only a few months later, while in England, that Moody heard Henry Varley's challenging words: "Moody, the world has yet to see what God will do with a man fully consecrated to him." Moody was prepared to be that man, and God used him to become the greatest evangelist of the late-nineteenth century.

Billy Graham was thirty years old when he reached a crossroad in his life. His good friend and colleague, Charles Templeton, had abandoned many of the beliefs that he and Graham had formerly shared. Now Templeton ridiculed Graham for his faith. Although Graham was a successful college president and itinerant evangelist, the core of his life and ministry had been shaken. If those who had been closest to him were abandoning their fidelity to the Bible and its teachings, was he naïve to continue trusting them as he had in his youth?

> As that night wore on, my heart became heavily burdened. With the Los Angeles campaign galloping toward me, I had to have an answer. If I *could not* trust the Bible, I could not go on. I would have to quit the school presidency. I would have to leave pulpit evangelism. I was only thirty years of age. It was not too late to become a dairy farmer. But that night I believed with all my heart that the God who had saved my soul would never let go of me. . . .

"O God! There are many things in this book I do not understand. There are many problems with it for which I have no solution. There are many seeming contradictions. There are some areas in it that do not seem to correlate with modern science. I can't answer some of the philosophical and psychological questions Chuck and others are raising." . . . At last the Holy Spirit freed me to say it. "Father, I am going to accept this as Thy Word—by *faith!* I am going to allow faith to go beyond my intellectual questions and doubts, and I will believe this to be Your inspired Word." When I got up from my knees at Forest Home that August night, my eyes stung with tears. I sensed the presence and power of God as I had not sensed it in months. Not all my questions had been answered, but a major bridge had been crossed. In my heart and mind, I knew a spiritual battle in my soul had been fought and won.[12]

It was the Los Angeles campaign shortly after this event that launched his career into international prominence. Before God elevated him into a prominent international figure, Graham yielded himself to God to a degree that many of his colleagues were unwilling to do. This deepened sense of yielding everything to the lordship of Christ has been the turning point for many of history's greatest spiritual leaders.

The common factor in the experience of Finney, Moody, and Graham was their total submission to God. They did not need to be more resolved to seek God's will; they needed to be more yielded in faith to trust God and to do his will. With their absolute submission to God came a profound assurance of God's presence. Their phenomenal success as spiritual leaders was not based on their superior oratorical abilities, or on their organizational genius. Rather, their amazing success as spiritual leaders can be traced to their consummate submission to Christ. These people went far deeper than the initial submission most Christians experience at their conversion. They, and many others like them, determined that if they were to follow Christ, they would do so with abandon. They determined to hold nothing back from Christ's absolute lordship over their lives. God was pleased with their humble submission and chose to exercise his power dramatically through their lives. Most spiritual leaders never reach this depth of submission to God. Many make commitments; few offer absolute submission. God continues to look for those who are radically yielded to him in every part of life so he may reveal his power to a watching world.

Character/Integrity

In previous generations, the public was not generally aware of their leader's personal life, and so leader's personal failures were not usually considered when evaluating their job performance. A drinking problem at home was considered a personal matter as long as the employee kept sober on the job. Prominent politicians could live immorally, yet their deceit was not widely known and not considered to significantly detract from their leadership ability. Today most leadership experts agree that character, or integrity, is foundational to business and leadership success.

Kouzes and Posner, in extensive studies of employees from across the United States, asked people what they most valued and admired in their leaders. Over the years, the trait that has consistently topped the list has been honesty.[13] Employees have counted honesty in their leaders as more important than vision, competence, accomplishments, and the ability to inspire others. We conducted an informal survey for this book; we asked various CEOs of major companies what they looked for in a potential employee. Almost every one cited integrity as the number one qualification. John Beckett of the Beckett Corporation explained: "The chief trait I look for is integrity. . . . I believe if this trait is embraced and in place, other qualities such as honesty, diligence, and a good work ethic will follow."

The fact that integrity is mutually desired by both employers and employees should come as no surprise. Leadership is ultimately based on trust. Since people choose to follow leaders they trust, their confidence must have a foundation. The foundation is honesty. In a follow-up book, Kouzes and Posner use another term to describe integrity in a leader: credibility. They claim that "credibility is the foundation of leadership. Period."[14] They go on to say, "The ultimate test of leaders' credibility is whether they do what they say."[15]

Spiritual leaders, of all people, ought to be known for their honesty. Yet many are not. In fact, there is a cynical suspicion among much of the public that most prominent spiritual leaders are hypocrites and charlatans. Media coverage continually exposes high-profile religious leaders who deceived the public about their finances and their moral lives. On a local level, many ministers think nothing of embellishing the truth or misrepresenting the facts to present their view to their congregation in the best possible light. They distort reality with the misguided justification that exaggerating the truth will impress people and will attract them to Christianity as well as to their leadership. When people see their leader stretching the truth or strategically glossing over problems, they lose confidence in that leader. Followers don't expect their leaders to be perfect, but they do expect them to be honest.

Both secular and Christian leaders realize that integrity must be paramount in the life of a leader. Max Depree claims: "Integrity in all things precedes all else. The open demonstration of integrity is essential; followers must be wholeheartedly convinced of their leader's integrity. For leaders, who live a public life, perceptions become a fact of life."[16] The dictionary definition of integrity is: "A firm attachment to moral or artistic principle; honesty and sincerity; uprightness; wholeness, completeness; the condition of being unmarred or uncorrupted, the original, perfect condition." Integrity means being consistent in one's behavior under every circumstance, including those unguarded moments. If leaders are normally peaceable and well mannered, but they throw violent temper tantrums when things go wrong, their lives lack integrity. If leaders are honest and moral in public, but discard those standards in private, their lives lack integrity. When leaders have integrity, their followers always know what to expect.

It is said of Robert E. Lee that "however hot the blood in the chase and in the fight, Lee remained the Christian soldier."[17] During professional sporting events, many athletes purporting to be Christians (and even some fans) have sacrificed their credibility through outbursts of anger. After Tom Landry was fired as the head coach of the Dallas Cowboys, the sports media paid tribute to the well-known Christian coach. One commentator, who was not a Christian, remembered interviewing Landry after the Cowboys had suffered a particularly humiliating defeat. Despite being embarrassed on the field that day, Landry answered every question for the press with grace and dignity. At the close of the interview, as the reporters were packing up their equipment, this newsman realized to his dismay that his camera had not properly recorded the interview. He had nothing for his station to broadcast that evening. In desperation, the frantic reporter chased after Landry as he walked down the hallway. When the weary coach heard the reporter's dilemma, Landry returned and completely refilmed the interview for this man's sake. As the reporter testified on national television during a tribute to Landry, he marveled at the Christian character of the man, who acted with equal grace and dignity regardless of whether his team had won or lost. That's integrity.

Scripture is filled with promises for the person of integrity:

He stores up sound wisdom for the upright; he is a shield to
     those who walk in integrity (Prov. 2:7).

He who walks in integrity walks securely, but he who perverts
     his ways will be found out (Prov. 10:9).

A righteous man who walks in his integrity—how blessed are his
     sons after him (Prov. 20:7).

Vindicate me, O LORD, for I have walked in my integrity; and I
     have trusted in the LORD without wavering. Examine me, O
     LORD, and try me; test my mind and my heart (Ps. 26:1–2).

The Bible also uses the term "blameless" to describe integrity. The apostle Peter urged Christians, in light of Christ's second coming to "be diligent to be found by Him in peace, spotless and blameless" (2 Pet. 3:14).

Why is a leader's personal life so important? Some people claim leaders who commit adultery can still lead their organizations effectively. They argue that one matter does not affect the other. The issue, however, is integrity. If a man can deceive his wife and children, break a vow he made to God in the presence of witnesses, and knowingly betray the trust of those who love him, what guarantee does his organization have that he will be honest in his dealings with them? People who prove themselves deceitful in one area of life are equally capable of being deceitful in other areas. Perhaps that is why when Warren Bennis and Burt Nanus surveyed sixty successful CEOs of major companies, almost all of them were still married to their first spouse.[18] These leaders valued their commitments and were living their married lives, as well as their business lives, with integrity.

An unmistakable sense of authority accompanies leaders with integrity. Leaders without integrity may promote worthwhile causes, yet fail to gain people's loyalty because their lives discredit the validity of their proposals. When people live lives of integrity, their followers assume they are trustworthy to lead. Leaders who are not haphazard with their own lifestyles, will be trusted to not be careless with their organizations.

Integrity alone is not sufficient to ensure successful leadership. A leader must also have competence. But integrity will gain a leader the benefit of the doubt from followers who do not yet see the vision as clearly as the leader does.

Integrity is not automatic. It is a character trait that leaders consciously cultivate in their lives. Early in Billy Graham's ministry, he met with his associates during a crusade in Modesto, California. They were troubled by the notorious vices of well-known evangelists and they feared that, if they were not careful, they, too, could fall prey to immorality. Graham led his group to identify those things most likely to destroy or hinder their ministry. Then they agreed upon a list of principles they would each follow in order to ensure the integrity of their lives and their ministry. Graham described this time as "a shared commitment to do all we could to uphold the Bible's standard of absolute integrity and purity for evangelists."[19] As a result of this early commitment to integrity, Billy Graham's evangelistic association became the foremost model of integrity for Christian organizations around the world. Integrity doesn't happen by accident. It happens on purpose.

A Successful Track Record

Few things bring a leader more credibility than consistent, long-term success. Success can be a sign that God is blessing a leader. God promised Joshua that he would be with him wherever he went and therefore, no enemy could withstand him. No enemy did. Joshua's consistent victories were direct proof of God's blessing. Kouzes and Posner claim: "Having a winning track record is the surest way to be considered competent."[20]

Leaders cannot demand respect. They can only earn it. The problem with many would-be spiritual leaders is that they want people's respect without first establishing a history of success. They are like the hopeful job applicant who commented on his application form, "Please don't misconstrue my fourteen jobs as 'job hopping.' I have never quit a job." People have the right to examine their leaders' record of achievement. If leaders failed in their two previous assignments, they should not be surprised when people are hesitant to follow them or to give them new assignments. This is why younger leaders cannot expect the same degree of respect and authority that more experienced leaders enjoy. There are no substitutes for experience. "You cannot lead out of someone else's experience" Kouzes and Posner point out, "You can only lead out of your own."[21] John Beckett of the Beckett Corporation observes, "I am wary of 'potential' without a supporting track record."

One of the biggest obstacles young leaders face is garnering respect among their followers when they do not yet have previous successes to their credit. We met with a sincere young pastor serving in his first church. This man obviously loved the Lord. He had a deep concern for a nearby town where there was no evangelical church, and he wanted his church to begin a mission church to provide a gospel witness to that community. Unfortunately, his church members were not supportive of his proposed mission project. He voiced his frustration that no one had volunteered to help reach out to that needy community. Several church members had openly questioned the wisdom of extending their ministry to another city when they had so many needs in their own church. The pastor was grieved because his people were unwilling to follow his leadership into this exciting ministry opportunity. He asked us what we thought he should do to get his people on to God's agenda.

We often encounter this kind of scenario, and it always creates an awkward situation. When spiritual leaders are already discouraged, it seems unkind to point to their leadership as the key to the problem. It is tempting to simply agree that the fault lies in their followers, or the downturn in the economy, or the unresponsive community, or the mistakes of the previous leader. But to shift the blame elsewhere would leave this struggling leader with the same shortcomings that were presently crippling his effectiveness. This sincere young pastor could not be faulted for his zeal to spread the gospel. He truly wanted to lead his church to do something effective for God's kingdom. However, the fact was his own church was in dismal condition. The church was running a deficit. The facilities were in desperate need of repair. There was a chronic shortage of Sunday school teachers. Yet he had been ineffective in addressing these needs. His church members saw their pastor struggling to organize and maintain one church, so they had every reason to question whether he could effectively lead in establishing and maintaining a mission church as well. Further discussion revealed that he was experiencing financial problems personally, due to poor money-management skills. He confessed that he had put on a great deal of weight because he paid little attention to his eating habits. He began to see that perhaps the problem was not with his people but with their leader. This pastor had not established a successful track record. He had not been able to organize his church to keep up their property or to run an educational program, yet he was asking his people to trust his leadership in a major venture in another city. Furthermore, both his financial and physical conditions demonstrated mismanagement in his personal life. As we talked, he confessed that although he was burdened for the unchurched people in the neighboring town, perhaps he was also seeking a distraction from the problems in his own church. Focusing on a new group of people would provide a diversion from the difficulties he experienced with the original group. His people had been wise to resist moving forward on his suggestion.

This situation magnifies the need for small accomplishments by leaders. New leaders are remiss if they immediately undertake large projects with their organizations. Better to first tackle smaller projects that can be completed successfully. When people experience a string of small victories with their leader, they will be more willing to attempt something larger. The first place to demonstrate small triumphs is in the leader's self-mastery.

Jesus told the story of three servants who were entrusted with large amounts of money to invest for their master. The first two servants invested their resources and doubled their investments. The third servant buried his assets and earned nothing for his master. Their master's response to the first two servants was: "Well done, good and faithful slave; you were faithful with a few things, I will put you in charge of many things" (Matt. 25:23). God's kingdom operates on this truth: Those who prove themselves faithful with little will receive more from God. Conversely, those who squander the initial responsibilities God gives them will not be trusted with more. They may even lose the little they had. The problem is, too many people want to bypass the small assignments and get right to the big jobs—the ones with the influence and prestige. But God doesn't work that way. God is sequential in the way he develops leaders. The biblical pattern is that God generally begins by giving leaders small assignments. When they prove themselves faithful, God trusts them with more weighty tasks.

Leaders who are frustrated that God is not blessing their zeal to do great things for him should examine their recent track record. Have they been faithful in the smaller assignments? They should also be sure they are measuring success the way God does. "More" in God's economy does not necessarily mean greater numbers of people, more money, or enhanced prestige. It may mean that God entrusts them with a more difficult assignment, or greater suffering. God's Son received the highest assignment and it culminated in a cross. Knowing and experiencing God is a progressive endeavor that depends on obedience. As God's servants obey him in each stage of their lives, no matter how humble the task, they will come to know God in a more intimate way and their faith in him will increase, giving them the spiritual maturity to handle whatever assignment God gives next.

Eventually, through this pattern of obedience and growth, spiritual leaders will attain a higher degree of influence among those they lead. Followers are much more motivated to support leaders who demonstrate faithful service to God. The evidence that God has honored such leaders serves to solidify their credibility. On the other hand, leaders who use political means to gain leadership positions have a tenuous credibility at best. They may experience short-term success, but God will not honor them as leaders and ultimately they may be discredited.

L. R. Scarborough, the second president of Southwestern Baptist Theological Seminary in Fort Worth, was disconcerted at how many aspiring pastors were aggressively pursuing prominent places of ministry. He issued this challenge to spiritual leaders: "If your place is not great enough to suit you, make it so. The minister who is unable to make a place great is too weak to hold a great one."[22] Leaders who fix their gaze on the horizon, hoping for something better rather than focusing on the tasks at hand, are unworthy to hold their current positions. Conversely, leaders who enthusiastically invest their energies into each new assignment God grants them will enjoy success where they are, but they will also develop the character God looks for to use for further, expanded service.

It is crucial for those in spiritual leadership to recognize what "success" means in God's kingdom, for it is not measured by the same standards the world uses. During the early years of the American Revolution, George Washington lost most battles he fought. But, considering the rag-tag group of untrained, ill-equipped soldiers he was leading, it was a major victory simply keeping his troops from starving or freezing to death. Sometimes a tactical retreat can be a success. God gauges success in terms of faithfulness and obedience, not in terms of dollars or status. The definitive measure of leaders' success is whether they moved their people from where they were to where God wanted them to be. This *may* be reflected in numbers, or even in financial growth, but it is expressly seen in the spiritual growth of the followers. The measure of leaders' success is whether or not they accomplished God's will. People often look for tangible results such as head counts or profit margins, but these only serve as partial indicators of what God considers success. The accomplishment of God's purposes is the only complete and infallible indication of success.

Organizations seeking a new leader should critically examine each candidate's history. A prospective leader may never have been a CEO or a pastor of a large church before, but if that person is a leader, there will always be evidence of successful leadership capacities. Emerging leaders may not yet have major accomplishments to their credit, but they should be accumulating a series of small successes. Perhaps they have demonstrated leadership capacity in sports or in various volunteer organizations. While they may not have held prestigious jobs before, they should have a track record of success in the jobs they *have* held. Leaders generally accumulate promotions and raises in whatever jobs they hold, regardless of how menial, because their leadership qualities quickly become evident. Success in previous, smaller ventures may indicate the emerging leader is now prepared for greater responsibility.

This does not mean that they do not experience failure, but that they learn from their failures and continue to be effective in their roles. As Warren Bennis observes: "Leaders, like anyone else, are the sum of all their experiences, but, unlike others, they amount to more than the sum, because they make more of their experiences."[23] In other words, experience is not the end factor; it is merely an avenue to reveal and develop character. It is character that enables a person to lead. The spiritual leader's personal growth is the accumulation of God's activity in his or her life.

Leaders who are faithful in every assignment God gives them enjoy a tremendous sense of peace and confidence. An observer of General Robert E. Lee at the close of the American Civil War concluded: "It must have been the sense of having done his whole duty, and expended upon the cause every energy of his being, which enabled him to meet the approaching catastrophe with a calmness which seemed to those around him almost sublime."[24] Leaders who have been faithful can even lose a war successfully! They can rest assured that God will reward them in his own way and in his own time. In addition, those who observe their lives will recognize the unmistakable qualities of leaders who have been faithful in every assignment they have been given, large or small. Few people expect perfection from their leaders, but when people perceive that their leader has been faithful to God, they will also acknowledge the spiritual influence that God has granted their leader. And they will follow willingly.

Preparation

At the close of his autobiography, Billy Graham listed several things he would do differently if he could live his life over again. He said, "I have failed many times, and I would do many things differently. For one thing, I would speak less and study more."[25] Billy Graham preached to more people and saw more conversions than any preacher in history, yet he acknowledged that if he had been better prepared, God might have used his life to an even greater extent!

Preparation brings profound confidence to leaders. The most successful leaders have been the ones who did their homework thoroughly. Winston Churchill would typically read nine newspapers every morning over breakfast. He would pour over reports, refusing to have his staff digest information for him. Abraham Lincoln was so anxious to be informed of events during the Civil War that he would often go to the telegraph office in order to obtain the latest information the instant it came in.

Harry Truman was not generally perceived as a brilliant man, but he was admired for always being prepared. When he took office at the death of Franklin Roosevelt on April 12, 1945, he faced an enormous task. He would meet with Joseph Stalin and Winston Churchill in July to discuss the world peace process and the treatment of Germany and Japan. Truman had not been in the earlier meetings with these two men, nor had his predecessor briefed him on what had been discussed. Furthermore, Truman had to confront the reality of the atomic bomb. The decision of whether or not to use it rested on his shoulders. Truman inherited a tremendous load of decisions for which he bore sole responsibility. Yet those who met with Truman found him to be thoroughly prepared. He would fastidiously examine every document and briefing until he understood the issues and was thoroughly equipped to make his decision. Truman became known for his decisiveness, but this decisiveness was borne of his meticulous preparation. Leaders can make momentous decisions with confidence if they are adequately prepared.

It is significant that so many great leaders of the past were well versed in history. Winston Churchill was a historian. This enabled him to put his nation's conflict with Hitler into historical perspective. Napoleon was a voracious reader, especially of history. Successful leaders invest time in learning the history of their organizations. Spiritual leaders carefully study their organization's past in order to identify the way God has been leading to date. History is particularly important for spiritual leaders new to their churches or organizations. When pastors arrive at churches, they are remiss to assume that God arrives with them! God was there at the church's founding, and he will be there when the pastor leaves. A wise pastor will scrutinize the church's history to see how God has led thus far in order to gain perspective on how God is guiding at present.

Preparation for leadership also involves training. Good leaders take time to learn. Many a zealous leader has charged off to serve the Lord, disdainfully neglecting opportunities to obtain an education or additional skills, only to face issues in their organization that far exceed their expertise. Leaders who make the effort to obtain proper training are not only better prepared for their leadership role; they also have more credibility with those they lead. As the writer of Proverbs extols: "Do you see a man skilled in his work? He will stand before kings; he will not stand before obscure men" (Prov. 22:29). Too often leaders prematurely end their training because a job opportunity is presented to them. By assuming that "getting to the task at hand" is more important than thorough preparation many leaders enter into their careers ill prepared for the inevitable challenges they will face. Emerging leaders who abort their educational preparation often demonstrate a character that is not committed to finishing what it starts. Those who cannot carry through with their training often prove they cannot stick with assignments and jobs later in their careers. The way people handle their preparation for leadership is a strong indicator of what kind of leaders they will eventually be.

Obviously not all learning comes through formal education, but a good education must not be discounted as an important means of preparation. The Old Testament leader who towers over the rest is Moses. But before Moses became a leader, he received a good education. He became a thinker, the systematic theologian of the Old Testament. Moses received his formal education from the finest schools in Egypt. His mind had been trained to think. Apart from Jesus, there is no more influential leader in the New Testament than the apostle Paul. He, too, was a thinker, the systematic theologian of the New Testament. Paul earned what today would be considered a Ph.D. in his field, studying under Gamaliel, who was considered to be one of the greatest minds of his day. Both Moses and Paul spent time learning how to think. This is the contribution formal education gives to leaders. Far beyond an arsenal of head knowledge, a good education trains leaders how to think for themselves. The ability to think will hold leaders in good stead regardless of what new or unforeseen challenges they encounter. Today's leaders do not always see the value in pursuing an education before undertaking their life's work.

In 1944, Leander McCormick-Goodheart, a recruiter for the Ford Motor Company, toured fifty universities across the United States to recruit the outstanding graduating student of each institution. At Lehigh University, he met a young man named Lee Iacocca and offered him a position at Ford. This was a dream come true for Iacocca. His greatest ambition was to one day work for Ford. Yet Iacocca asked if he could delay the starting date of his employment for one year. He had the opportunity to earn a masters degree from Princeton University. Even though the ambitious and talented Iacocca had the opportunity to launch his meteoric automaking career immediately upon his graduation, he determined to be fully prepared for whatever opportunities might come his way in the future. While there are some well-documented stories of college dropouts who "made it big," these are the exception. Most of the great leaders have taken the time to properly prepare themselves at the outset of their careers.

Howard Gardner, in his book *Leading Minds*, suggests that there are both direct and indirect forms of leadership. Whereas Franklin Roosevelt, Winston Churchill, and Joseph Stalin wielded direct influence over others, thinkers such as Albert Einstein exercised indirect influence over people that in many ways was more profound and long-lasting than direct leadership. Thinkers lead with their minds. They cut new paths through traditional ways of thinking and solving problems. They envision new paradigms. They break through stereotypical, limiting traditions and offer fresh insights into organizational effectiveness.

Consider Jesus, the perfect model of leadership. This is how he led. Although he had a small coterie of disciples, he exerted tremendous influence through his teaching. Jesus spent great amounts of time studying Scripture and praying. Jesus told his disciples, "All things I have heard from my Father I have made known to you" (John 15:15). As a result, Christ radically challenged the commonly accepted beliefs and customs of his day. He presented a profoundly different view of God and of salvation than was commonly held. In his Sermon on the Mount, he put forth a standard of living that was breathtakingly fresh and different than anyone had ever imagined. Jesus commanded no armies; he controlled no organizations; he had no access to large treasuries; yet his influence has endured and multiplied for over two thousand years.

It has been the thinkers who have exerted the longest-lasting influence on world history. In fact, the timeline of history can be divided according to the emergence of leaders who envisioned reality differently than people had previously understood it. Historians mark the beginning of the Protestant Reformation from the time an insignificant German monk named Martin Luther questioned the commonly accepted thinking about God and man. Likewise, his namesake, Martin Luther King Jr. dared to challenge the commonly accepted status quo of his generation.

Such significant leadership does not come primarily by doing, but by thinking. Society-shaking, world-changing, history-making thought is not produced by lackadaisical, lazy minds. Warren Bennis laments that too many of today's leaders suffer from what he calls "celibacy of the intellect."[26] These are people of action who seldom stop to consider whether their actions are appropriate or effective.

Legitimate Sources of Influence

- God's authentication
- Encounters with God
- Character/integrity
- A successful track record
- Preparation

Detractors of Christianity like to denigrate it as a religion that discourages thought and asks only for faith. Historically this has been proven blatantly untrue. The greatest scientific advances in history have been made in countries where Christian thinking was widely accepted. Many of history's great scientific advances have been made by Christians, such as Isaac Newton, who disciplined his mind in order to bring glory to God. Spiritual leaders who have made a lasting difference in their society have been those who have diligently studied the Scriptures. They have persistently sought to know God. They have relentlessly pursued his will for themselves and for their society. They have taken advantage of opportunities to discipline their minds to think.

These spiritual leaders have come to understand that their ways are not God's ways (Isa. 55:8–9). Out of their intimate relationship with Christ, God chose to reveal to them what was on his heart for their generation. These leaders have made enormous contributions to their world. Because they took the time to prepare themselves spiritually and mentally, they have left a lasting mark on human history.

CONCLUSION

Whether you are a CEO, a pastor, a school principal or a committee chairperson, every leader should periodically take a leadership inventory. No matter what leadership capacity you hold, you need to ask yourself these questions: "Why are people following me?" Is it because they are paid to do so? Is it because they can't find a better job? Is it because they believe it is their duty? Or, do they see the activity of God in my life? Do they recognize in my character and integrity the mark of God? Do they sense that God is with me? Do I have a track record of success? If my employees received more lucrative job offers, would they choose to remain with me? If a larger church with more extensive programs were located near my church, would my people wish to remain where they are? What is it about me, if anything, that causes people to want to follow me? Spiritual influence does not come automatically, haphazardly, or easily. It is not something upon which leaders can insist. It is something God must produce in you.

CONCEPTS AND SCRIPTURES FOR CONSIDERATION

- It has never been easier to create the image of a leader than it is today.
- "Should it not be the office that seeks the man, rather than the man the office?"
- Spiritual leadership is based on the work of the Holy Spirit.
- It is the epitome of arrogant and brutish leadership to say, "God has spoken to me. Now you must follow."
- A leader must bring more to his people than a bright smile.

- Leaders do not have to prove God is guiding them. God's presence will be unmistakable.
- The great leaders of Scripture never had to insist on the people's respect. God saw to that.
- You cannot skip steps with God.
- "If your place is not great enough to suit you, make it so. The minister who is unable to make a place great is too weak to hold a great one."
- The definitive measure of leaders' success is whether they moved their people from where they were to where God wanted them to be.
- Leaders can make momentous decisions with confidence if they are adequately prepared.
- Society-shaking, world-changing, history-making thought is not produced by lackadaisical, lazy minds.

Joshua 1:5–9
Matthew 25:23
2 Corinthians 5:10
Proverbs 2:7; 10:9; 20:7; Psalm 26:1–2
2 Peter 3:14
Isaiah 55:8–9
Romans 8:29
John 15:15
Mark 6:45–52

CHAPTER SIX

The Leader's Goal
Moving People On to God's Agenda

WHEN MEL BLACKABY, THE THIRD SON
in our family, was a young seminary student, he was delighted to be
called as pastor to a small rural church in Texas. His first pastorate!
Before long he was required to conduct his first funeral. To his relief,
the service went smoothly. Then it was time to drive to the cemetery for
the graveside service. Mel was instructed to drive his car at the front of
the procession, just behind a police car. Mel had not yet been to the
cemetery, but he assumed the policeman would lead the way. The
mourners moved slowly forward, forming a line of vehicles a mile long.
Mel felt exhilarated to be ministering to such an impressive group of
people in his small town. All was well until the procession came to an
uncontrolled intersection. The policeman driving the lead car dutifully
pulled over and, after waving the bewildered minister forward, stayed
behind to direct traffic. Poor Mel was leading a mile-long group of
mourners to a place he had never been. He had absolutely no clue
where he was going! What should he do? As he tells it, "I drove as
slowly as possible hoping that someone would figure out that I didn't
know where I was going and come to my rescue!"

Leaders who take on a new position must ask themselves: Where
should this organization be going? This question may seem ridiculously
simplistic, but it is amazing how many leaders become so focused on the
journey they lose sight of the destination. It's not that these leaders have

no agenda for their organization. They may in fact have high aspirations and detailed plans of what they hope to achieve. The problem is that they fail to examine whether these plans will lead them to results that are truly best for their organization. Some leaders confuse the means to the end with the end itself. If leaders do not clearly understand where their organization is and where it should be going, they will be unable to lead effectively. The following are three of the most common, and perhaps most subtle, organizational goals that can disorient leaders to their true purpose.

UNWORTHY GOALS

"Bottom Line" Mentality

What do people want to see happen when they choose a new leader? *Results.* In the marketplace, effectiveness is based on sales and profit. The larger the market share, the greater the increase in sales; the more new products, or new customers or new stores there are, the more successful the leader is deemed to be. It is human nature to look for tangible measures of success. Even in religious circles, people establish goals to measure their organization's success. For example, churches determine their effectiveness by focusing on things they can count: number of seats filled in the auditorium, number of dollars in the offering plate, number of ministries conducted throughout the week. Peter Drucker says the ultimate measure of leadership is "results."[1] Successful leaders must be people who get things done! This demand for measurable results from leaders puts pressure on people to focus on their accomplishments. What better way to appear successful than to set a goal and then meet it. According to Drucker, a person hasn't led unless results have been produced.

This result-oriented philosophy has motivated many leaders to arrive at new positions with lists of goals already in hand. They are inadvertently putting the cart before the horse. Setting goals has become a popular way for leaders to motivate their followers as well as to measure their success. The popular trend is to focus entirely on achieving goals; increasing sales by 25 percent, constructing the building on budget, boosting attendance by 10 percent, cutting costs by 15 percent.

When goals are met, leaders consider themselves successful. But what about the price their organizations pay in achieving the goals? If meeting a cost-reduction goal is the bottom line, what is to prevent massive layoffs and arbitrary firings? Interestingly, secular writers realize that organizational leadership involves far more than merely reaching goals. James Collins and Jerry Porras, in their book *Built to Last*, argue that great leaders do not focus on achieving their goals. Rather, they concentrate on building great organizations. Leaders can achieve their goals for a time but destroy their organizations in the process. A healthy organization will meet its goals year after year.

In the past, organizations were generally built on the goals and dreams of the leader. The leader made the plans; everyone else followed them. But as Peter Senge contends in *The Fifth Discipline:*

> It is no longer sufficient to have one person learning for the organization, a Ford or a Sloan or a Watson. It's just not possible any longer to "figure it out" from the top, and have everyone else following the orders of the "grand strategist." The organizations that will truly excel in the future will be the organizations that discover how to tap people's commitment and capacity to learn at *all* levels in an organization.[2]

Society has changed. Modern leaders cannot and should not do all the thinking for their organizations. New leaders cannot simply arrive at an organization and begin imposing their preset goals and agendas. It is critical that today's leaders develop their personnel in order to build healthy organizations.

Max Depree, former chairman of the board of Herman Miller, Inc., suggests that leadership is a "posture of indebtedness."[3] Leaders are morally obligated to provide certain things for those who work for them. Depree claims that followers have a right to ask the following questions of their leaders:

- What may I expect from you?
- Can I achieve my own goals by following you?
- Will I reach my potential by working with you?
- Can I trust my future to you?
- Have you bothered to prepare yourself for leadership?
- Are you ready to be ruthlessly honest?

- Do you have the self-confidence and trust to let me do my job?
- What do you believe?[4]

People are no longer unquestioning followers. They don't have to be. They have more options, so they will choose to follow leaders whose answers to the above questions best satisfy them. How leaders answer will determine the quality and loyalty of their followers.

If this is true for secular businesses, it is even more so for religious organizations that rely largely on volunteers. When there is no paycheck to motivate followers, what is it that influences people to invest their valuable time, money, and energy? Will they be galvanized to action by a list of goals? The primary purpose of spiritual leaders is not to achieve their goals but to accomplish God's will. Depree says, "Reaching goals is fine for an annual plan. Only reaching one's potential is fine for a life."[5] Leaders can achieve their goals and yet be out of God's will. Reaching goals is not necessarily a sign of God's blessing. Spiritual leaders do not use their people to accomplish their goals; their people *are* the goal. Spiritual leaders have a God-given responsibility to do all they can to lead their people on to God's agenda.

According to Depree, both religious and business leaders should enter a "covenantal relationship" with their employees. Depree describes this as a "shared commitment to ideas, to issues, to values, to goals, and to management processes. Words such as *love*, *warmth*, and *personal chemistry* are certainly pertinent. Covenantal relationships are open to influence. They fill deep needs, and they enable work to have meaning and to be fulfilling. Covenantal relationships reflect unity and grace and poise. They are an expression of a sacred nature of relationships."[6] Kouzes and Posner argue convincingly in *Encouraging the Heart* that business leaders cannot afford to neglect regularly giving their employees positive feedback if they want to gain maximum performance.

Depree described his desire for his company: "My goal for Herman Miller is that when people both inside and outside the company look at all of us, not as a corporation but as a group of people working intimately within a covenantal relationship, they'll say, 'Those folks were a gift to the spirit.'"[7]

Leaders who strive for and even achieve their goals, but whose people suffer and fall by the wayside in the process, have failed as leaders.

Using people to achieve organizational goals is the antithesis of spiritual leadership. Firing personnel can be a symptom of failed leadership. Occasionally, a leader may have no choice but to dismiss personnel, but too often firing people is merely a more expedient way to achieve desired ends than investing time and energy to help employees develop to their potential. If a company meets its annual sales goal but three of its key management personnel lose their marriages because of the stress of the sales campaign, the leadership has failed. If a church succeeds in building a new worship center but loses members in the process through bickering and bitterness, the church has failed. If costs have been cut by 15 percent but loyal, long-term employees have been abruptly downsized as part of the cost-saving effort, the success is tainted. In God's eyes, how something is done is as important as what is done. The end does not justify the means in God's kingdom. Getting results can make leaders look good. God's way magnifies God's name.

Perfectionism

"God expects the best!" "Nothing but excellence is good enough for God!" How often we hear these emphatic assertions, expressed out of the sincerity of a leader's heart. They sound noble and right, yet there is a subtle danger inherent in the philosophy that everything done in an organization must always be done with excellence.

Indeed, God does have high expectations for his people. For one, he commands them to be holy, as he is holy (1 Pet. 1:15–16). For another, God wants his followers to be spiritually mature and complete (Matt. 5:48). God expects people to give him their best (Mal. 1:6–14). God commands employees to work as if they were laboring for their Lord (Eph. 6:7). But leaders must be careful how they use the term *excellence*. If excellence is understood to mean perfection in everything one does, then that is not God's standard. If excellence refers to doing things in a way that honors God, then all leaders should strive for it. There is a difference between giving God your best and giving God the best. Excellence generally describes tasks, and tasks are usually a means to an end. People are the end. Churches that concentrate more on their tasks than on their people are missing what God considers most important.

This is true in all aspects of spiritual work. The apostle Paul did not claim that his purpose was to do everything perfectly. Instead, he declared his aim was to "proclaim Him, admonishing every man and teaching every man with all wisdom, that we may present every man complete in Christ. And for this purpose also I labor, striving according to His power, which mightily works within me" (Col. 1:28–29).

Paul's focus was on developing people. He sought to take them from their spiritual immaturity and to bring them to spiritual maturity. He led them from disobedience to obedience. He brought them from faithlessness to fruitfulness. His joy was in seeing those he led blossom into the people God wanted them to become. In other words, his approach was completely contrary to that of many modern Christian organizations.

Misguided Excellence. Let's examine a church that embarks on a misguided quest for excellence. As the church leaders look at the music program, they discover several of the singers have less than excellent voices. These people are discreetly removed from the music program. It becomes apparent that the pianist cannot master the more difficult musical pieces, so a professional accompanist is hired. When the volunteer running the sound equipment makes one too many mistakes, a sound technician is hired to operate the equipment. When those volunteering to work with the youth seem unable to expand the youth program, staff is hired to take their place. As time passes, the standard of excellence is brought to bear on every aspect of church life. In each case, when people do not measure up, they are replaced with someone who meets the toughest scrutiny of critics. Volunteer-led programs are gradually taken over by professionals with specialized training in their fields. As new people come to the church and look for ways they can serve, they notice that a large professional staff conducts most of the ministries of the church. They also see that only the most highly skilled people are ever called upon to serve in the church because the church values, above all else, excellence. So, knowing they are far from excellent themselves, they settle in to a comfortable seat and let the professionals serve them excellent program after excellent program. And the church grows but THE CHURCH doesn't.

Perhaps it was this type of attitude that prompted the risen Christ to accuse the church at Laodicea as he did: "Because you say, 'I am rich, and have become wealthy, and have need of nothing,' and you do not know that you are wretched and miserable and poor and blind and naked" (Rev. 3:17). The primary goal of spiritual leadership is not excellence, in the sense of doing things perfectly. Rather, it is taking people from where they are to where God wants them to be. There is a tension here, for surely leaders want to motivate their people to develop their skills/talents/gifts to the glory of God and never settle for less than their personal best. But in order to help people develop spiritually, leaders may have to allow them to make mistakes, just as leaders make mistakes on their road to maturity as leaders. Developing people to their potential is not tidy. Often church staff could do a better job than volunteers could. Allowing amateurs to attempt things may not always be efficient in the short term, but good leaders recognize the long-term benefits. Both the people in training and the organization benefit when their leaders value developing people over doing everything perfectly. This phenomenon can be especially seen in small churches. It is easy for megachurches to proclaim "excellence" as the only standard worthy of God. After all, they have multiple staffs, huge budgets, spacious facilities, and high-tech equipment. If "excellence" is understood to mean flawless, world-class productions in everything the church does, then the small, single-staffed, talent-challenged church might as well close its doors. If "excellence," however, means following God's will and honoring him through our best efforts, any church can be an "excellent" organization!

Bigger, Faster, More

The Western world has been seduced by size. Size can justify almost anything. Leaders of the largest churches or companies are automatically viewed as experts. If a leader has grown a religious organization to a significant size, people take this as a sign of God's blessing. It may not necessarily be so.

In the business world, the primary attraction for consumers used to be the low cost of the product. Soon, giant low-cost stores swallowed up smaller businesses. Today, sociologists claim people are more concerned with service than cost. Time is often more precious than money for modern shoppers. So, smaller businesses that concentrate on service will have a key role to play in today's market. In other words, bigger is not always better.

In the religious sector, leaders who are able to grow megachurches are treated as spiritual heroes. They are encouraged to write books chronicling their success, and they regularly appear on the speaking circuit for church growth conferences. Even if these leaders fall into immorality, churches may be reluctant to relieve them of their duties because it appears God still has his hand of blessing upon them. We have often heard people ask, "If what our pastor did was so wrong, why has God blessed him so?" This question equates growth with God's blessing. That's not always the case. Certainly church growth is inevitable in a healthy church, as the Book of Acts clearly exemplifies. But it is also entirely possible for a church to grow in numbers apart from God's blessing. There is a significant difference between drawing a crowd and building a church. Marketers can draw a crowd. They can't grow a church. Cults can draw a crowd. They can't build God's kingdom. If growth in numbers is a sure sign of God's blessing, then many cult groups are enjoying God's blessing to a far greater extent than many churches.

The seduction is in believing that God is as impressed with crowds as people are. He is not. The essence of Satan's temptations for Jesus was trying to convince him to draw a crowd rather than build a church (Matt. 4). When Jesus fed the five thousand, he became so popular that the people wanted to forcibly make him their king. In response, Jesus began teaching them about true discipleship. Jesus knew that, even though there was a large crowd following him, many of them were not believers. They were simply wanting their physical needs met. So Jesus preached to them about the cost of discipleship. "As a result of this many of His disciples withdrew, and were not walking with Him anymore" (John 6:66). So quick and so vast was the exodus of would-be disciples that Jesus turned to the Twelve and asked if they, too, intended to abandon him (v. 67). Jesus was never enamored with crowds. In fact, he often sought to escape them (Mark 1:37–38).

Churches often use the world's methods to draw a crowd. A grand performance done with excellence, using high-tech sound equipment, professional lighting, eye-catching brochures, and charismatic leadership, can draw a crowd. It will not, however, build a church. Only Christ can do that. Does this mean that churches should not seek to do the best they can? Should churches never compose attractive brochures or invest in quality sound and lighting equipment? Of course they should. But leaders must be diligent that they never shift their trust from the Head of the church to the tools of the world. They should never assume that, because attendance is growing, their church is healthy and pleasing to God. Leaders must continuously measure their success by God's standards and not by the world's.

Misguided Goals

1. Bottom-line mentality
2. Perfection
3. Bigger, faster, more

THREE WORTHY GOALS

Assuming leaders do not succumb to misguided goals for their organizations, what should their goals be? There are at least three legitimate goals spiritual leaders ought to have for their people regardless of whether they are leading a committee, a church, or a corporation.

Leading to Spiritual Maturity

The ultimate goal of spiritual leadership is not to achieve numerical results alone, or to do things with perfection, or even to grow for the sake of growth. It is to take their people from where they are to where God wants them to be. God's primary concern for all people is not results, but relationship. People's call to be in a right relationship with God takes precedence over their occupation. Calling comes *before* vocation. There is a profound comment on this issue in Exodus 19:4: "You yourselves have seen what I did to the Egyptians, and how I bore you on eagles' wings, and brought you to Myself."

At first glance, this verse can seem confusing. It refers to the Israelites who were rescued from slavery in Egypt. We tend to assume that God delivered the Israelites so that he could bring them to the Promised Land in Canaan. But that is not what God said. The key for God was not the *region* but the *relationship*. God delivered the Israelites so they could be free to develop an intimate relationship with him, a relationship of faith and obedience. The location was simply a means for that relationship to be developed. The reason the Israelites spent forty futile years wandering in the wilderness was not that God could not give them victory in Canaan. He could have easily done that. However, God took them into the wilderness for forty years in order to establish a proper relationship with them. The place was accessible, but the relationship was not yet where God wanted it to be. Unfortunately, once the Israelites entered the Promised Land, they came to see the land as an end in itself rather than a means to a relationship with God. As a result, God ultimately took their land away from them.

One of the issues regarding spiritual leadership is whether spiritual leaders can take people to places they themselves have never been. That depends on one's definition of spiritual leadership. If spiritual leadership is understood as taking people to a *location* or completing a *task*, then leaders can lead people to places they have never been. But if the goal of leadership is a *relationship*, then leaders will never move their people beyond where they have gone themselves. Leaders can lead people to relocate their organization or to build a building or to grow in size without prior experience in these areas. But leaders cannot take their people into a relationship with Christ that goes any deeper than they have gone themselves. Followers may grow deeper spiritually in spite of their spiritually immature leaders, but they will not grow deeper because of such people. Thus, spiritual leaders must continually be growing themselves if they are to lead their people into a mature, intimate relationship with Christ. Leaders will not lead their people to higher levels of prayer unless they have already ascended to those heights themselves. Leaders will not lead others to deeper levels of trust in God unless they have a mature faith themselves.

A spiritual organization will reach its maximum potential only when every member knows how to hear clearly from God and is willing to respond in obedience. It is not enough for leaders to hear from God and then relay the message to the people. Each believer must learn to recognize God's voice and understand what he is saying. When this is true of an organization, leaders will not need to "sell" their visions; they will simply share with their people what God has said to them and then allow their people to seek confirmation themselves.

According to Max Depree, the first responsibility of leaders is to "define reality" for their organizations.[8] People do not always readily understand the full implications of what their organization is experiencing. The people may be so immersed in day-to-day routines or in their own particular area of responsibility within the organization that they do not see the big picture. It is a spiritual leader's responsibility to help people understand God's activity in the midst of the daily challenges they are facing.

A Ship Captain. A spiritual leader is like the captain of a sailing ship. As the ship approaches its destination, the crew begins its lookout for the first sight of land. The captain has sailed the seven seas and has experienced every possible kind of sailing condition. His crew, on the other hand, is much less experienced than the captain. At one point a sailor excitedly cries out, "Land ho!" But all he has seen are vapors coming off the water from the hot sun. Presently, another sailor yells out that he has spotted land, but it is another false alarm. The "land" proves to be only a herd of whales. As the captain casts his careful gaze about the sea, he detects the unmistakable shape of land to the east. Although it is but a slight bump on the distant horizon, the captain knows it is land.

What happened? The crew had the same capacity to see as their captain had. But their inexperience at sea caused them to be confused. What does the captain do with his crew? Does he say, "Don't worry. Seeing where we are going is my duty as captain. I'll do all the watching and announce when we are approaching land"? Or does he chastise his crew for being so blind that they could not see what lay before them? No. The captain understands that he has had more time at sea to learn how to recognize land on the horizon. He realizes that, due to the nature of their jobs, the deck hands do not always have as much time to look out to sea as the captain does. He also knows that his eyesight is no better than his crew's. They can learn to see land just as well as he can, if they are taught how. So he teaches them. He helps them learn to discern if a distant shape is a rock or a whale. He shows them how to scan the horizon and how to recognize when their eyes are playing tricks on them. Eventually the captain no longer needs to be on the deck watching for land. His crew knows how to do that too.

Spiritual leaders often have an advantage over those they lead. Leaders may have walked with God for many years. They have come to recognize when the Spirit's still, small voice is speaking. They recognize when an opportunity has the mark of God upon it. It is not that they are any more gifted or talented than the people they lead. They have just had more experience walking with God than their people have. So, like the sea captain, leaders do not resign themselves to always being the one who sees where God is at work. Instead, spiritual leaders realize that people tend to be disoriented to God, so they teach their people how to know him better. Once people in an organization know how to recognize God's voice and once they are able to determine his leading, the organization will have enormous potential for serving God. The ministry of the organization will not depend on one overworked leader always having to decide what God is guiding them to do. The entire organization will be excitedly scanning the horizon for the first glimpse of what God has in store next. When spiritual leaders have brought their people to this point, they have truly led.

Missions in Canada
A Personal Example from Henry Blackaby

When I was the pastor of Faith Baptist Church in Canada, my goal was not to set the direction for the church but to bring the people into such an intimate relationship with Christ that Christ could lead the church and the people would follow. It was not an issue of selling a vision. It was a matter of helping the people learn how to recognize God's voice. It wasn't easy. At first the people were so disoriented to the ways of God that they had difficulty recognizing his working right in their midst. Len Koster, the pastor of missions, would report to the church that he had discovered a group of people in a nearby town that had been praying for several years for a church to be started in their community. Initially, our church members would immediately focus on their limited resources and the difficulties involved in providing a ministry to that place. As the people grew to know and trust God more, however, their receptivity to what God was doing greatly increased. After they had walked with God and had seen how he worked in people's lives and had witnessed his miraculous provision of resources to meet every need, the people became eager to get involved in what they saw him doing next.

In subsequent situations, when Len Koster reported that he had found another community in need of a church, the Holy Spirit would confirm with the membership whether this was God's invitation for our church to join him in his work. The people would recognize the opportunities that had the mark of God's presence upon them. The people of the church no longer needed their pastor to explain everything to them. They now had a mature relationship with God themselves. They had the same ability to hear from God as their spiritual leader did. If the success of the church had depended solely upon what I was able to see, the church would not have accomplished very much. But when the entire membership began responding in faith and obedience to God's direction, the effectiveness of the church multiplied.

In churches we have led, we have always instituted a regular time of sharing by the people. Often during the evening worship service or during a prayer meeting, people would be asked to share with the church family what they had seen God doing around them during that week. One person might relate that he had an opportunity to minister to an inmate in the local prison. The members would then pray to see if God was leading the church to become involved in a prison ministry. Another might report that when she volunteered in a local school, God alerted her to a hunger among the staff for spiritual guidance. The church would then seek to understand if God was leading our church to minister in some way to that school. Most of the ministries in our churches did not come from suggestions by the pastoral staff, but rather they grew out of God's activity in and around the lives of our church members.

The key was not for the pastor to constantly cast visions of what the church should do next. The key was to bring the people of the church into such an intimate relationship with Christ that they knew when he was speaking to them and guiding the church as his body. Then Christ would use that church to impact the world.

Business leaders must understand that their preeminent task is to equip their people to function at their God-given best and not simply to accomplish organizational goals. From a secular perspective, Peter Senge calls this a "learning organization." That is, every member of the organization is responding to new opportunities and developing personal abilities so that the organization is thinking and growing and learning at every level, not just at the top. When employees are set free to respond to opportunities that present themselves, the entire organization will be mobilized to be far more effective than if everything depends upon the creativity and ability of the leader.

Spiritual leaders in the workplace must also understand that their calling is first to please their heavenly Father, then to satisfy their board of directors. It is appropriate to provide spiritual guidance and encouragement to employees as well as to clientele. CEOs have a responsibility to care for the spiritual well-being of their employees. This should include praying regularly for their salvation. It may also involve seeking opportunities to provide a simple Christian witness to employees. One CEO who responded to our survey indicated that he had been praying for God to show him how he could serve him in a greater capacity. God led him to start a Bible study at work. This proved to be one of the greatest challenges this executive had faced during his eventful tenure at his company! Yet people encountered God in powerful ways there in his workplace.

Spiritual Leadership on the Job
A Personal Example from Richard Blackaby

Several years ago I was leading a series of meetings in a church in one of the Midwest states. I challenged the people to watch throughout the next day to see what God was doing in their workplaces. A businessman in attendance that night took the challenge to heart. The next morning he prayed that God would reveal to him where he was at work in his company. By noon the man had not observed anything unusual. But as he sat in the lunchroom eating his lunch, he noticed, over in a corner, a man sitting alone eating his meal. The Holy Spirit prompted the Christian to join his associate and to ask him how he was doing. He soon discovered that his fellow employee was in crisis. His marriage had been under great strain and that morning he and his wife had undergone a bitter argument. As the man drove to work he had decided that when he returned home that evening he would pack his bags and leave. As this hurting man shared his plans for that evening, the Christian knew God was at work and that this was God's invitation for him to become involved. The Christian was not sure how to help him, but he felt the man would surely abandon his family if he were to go straight home after work. He invited his colleague out for dinner that evening and asked if he would join him for the special meetings being held at his church. To his relief, the man agreed. That evening, as the Christian sat beside his troubled coworker at church, he prayed that God would work powerfully in his life and heal his broken relationship. After the service, the Christian drove his friend back to the company parking lot to pick up his car. As the two men sat in the car, he asked his friend to share his thoughts about the worship service. As the man responded, he confessed that he knew leaving his wife and children was wrong, but he did not know what else to do. The Christian shared that Christ was the answer to his situation. He urged his friend to let Christ bring forgiveness and healing and to help him be the godly husband and father his family needed him to be. There in the darkened company parking lot, the Christian businessman led his associate to the Lord. In tears, the new convert pledged to go home and ask his wife to forgive him.

What happened? A Christian businessman asked God to reveal his agenda for his workplace. On that particular day, God's agenda included saving a man and his family from brokenness. This Christian business-man's pastor was not present in his workplace to discern God's activity for him. It had been imperative that the Christian learn how to hear God's voice for himself.

Leading Others to Lead

Leaders lead followers. Great leaders lead leaders. One of the most tragic mistakes leaders commit is to make themselves indispensable. Sometimes insecurity can drive people to hoard all the leadership opportunities for themselves so that no one else appears as capable or as successful. Other times leaders get so caught up in their own work that they fail to invest time in developing other leaders in the organization. If some leaders were to be completely honest, they would acknowledge that they enjoy being indispensable. They like being the only person in the organizational limelight. Failing to develop leaders in an organization is tantamount to gross failure by the leader, whether by design or by neglect.

It has been said that Napoleon's greatest failure at the Battle of Waterloo was not having trained his generals to think independently of him. When victory hung in the balance and Napoleon was counting on General Grouchy, with 34,000 men and 108 guns, to engage the enemy, Grouchy remained immobilized. Felix Markham, Napoleon's biographer, comments: "Lacking initiative, authority and energy, Grouchy took refuge in a literal obedience to orders. But the orders he received from Napoleon were lacking in precision and too late."[9] Markham suggests, "Napoleon frequently criticized his Generals' mistakes, but he never made any systematic attempt to teach them his methods, or to form a Staff College. He relied entirely on himself."[10] Napoleon's failure to develop leaders around him cost him his empire.

Many famous leaders have failed in this essential element of leadership. When Franklin Roosevelt won his fourth term as president in 1944, many suspected he would not live to finish his term and that the presidency would inevitably fall to the vice president, Harry Truman. This was one of the most critical periods in American history. The world's first nuclear bomb was nearing completion, and an executive decision would soon be required regarding whether to use it. As the most devastating war in human history drew to a close, Europe lay in ruins. The Allied powers would have to decide what to do with the defeated nations. The Soviet Union was now a world superpower, spreading its communist tentacles all over the world. No U.S. president had ever confronted so many monumental decisions as Harry Truman would face, yet Roosevelt never briefed his vice president. In fact,

Roosevelt met briefly with Truman only twice during the 86 days of his vice presidency. Roosevelt failed to develop his successor and, in this respect, he failed as a leader.

In comparison, General George Marshall kept a "black book" of all the soldiers he believed showed promise for future leadership. Whenever he encountered someone who demonstrated leadership ability, he added his name to the book. When a vacancy came up in the officer corps, he referred to his book, where he kept track of an ample supply of qualified candidates. This system enabled Marshall to develop a large military organization filled with talented and effective officers.

One of the most common failures of leaders is that they spend little time or effort preparing their organization for their departure. Many leaders work extremely hard at their jobs and they may enjoy remarkable success during their term as leader. But one test of great leaders is how well their organizations do after they leave. This phenomenon can be clearly seen in the life of Samuel. Samuel was one of the most godly leaders Israel ever had. At the time of his "retirement," no one with whom he had worked could find any fault with him (1 Sam. 12:1–5). Nevertheless, Samuel ultimately failed as a leader, for he did not prepare a successor.

> And it came about when Samuel was old that he appointed his sons judges over Israel. Now the name of his first-born was Joel, and the name of his second, Abijah; they were judging in Beersheba. His sons, however, did not walk in his ways, but turned aside after dishonest gain and took bribes and perverted justice.
>
> Then all the elders of Israel gathered together and came to Samuel at Ramah; and they said to him, "Behold, you have grown old, and your sons do not walk in your ways. Now appoint a king for us to judge us like all the nations." But the thing was displeasing in the sight of Samuel when they said, "Give us a king to judge us." And Samuel prayed to the LORD (1 Sam. 8:1–6).

Samuel failed on two counts: as a parent and as a leader. As long as the Israelites had the noble Samuel for their leader, they followed him without protest. But when Samuel became older and appointed his sons, Joel and Abijah, to replace him, the Israelites resisted. Later generations have castigated the Israelites for rejecting God's leadership at this time and asking for a king. The fact is, the spiritual leaders available to them were so inferior that they saw a secular king as a preferable option. If Samuel had groomed an acceptable replacement, the people might not have clamored for a king. The people's failure stemmed from their leader's failure to do his job.

Samuel's mistake was very costly but, sadly, very common as well. Samuel's example demonstrates that a leader's failure carries with it significant ramifications for everyone in the organization, present members and future members alike. The following are some of the principles leaders follow as they develop leaders around them.

Developing leaders must be a core value of any leader. Unless leaders are intentional about developing leaders within their organization, it will not happen. While there are many ways leaders can enhance leadership skills in others, there are at least four habits leaders must regularly practice if they are to produce a corps of leaders around them.

1. *Leaders delegate.* This is often difficult for leaders. Leaders are generally highly skilled individuals who can do many things well. In addition, if they are perfectionists, as many leaders are, they will be tempted to do more than they should so things are "done right." The inherent danger, of course, is that the growth of the organization is directly tied to the amount of time and energy the leader has. Leaders are, by nature, decision makers. However, it is not wise for leaders to make all the decisions. Doing so impedes the growth of emerging leaders in the organization. As Peter Drucker suggests, "Effective executives do not make a great many decisions. They concentrate on the important ones."[11]

Deciding Not to Decide
A Personal Example from Richard Blackaby

I had to learn this when I became president of the Canadian Southern Baptist Seminary. There were numerous decisions to be made. So I made them. The seminary had a well-educated, talented, and bright business manager named Laurel Miller. She would regularly stop by my office to ask my opinion regarding various financial matters. Because I was the leader, I would always make a decision and Laurel would promptly put the decision into action. One day it dawned on me what was happening. Laurel was working on her master's degree in business management and accounting. I had no financial training. Laurel had dealt with these kinds of issues for many years. I had not. Why was I making these decisions? I decided that the next time Laurel asked for my opinion, I would not give it until she had given hers. When she came by the next time, I asked her, "What do you think?" She was caught by surprise, but she readily gave her response. "Excellent idea!" I replied. "Let's do that!" And we did. From that point on, Laurel has generally only come to me for a second opinion after she had formulated a solution. I began to use this approach with all my staff. At first, I thought I was being a decisive leader but in fact, by making decisions I didn't need to make, I was unknowingly fostering a corporate culture in which people came to me for approval on almost everything. The advantages to my new approach were soon obvious. First, the most qualified personnel were now making the decisions. Second, the faculty and staff took more ownership of their responsibilities. Third, I was freed up to spend more time performing my legitimate role as leader.

---

2. *Leaders give people freedom to fail.* If leaders are going to develop other leaders, they must delegate. But when they delegate, they must not interfere. Nothing will demoralize staff faster than leaders who constantly meddle in their work. Once a task has been assigned to someone, it needs to belong to that person. If leaders continually second-guess decisions their staff make, their staff will stop making decisions. Inevitably, employees will propose ideas and methods that differ from what the leader would have preferred. At this point, leaders must weigh the value of having work done by others against the value of having things done exactly as they would do it themselves. It is impossible to have both.

Business history provides a famous example of the hazards of interference by leaders. Henry Ford gave his only son, Edsel, the responsibility for overseeing his automotive business. The younger Ford had some innovative and practical ideas that would have made the company more efficient in the face of growing competition. Yet as Edsel moved to implement his ideas, the elder Ford constantly countermanded his son's orders and proceeded to undermine Edsel's authority in every way possible. The relationship between father and son was irreparably damaged. Finally, Edsel's fragile health broke down, and the Ford Motor Company languished under the administrative quagmire.

Ford Sr. sacrificed the development of a promising leader to make sure things were always done the way he wanted them to be. At times it is better to sacrifice perfection if doing so will develop leaders in the process. Leaders must regularly resist the temptation to interfere in their people's work. Leaders whose people are reluctant to work for them or leaders who experience difficulty recruiting volunteers should consider whether this is because they have developed a reputation for meddling.

3. *Leaders recognize the success of others.* A sure way to stifle initiative from staff and volunteers is to take the credit for something they have done. Good leaders delegate. They resist interfering. Then, when the job is done, they give credit where it is deserved. One of the greatest rewards a leader can give people, even more than remuneration, is recognition. Leaders ought to be constantly praising their people for their accomplishments and acknowledging their contributions to the organization. At staff gatherings and special occasions, leaders ought to be known for praising their people for their work rather than for blowing their own horns. Although few leaders deliberately steal credit, this can happen inadvertently. If the leader fails to point out an employee's contribution, the assumption is that the leader is responsible for the success. If leaders continually take the credit for work their people have done, or if they consistently ignore people's hard work, people will grow to resent their leader and will be reluctant to give their best effort. The fact is, when the people are successful, so is the leader.

This need for affirmation and a show of gratitude is especially acute in voluntary organizations. Volunteers don't receive year-end bonuses or increases in pay as rewards for their efforts. That's why leaders should be especially diligent to find ways of showing appreciation. At times, leaders can "spiritualize" the work done by volunteers in their organizations with absurd statements such as, "They were doing it for the Lord. They don't need my recognition." Certainly some people's only motivation for serving is the recognition they hope to receive, but wise leaders leave people's motivations for God to judge. True spiritual leaders assume the best of their volunteers. They understand that people want their sacrifice of time and energy to be worth the effort. Volunteers need to know they are making a positive difference. The leader can assure them of this. By publicly recognizing and thanking them, the leader is alerting the entire organization that volunteers make a valuable contribution and that they are appreciated. Never will a leader regret having said thank you, but an attitude of ungratefulness will eventually cost the leader dearly.

While Harry Truman was in the White House, the kitchen staff baked him a birthday cake. After the meal, Truman excused himself from the table and went to the kitchen to thank the cook. This was the first time any of the staff could remember a president entering the kitchen for any reason, let alone to say thank you. On a much larger scale, Truman knew that Europe would need to be reconstructed after World War II. Truman's secretary of state, George Marshall, presented a seventeen-billion-dollar European Recovery Program plan that would help to rebuild Europe and would hurtle the United States into world prominence. Truman's advisors encouraged him to dub it the "Truman Plan," named after the president who authorized it. Truman deferred, insisting that it be called the "Marshall Plan" after the man who had helped develop it. Truman would often be quoted as saying, "It is remarkable how much could be accomplished when you don't mind who receives the credit."[12] Such self-effacing leadership endeared Truman to people.

4. *Leaders give encouragement and support.* Once leaders delegate tasks, they ought to avoid interfering at all costs. This does not mean they should abandon their people. Every time leaders delegate, they must do so with the clear understanding that, to use Truman's vernacular, "the buck stops here." Delegation is a hazardous, albeit necessary, task of leaders. If the people are successful, the people receive the credit. If the people fail, the leaders shoulder the responsibility. In leadership, this fact goes with the territory.

Coaches of professional sports teams are well acquainted with this reality. If the team wins the championship, the athletes assume much of the credit and often demand more lucrative contracts. But when the team performs poorly, the coach is usually the first person to be fired. Mature leaders know this. Good leaders don't make excuses. Great leaders understand and accept that the performance of their organization will be viewed as equal to their own performance.

Weak leaders cast blame upon their subordinates when things go wrong. It is an abdication of leadership for a CEO to fire management when the company has a bad year. It is a sign of deficient leadership when a pastor blames his people for the declining condition of his church.

When people fail in the task they were assigned, this might point to one or more possible problems. Perhaps the leader made a poor choice in assigning a job to someone who was not prepared to handle the responsibility. Maybe the leader did not provide enough support, training, or feedback. Sometimes problems can be traced back to the leader's communication skills and how clearly the assignment was explained in the first place. Of course there are times when individuals simply do not perform well despite all the help their leader provides. Nevertheless, regardless of the reason for failure, good leaders will support their people even when they fail. Often, they use the failure to help the person grow.

During the crucial battle of Gettysburg, General Lee ordered General Longstreet to move his forces forward. For some inexplicable reason, Longstreet delayed. For many precious hours when the Confederate forces might have gained a victory, Longstreet held his forces in check. When Lee finally prevailed upon his reluctant general to proceed, it was too late. The Union troops were now prepared to repel the Confederate attack, and they won the decisive battle of the war. Lee had every right to castigate Longstreet for his insubordination. But he did not. Lee took full responsibility for the defeat. Lee knew that, despite his deficiencies, Longstreet was the best general he had available and that to alienate or lose him at this juncture of the war could be devastating. More importantly, Lee understood that, as the leader, he must always bear responsibility for the performance of his troops even when his subordinates disobeyed his orders.

People need to know that their leader will stand by them when they fail. Church members want the assurance that when their pastor gives them responsibility, he will also back them up if things get difficult. When leaders fail to support their followers, everyone else grows anxious because they rightly assume their leader would abandon them as well. When leaders come quickly to the aid of a struggling follower, everyone else can relax in the assurance that their leader would do the same for them.

The people Moses led failed miserably. Even Aaron, the high priest, shirked his responsibilities. Consequently, the Israelites were sentenced to spend the rest of their days meandering across the desert, shut out of the Promised Land. Moses was not the one who had disobeyed in that instance. He had been faithful, yet God did not release Moses from his people. He was their leader. If ever God's people needed a leader, it was during this period of affliction. Moses spent the remaining forty years of his life wandering in the wilderness, not because of his own failure, but because of the failure of his followers. Too many leaders abandon their people once they fail. Many leaders have justified their abandonment, claiming, "I had to leave that church because no one there wanted to be on mission with God." Or, "My company was hostile to Christianity so I found a more tolerant place to work." The only valid reason for leaving one's leadership position is that God clearly guides a person to do so. Often, however, leaving one's leadership position is nothing short of abandoning the people God gave to a leader.

Bringing Glory to God

There is a third goal leaders should have for their organizations, one which is the ultimate goal of any organization and the reason behind the first two goals of leadership—to bring God glory. Whether people lead Christian or secular organizations, their goal ought to be to glorify God by the way they lead their organization. Although one would assume that Christian organizations would embrace this goal wholeheartedly, this is not always the case. Christian organizations affirm their desire to glorify God, but they can become sidetracked in many subtle ways. Churches can become so preoccupied with growing in numbers or erecting buildings or running programs that they incorrectly assume that everything they are doing honors God. Schools can become distracted by educational concerns and assume that academic respectability is equal to honoring God. Christian charities can become so consumed with funding issues that they stop seeking God's will. As the media is eager to point out, some Christian leaders are more concerned with developing their own name than they are with honoring God's name. While Christians regularly give lip service to their desire to glorify God, not everything they do necessarily accomplishes this goal. God's desire is to reveal himself to the world through people and organizations that believe him and obey him. God is not concerned with bringing glory to people. He wants to reveal his glory through people. Christian organizations do not do this spontaneously. It is the leader's goal to keep this task at the forefront of their organization's agenda. A leader's assignments and positions will change over time, but the goal of bringing glory to God must always be the impetus behind the efforts of every Christian.

When charismatic, worldly leaders achieve great accomplishments, they earn people's praise. In 1978, the Chrysler Corporation faced a seemingly insurmountable crisis. Having suffered millions of dollars in losses and facing the potential layoff of 150,000 employees, Chrysler was in dire straits. Enter Lee Iacocca. Chrysler hired him as president, and his success is legendary. His name has become synonymous with dramatic corporate turnarounds and management genius. He has written best-selling books and was even considered as a presidential candidate. Iacocca received the glory.

That is not the way spiritual leaders operate. Spiritual leaders seek to bring God glory. They strive to honor God through their personal lives as well as by the conduct of their businesses. Spiritual leaders understand they cannot relentlessly pursue their own personal goals and glorify God at the same time. They know it is possible to bring their organizations to the apex of success, but still dishonor God in the process, or at best, neglect to give him the glory. True spiritual leaders value glorifying God more than they do personal or organizational success.

John Beckett is CEO of Beckett Corporation, North America's leading producer of residential oil burners. Beckett is a committed Christian with a desire to apply his Christian faith in the business world. He seeks to operate all aspects of his business in a Christlike manner. His business is not a Christian organization, but this does not stop him from operating his company on Christian principles. How does he do this? He gives priority to the needs of his employees and their families. When an employee is expecting a baby, his company provides a generous paid maternity leave and offers three years off while she cares for her baby. The Beckett Corporation encourages younger employees to go back to school by helping provide tuition money.

Beckett's company is so unusual that it caught the attention of the national media. Peter Jennings of ABC News sent a news team to the Beckett Corporation to investigate the story. The newscast opened with this introduction written by Jennings himself: "Tonight we are going to concentrate on the growing tendency of business leaders in America to have their personal faith make an impact in their companies. In other words, they are using the Bible as a guide to business." When Beckett was asked on national television about his life's purpose, he responded, "My main mission is to know the will of God and do it."[13] The Beckett Corporation is a secular organization in the business sense of the word, but that has not hampered John Beckett from using his business as God's instrument in bringing God glory. In that regard, his company is as much a spiritual organization as, say, a Christian bookstore.

Truett Cathy, well-known Christian businessman and owner of the fast food chain Chick-fil-A, has maintained a longstanding policy that his stores remain closed on Sundays, even though Sunday is a high-volume day in terms of business profit. Even when the shopping malls in which Chick-fil-A leases space require stores to be open on Sunday, Cathy has not budged. Whenever Sunday shoppers walk past a closed Chick-fil-A store, they receive a testimony to the convictions of a Christian CEO. The company also sponsors employees' spouses to attend special company training events in exotic locations as a way to demonstrate that it values the family. Cathy generously uses company profits to support many charitable projects such as providing recreational experiences for children.

We are aware of numerous Christian business people who are choosing to glorify God through their jobs. A friend of ours, Carol Parkin, is a real estate agent. She lives in one of the hottest real estate markets in the country. Even though many of the closings on houses take place on weekends, Carol was convinced that God did not want her to do business on Sundays. She stopped carrying her pager to church on Sunday. Rather than her business drying up, she became one of the most successful salespeople in her region. She is highly respected in her town and has been recognized by her peers as the outstanding real estate agent of the year. Her town newspaper carries her picture every Christmas with an article she writes that details the true meaning of Christmas. Carol doesn't work for a Christian organization, but she brings her Christianity *to* her organization and God receives the glory.

A Christian MVP
A Personal Example from Henry Blackaby

The sports world has enticed countless athletes and coaches to sacrifice their principles in order to win and to become successful. Yet a Christian leader knows life holds a greater purpose than simply leading one's team to victory. I served as chaplain to the St. Louis Rams football team on the day they won the Super Bowl in January 2000. Kurt Warner, the quarterback, had won the MVP of the league for the NFL that year. He would win the MVP of the Super Bowl before the day was over. Yet the day of the big game he met with me and, along with many others, fervently prayed that God would receive the glory for whatever would occur that day. Warner was interviewed after the game, and he reverently gave God the credit for his success. Warner developed a sports card that he autographed and handed out to fans. It reads: "The greatest day of my life had nothing to do with throwing forty TD passes in a season, being invited to the Pro Bowl, or being named NFL MVP. It was the day I asked Jesus into my heart. Now my life is dedicated to living out God's will and telling others about him." Christian leaders who impact their society understand that their first calling is not to be successful in the business world, or the sports world, or the medical or legal profession but to be a success in the kingdom of God.

It is no accident that, when Jesus was seeking twelve disciples, he bypassed the professional religious establishment and sought businessmen. Among those he chose were two pairs of fishermen and a tax collector. He found people who understood how the world operated and who were not afraid of working right in the middle of it. He chose people who spoke the language of the marketplace. These businessmen were strategically chosen to turn the world upside down. God does nothing by accident. When God places someone in a leadership position, he has a purpose. A Christian's first calling is to bring honor to the heavenly Father.

Bringing glory to God is not complicated. People bring God glory when they reveal God's nature to a watching world. When Christian leaders forgive others, people come to understand that God is a God who forgives. When Christian leaders are patient with those who fail, people come to understand that God is, by nature, long-suffering. When Christian leaders live with holy integrity, people gain a glimpse of God's holiness. The first glimpse of the true God that many people see will be reflected in the Christians who work alongside them week by week. To accurately reflect God's nature to others is to bring him glory.

God has a specific agenda for every person and every organization. Leaders can only discover God's will as he reveals it to them through their personal relationship with him. There are, however, spiritual goals that should guide every leader. Bringing people to spiritual maturity, developing leaders and, most importantly, bringing glory to God ought to be basic objectives of every leader.

CONCEPTS AND SCRIPTURES FOR CONSIDERATION

- Leaders can achieve their goals for a time but destroy their organizations in the process.
- Leaders can achieve their goals and yet be out of God's will. Reaching goals is not necessarily a sign of God's blessing.
- Excellence generally describes tasks, and tasks are usually a means to an end. *People* are the end.
- In God's eyes, *how* something is done is as important as *what* is done. The end does not justify the means in God's kingdom.
- There is a difference between giving God *your* best and giving God *the* best.

- The primary goal of spiritual leadership is not excellence, in the sense of doing things perfectly. Rather, it is taking people from where they are to where God wants them to be.
- There is a significant difference between drawing a crowd and building a church. Marketers can draw a crowd. Cults can draw a crowd. They can't build God's kingdom.
- One of the issues regarding spiritual leadership is whether spiritual leaders can take people to places they themselves have never been.
- It is not enough for leaders to hear from God and then relay the message to the people.
- Weak leaders cast blame upon their subordinates when things go wrong.
- God is not concerned with bringing glory to people. He wants to reveal his glory through people.
- God has a specific agenda for every person and every organization.

---

1 Peter 1:15–16
Matthew 5:48
Malachi 1:6–14
Colossians 1:28–29
Exodus 19:4

CHAPTER SEVEN

The Leader's Influence

How Leaders Lead

THE FUNDAMENTAL QUESTION FOR leaders is, "How can I move people to do what needs to be done?" For some people, exerting influence seems to come naturally. We all know people like that. When they merely enter a room, they immediately become the focal point. Others defer to them automatically as though instinctively bestowing leadership status upon them. Then there are those who struggle desperately to be heard and followed. They do all they know to do to wield influence on others, but their efforts are in vain. They grow more and more frustrated because no one listens to them. No one seems to value the expertise and wisdom they have to offer. James MacGregor Burns poignantly observes: "Much of what passes as leadership—conspicuous position-taking without followers or follow through, posturing on various public stages, manipulation without general purpose, authoritarianism—is no more leadership than the behavior of small boys marching in front of a parade, who continue to strut along main street after the procession has turned down a side street toward the fairgrounds."[1]

The ability to influence others is undoubtedly a pivotal requirement for leadership. To quote Oswald Sanders: "Leadership is influence, the ability of one person to influence others."[2] Chapter 5 outlined certain leadership qualities that generate respect from followers: God's authentication of leaders, leaders' character and integrity, leaders' track record of success, and leaders' preparation. These are qualities leaders bring with them when they arrive at new organizations. But what do leaders do to influence people once they assume a new leadership position? In other words, *how* do leaders lead?

When Lee Iacocca arrived at the Chrysler Corporation, Chrysler had just reported a third quarter loss of $160 million. Yet they had hope for the future. Iacocca arrived with years of successful experience at Ford. His training was impeccable. His track record was impressive. People at Chrysler naturally granted him the respect that was due him. All of that was great, but it wasn't enough. At a certain point, Iacocca had to begin leading Chrysler. His reputation was not enough. Leadership begins with "being" but ultimately turns to "doing." It is not one's credentials, but one's performance that ultimately confirms a person as a leader.

A spiritual leader, no matter how gifted or qualified, has not led unless people have shifted to God's agenda. How do spiritual leaders accomplish this? First, they need to know what God's agenda is. Spiritual leaders must take very seriously the weighty responsibility of learning to hear from God themselves before they can hope to equip others to do so. In this regard, the first thing leaders should do is, sadly, the last thing many leaders actually do. The single most important thing leaders should do is pray.

LEADERS PRAY

The leader's prayer life is critical for several reasons. First, nothing of eternal significance happens apart from God. Jesus said it clearly: "Apart from Me you can do nothing" (John 15:5). Leaders who neglect a close relationship with Christ will be unable to accomplish God's will through their organizations. It's that simple. Yet many leaders struggle in their prayer lives. Leaders are doers. The challenge for many is that they think of prayer as too passive. We know a pastor who exclaimed, "It's fine to pray and ask God what he wants to do through your church. But I prefer to be proactive rather than reactive." May God have mercy on his church! Leaders are men and women of action. They are programmed to get results. They are also very busy people on tight schedules. Taking time to pray can seem like wasting precious time. Even pastors of churches can grow to resent the time they spend praying, because they have so many things to do! Prayerless leaders can keep full schedules, but they will look back over their activity and realize that, despite their best efforts, nothing of eternal consequence occurred. Biblical praying can be the most challenging, exhausting, laborious, and yet rewarding thing leaders ever do.

Second, prayer is essential because to be a spiritual leader, one must be filled with the Holy Spirit. Leaders cannot fill themselves with the Spirit. Only God can do that (Eph. 5:18). While all Christians have the Holy Spirit's presence in their lives, the condition of being filled by the Holy Spirit comes through concentrated, fervent, sanctified prayer. God's promise is: "You will seek Me and find Me when you search for Me with all your heart" (Jer. 29:13). Without the Spirit's activity, people may be leaders, but they are not spiritual leaders.

God's wisdom is a third reward for dedicated praying. God is the leader of spiritual leaders: he knows far more than even the best-informed leader. God is infinitely wiser than the most astute leader (Rom. 8:26–27; 1 Cor. 2:9). He knows the future. He knows what the leader's opponents are thinking. He knows what the economy will be like. God knows what he wants to accomplish and how he intends to do it. God's invitation to leaders is "Call to Me and I will answer you, and I will tell you great and mighty things which you do not know" (Jer. 33:3). For leaders to have this kind of relationship available to them and then choose not to communicate with the one who wants to guide them is a gross dereliction of duty (Luke 18:1–8).

God is all-powerful. That is a fourth reason leaders should pray. God can do far more than even the most resourceful leaders. God's promise is open ended: "Ask, and it will be given to you; seek, and you will find; knock, and it will be opened to you" (Matt. 7:7 NIV). If someone is angry with a leader, reconciliation might look impossible. But God can melt the hardest heart. Leaders can be stymied when people refuse to cooperate. But God can change people's attitudes overnight. There are times when even the most powerful CEOs in the world can do nothing but retreat to the privacy of their executive office, pray, and let God work. When Nancy Reagan was diagnosed with a malignant tumor and had to undergo a mastectomy, her husband, though he was President Ronald Reagan, realized that even being the most powerful executive in the world had its limits. Commenting on that day, Reagan confessed: "For all the powers of the president of the United States, there were some situations that made me feel helpless and very humble. All I could do was pray—and I did a lot of praying for Nancy during the next few weeks."[3] The stark truth of life is that it is filled with situations that can only be overcome by God's power. The most powerful position leaders assume is when they kneel.

A fifth reason to pray is that prayer is the leader's best remedy for stress. Leaders are intimately acquainted with stress. Leadership and pressure go hand in hand. Scripture encourages leaders to cast "all your anxiety on Him, because He cares for you" (1 Pet. 5:7). Because of their position, most leaders carry a heavy load of responsibility. It may be difficult to find someone with whom they can share their concerns and fears. Sometimes circumstances dictate the need for complete confidentiality, so the leader bears the weight of responsibility alone. But there is one who is always ready to carry the burden for them. Christ said his yoke is easy and his burden is light (Matt. 11:28–30). When leaders allow Christ to carry their emotional and spiritual loads, this takes enormous pressure off them and allows them to face even the most difficult assignments with peace.

Finally, God reveals his agenda through prayer. Jesus modeled this truth in his life (Mark 1:30–39). At the outset of his public ministry, when Jesus was staying in Peter and Andrew's home, crowds of sick and demon-possessed people came to the house seeking healing. In fact, the Bible says the entire city turned out to see Jesus. Jesus healed many people until late into the evening. Early the next morning, Jesus rose and went to pray. The people wanted to keep Jesus in their city as the "resident healer," and they were reluctant to let him go. If Jesus had been a modern leader he might have reasoned, "I am obviously having success here and receiving a good response from the people. Perhaps I should stay here for a while until my reputation is firmly established." Instead, Jesus sought his Father's will. As Jesus prayed that morning, the Father helped Jesus understand what the agenda of the crowd was and he reaffirmed his agenda for his Son—to preach and teach in all the towns and villages and eventually to be crucified in Jerusalem. When the disciples found Jesus and told him the entire town was looking for him, Jesus responded, "Let us go somewhere else" (v. 38). Jesus would not be side-tracked from his Father's agenda because he was in regular communion with him in prayer.

More than any other single thing leaders do, it is their prayer life that determines their effectiveness. If leaders spend adequate time communing with God, the people they encounter that day will notice the difference. When pastors preach sermons, their people can soon tell whether or not they are speaking out of the overflow of their relationship with God or whether they are merely preaching a sermon. When leaders give counsel to others, the wisdom of their words will reveal whether or not they are filled with the Spirit. The holiness of leaders' lives is a direct reflection of the time they are spending with holy God. When spiritual leaders take their task of leading people seriously, they will be driven to their knees in prayer. They will recognize the magnitude of their responsibility to lead people. This truth is evident in the life of Moses. When the Israelites sinned against God and built a golden calf as an idol, God intended to punish them for their sin. In one of the greatest intercessory prayers in the Bible, Moses pleaded: "Alas, this people has committed a great sin, and they have made a god of gold for themselves. But now, if Thou wilt, forgive their sin—and if not, please blot me out from Thy book which Thou hast written!" (Exod. 32:31–32; cf. Deut. 9:4–21).

What an incredible testimony to the integrity of a spiritual leader! Moses recognized his people's failure as being his failure, because he was their leader. He could not stand by and watch them be destroyed, even if they deserved it, so he offered a sacred plea—his own life for theirs. Such sacrificial, earnest, heart-wrenching prayer is characteristic of great spiritual leaders.

There will be times when leaders will come to the end of their own resources. In those times they will understand there is nothing more they can do for their people. Giving speeches will not fix the problem. Issuing memos will change nothing. Calling in consultants will be futile. There are simply some things that can only be achieved through prayer (Ps. 50:15).

How fortunate are the people who are led by praying leaders. Leaders should regularly ask their people how they can pray for them. When prayers are answered, leaders can rejoice along with their people. This is true of secular businesses as well as Christian organizations. Christian CEOs ought not to force their beliefs on their staff, but even unbelieving employees can be effected by a leader who is a person of prayer. In the right setting, it can be very appropriate for Christian business leaders to ask their employees if they might have the liberty to pray for them. It is an awesome thing to have a secular business led by a Christian leader who diligently prays for every employee.

LEADING AN ORPHANAGE

George Mueller's name will forever be associated with effective prayer. Through fervent prayer, Mueller established an orphanage in Bristol, England in the 1800s. Mueller saw that ministry grow to include the care of two thousand orphans in five orphanages. Mueller traveled over 200,000 miles to share the gospel in forty-two countries. In all of this, he never once asked for money; he based his enormous ministry solely on prayer. Mueller also faithfully prayed for people's salvation. At one point in his life he observed:

> In November, 1844, I began to pray for the conversion of five individuals. I prayed every day without a single intermission, whether sick or in health, on land or at sea, and whatever the pressure of my engagements might be. Eighteen months elapsed before the first of the five was converted. I thanked God and prayed on for the others. Five years elapsed, and then the second was converted. I thanked God for the second, and prayed on for the other three. Day by day I continued to pray for them, and six years passed before the third was converted. I thanked God for the three, and went on praying for the other two. These two remained unconverted . . . . The man to whom God in the riches of his grace has given tens of thousands of answers to prayer in the self-same hour or day in which they were offered has been praying day by day for nearly thirty-six years for the conversion of these individuals, and yet they remain unconverted.

But I hope in God, I pray on, and look yet for the answer. They are not converted yet, but they will be.[4]

It was not until after Mueller's death that the last man accepted Christ as his Savior, but each one did. Such was Mueller's trust in God and tenacity in prayer.

The executive office ought to be a prayer center from which fervent intercession emanates on behalf of each person in the organization. As God in his grace responds to the prayers of leaders, things will happen in the organization that can only be attributed to God. People may not understand why certain dynamics are happening in the workplace, but the leader will know.

Why Should Leaders Pray?

1. Prayer is an essential leadership activity.
2. Prayer brings the Spirit's filling.
3. Prayer brings God's wisdom.
4. Prayer accesses God's power.
5. Prayer relieves stress.
6. Prayer reveals God's agenda.

Leaders should be known as men and women who pray. They should also be known as people who work hard. The two are not mutually exclusive.

LEADERS WORK HARD

Leaders dramatically influence the culture of their organizations through their own work habits. Being a leader does not mean one has "made it" and is now exempt from hard work. Rather, leaders should set the pace for others. Few things discourage employees and volunteers any more than lazy leaders. Leaders should not ask their people to undertake tasks they are unwilling to perform themselves. While the role of leaders does not allow them to spend all their time laboring alongside their people, they can seek to encourage their followers by their example of hard work. Leaders should ask themselves, "If the people in my organization worked with the same intensity as I do, would they enhance the operations of this organization or would they reduce it to a crawl?"

This means that if the pastor urges his members to participate in a workday at the church on Saturday, the pastor is there in his work clothes, not in his study finishing off Sunday's sermon. It means that if a company is forced to ask employees to take a reduction in pay, the CEO is the first one to make a sacrifice. It means that when a Bible teacher assigns a passage to be memorized, she learns the verses herself. A leadership position does not provide immunity from sacrifice; rather, it often provides occasions for an even greater effort.

Jesus was his disciples' leader, but no one worked harder than he did. After Jesus fed the five thousand, he allowed the disciples to get away for a much-needed rest while he remained to send away the multitude and then to pray (Mark 6:45–46). On another occasion, Jesus ministered to the crowds until he was so exhausted that even a raging storm at sea could not awaken him as he slept in the back of a fishing boat (Luke 8:22–24). At other times Jesus would forgo meals with his disciples so that he could continue ministering to people (John 4:31–34). Jesus taught his disciples not just with his words but always by his example. Even when Jesus' disciples suffered persecution, they knew Jesus had provided them with the model for suffering (Matt. 10:24–25).

Great military leaders have understood that there are times when they must lead their troops by example rather than by command. Alexander the Great, Robert E. Lee, and George Washington were all known for charging to the front of their troops when their men began to waver and lose heart. George Washington miraculously survived many close calls from the enemy when he refused to retreat to safety while his men were under fire. When Alexander the Great was advancing upon a city, his troops grew fatigued and became reluctant to scale the walls of the enemy city. So Alexander chose to lead by example. When he leaped over the wall and began fending off enemy soldiers, his embarrassed troops frantically scaled the wall to save their overzealous king. An enemy arrow seriously wounded Alexander, but his troops won another decisive victory. While his actions were not necessarily conventional for a commanding general, Alexander knew the power of motivating by example, and such leadership inspired his troops to follow him in conquering the known world.[5]

On May 28, 1970, Colonel Norman Schwarzkopf landed his command helicopter at the site where one of his companies had inadvertently wandered into a minefield. As a wounded soldier was being airlifted to base, a second soldier set off a mine and began screaming out in pain, unable to escape the minefield. The soldiers in the company began to panic as they realized they were in great peril. Schwarzkopf assumed responsibility for rescuing the endangered company and entered the minefield to rescue the wounded soldier. Another mine was detonated twenty yards away, severely wounding a third soldier and injuring Schwarzkopf. Schwarzkopf managed to get both wounded soldiers back to safety. Schwarzkopf clearly understood a truth that Jesus perfectly modeled: true leadership comes through personal sacrifice.[6]

A willingness to sacrifice gives leaders much more authority with their people than does their position in the organization. Mahatma Ghandi's readiness to suffer for the sake of his cause gave him an international influence that he would never have achieved by simply commanding his people to march into danger. Martin Luther King Jr.'s letter, written while he was confined in a Birmingham jail cell, gained him the attention of his nation. Nelson Mandela spent over twenty-seven years in the formidable prison on Robben Island before he was ultimately awarded the Nobel Prize, and later, his nation's presidency. History is filled with examples of great leaders who enjoyed ultimate success only after enduring great suffering. Life offers few shortcuts to greatness.

If leaders want their people to arrive at work on time, leaders must set the standard for punctuality. If leaders want their people to go an extra mile, leaders must go two. If leaders need their people to work late to complete a project, their people should not see their leaders leaving the parking lot promptly at quitting time. If leaders find that their organizations are filled with selfish, lazy employees, they need to understand that each employee is ultimately a microcosm of the organization, and a reflection of its leader. Leaders influence others by their example.

Wise leaders are sensitive to model a good example before their people. This is not because they are hypocrites or because they are seeking to impress people. It is because astute leaders understand that one of their greatest sources of influence over their followers is their example. Conscientious leaders ask themselves, "What do my people see when they watch me at work?"

A hard working leader may rise at five every morning in order to spend time with God in her office at home and then to prepare for the meetings she will participate in that day. By the time she gets to work, she may have already spent three hours doing her job. But that is not what her staff sees. They see their leader strolling in an hour after everyone else is obligated to be there. They may think, "It must be nice to be the boss and only work a couple of hours each day." The staff may not realize that their leader has already put in two hours working before they even arrived at work. And they *should* be aware of that. The point is not that the leader needs praise for working hard, but that she motivates others by her example. If leaders want their people to work hard, they must set the example. That's what leaders do. Leaders must realize that their employees will model what they see, not what they don't see. In this case, the employer may want to begin coming in to work earlier in the morning instead of working at home first. Then when employees arrive, they will see her office light already on and her car the first vehicle in the company parking lot. Because her employees know their leader works hard each day, they will be more motivated to be diligent in their jobs as well. This can be an enormous boost to company morale. Leaders must understand that they are responsible for the model they are giving to their people. In this sense, leadership is like parenting . . . "do as I do" is much more compelling than "do as I say."

Contemporary pastors must be particularly concerned about the model they are providing their people. Society is generally skeptical of today's church leaders and their work ethic. Pastors have long endured the critique that they only work one day a week. As a result, pastors need to maintain rigorous work habits, and their people need to know that they are doing so. Many pastors spend the early hours of each day studying and preparing their sermons because this is when their minds are fresh and they are less likely to be interrupted. In order to ensure that their study time is uninterrupted, some pastors choose to work at home during the mornings. Some pastors head straight into their study at home first thing in the morning before even showering or dressing. While this may be an efficient use of study time, it can also create perception problems for church members. We know a pastor who was at home when the church treasurer stopped by his house near the end of the morning to have a check signed. To her surprise, she was greeted at the door by her disheveled and unshaven pastor. He was wearing an old pair of sweat pants and a ragged T-shirt. The treasurer was using the lunch hour from her job to carry out this task as a church volunteer. Could she be faulted for feeling slightly dismayed? Needless to say, the pastor's reputation as an early-rising, hard-working minister was jeopardized.

This brings up another caution for leaders of Christian or charitable organizations. Leaders' work habits are particularly important in organizations that depend on volunteers. If volunteers are going to donate their time to an organization, they want to know that their leaders work as hard as they do. We recall a church staff person who went home two hours early every Wednesday to "make up for" the time he would spend attending the prayer meeting that evening. He didn't lead the meeting, but his rationale was that he "had" to go to it. It is highly unlikely that the accountant, secretaries, teachers and storekeepers in his church left their jobs early to account for the time they spent teaching children at the church on those same Wednesday evenings. If pastors want to have credibility with the businessmen in their church who rise at 6:00 every morning in order to be at work downtown, then they must demonstrate that they are equally as diligent in their calling. We are aware of pastors who liked to keep irregular hours. They were night owls who loved to work late at night and then sleep in until 9:30 in the morning. When their parishioners called them at home at 9:30 and got them out of bed, the callers were less than impressed. When people perceive that their leaders are not working as hard as they are, the people will lose any motivation to make sacrifices for the organization themselves. Leaders also need to be mindful of their appearance.

Some pastors pride themselves on wearing jeans and a T-shirt when they are not in the pulpit. They do not dress like the average professional dresses in their city, but they want to be treated like one. Just as Christians are aware that a worldly lifestyle can discredit their Christian witness to others, so leaders know that a careless lifestyle can diminish their credibility in the eyes of their followers.

A leader's reputation is developed over time. Destroying a reputation only takes an unguarded moment. As people observe their leader, they gradually come to conclusions about what he or she is really like. Some pastors, when making conversation, talk more about their golf games than they do about God's kingdom. Some ministers seem more excited about the newest restaurant in town than they are about answered prayer. People will naturally conclude that whatever their leader talks about the most is what they consider to be the most important.

The bottom line is this: *Leadership is hard work.* There are no short-cuts. Some people look for easy paths to leadership positions. They want positions of influence, but they don't want to put in their time in the trenches. They are the ones who refuse to take a turn in the church nursery but they are more than willing to run the preschool program. They are the ones with little Bible knowledge, yet they lobby to be a Bible Study leader; they should be helping in the children's department, but they want to teach adults because that has more status. They are the ones who seek jobs that require minimum effort but provide the maximum pay. They revile sacrifice. They flee from hard work. They are dreamers who want others to pay the price for their dreams. Such people are certainly not qualified to be spiritual leaders.

As Oswald Sanders observed: "If he is not willing to rise earlier and stay up later than others, to work harder and study more diligently than his contemporaries, he will not greatly impress his generation."[7] The reason there are not more great spiritual leaders in our day is that there are not more men and women willing to pay the price. Spiritual leaders are people who serve the King of kings. Their work is kingdom work. The results of their work are eternal. Having such a responsibility ought to compel them to labor far more diligently than those whose labors are only for the temporal.

One discipline leaders should work diligently to master is the art of communication. Jesus was an adept communicator.

LEADERS COMMUNICATE

Howard Gardner, in his book, *Leading Minds*, observed that most leaders exhibited "linguistic intelligence."[8] Not all leaders, however, are blessed with equal mastery of communication skills. Harry Truman's biographer noted that when Truman began making political speeches, "The most that could be said for his early speeches was that they were brief."[9] Jonathan Edwards, early in his ministry, preached his lengthy sermons from manuscripts that had to be held close to his face for him to read. Yet his sermon, "Sinners in the Hands of an Angry God," electrified his listeners and was a spark plug for the First Great Awakening. Conversely, it has been said of Winston Churchill that "Churchill mobilized the English language and sent it into battle."[10] Churchill understood that choosing the right word was crucial to a leader's success. Such famous phrases as: "I have nothing to offer but blood, toil, tears, and sweat" became famous rallying points for his entire nation. Yet, despite his obvious giftedness, Churchill's oratorical success came as a result of hard work. Churchill suffered from a speech impediment as a young man and had to work hard at the craft of speaking before he was able to be an effective communicator. At an early age he immersed himself in the English classics including Shakespeare and the King James Bible. Churchill's friend F. E. Smith once quipped, "Winston has spent the best years of his life writing impromptu speeches."[11] Churchill understood, as have other great leaders, that not all words are equally potent. Some words and phrases ignite people's passions and lodge themselves deeply into people's minds. Kennedy's "Ask not what your country can do for you" speech and Martin Luther King Jr.'s "I have a dream" speech both had a powerful effect upon their audiences and are cited by today's orators because of their oratorical brilliance.

Most leaders may not have the eloquence of Churchill or Martin Luther King Jr., but they can still be effective communicators. The key to successful communication is clarity, not verbosity. Robert Greenleaf suggests this poignant self-check for speakers: "In saying what I have in mind will I really improve on the silence?"[12] Greenleaf also cautions, "From listening comes wisdom, from speaking comes repentance."[13] Leaders ought to be students of language and communication. They ought to seek ways to expand their vocabulary so they have more words at their disposal when communicating important truths to others. Public speakers, such as pastors, ought to beware of falling into verbal ruts lest their sermons become predictable and monotonous. Leaders ought to immerse themselves in the Scriptures and the writings of great thinkers. A dynamic and growing mind is better able to germinate fresh insights than a dull, lazy one. Conscientious leaders will also enlist confidantes to evaluate and critique their communication skills. Many pastors have admitted that their loving, candid wives have done more to enhance their speaking ability than the pastor's seminary preaching professor ever accomplished!

Effective leaders are sensitive to the nuances of their words. Jesus was adept at tailoring his words to his audiences. He called James, John, Peter, and Andrew to be "fishers of men." He spoke to rural audiences in terms of sowing, reaping, and harvest. Buzzwords come and go. While the use of popular terms can bring a sense of relevance to an organization, the important thing is to consider the connotations of such words and phrases. For example, the word *team* is popular in contemporary management theory. Team-building exercises are in vogue, even for religious organizations, and many churches now use the words *coaching* or *mentoring* in place of the term *discipling*. Certainly the word *team* invokes positive connotations. The image of working together toward a common goal is appealing. Several healthy qualities can be developed by participating in a team, but spiritual leaders must be sensitive to any unbiblical implications attached to the word. For example, the primary goal of a team is usually to win. Teams foster competition for positions as candidates try to make the cut. Most teams have a hierarchy of first, second- and third-string players. Teams often have star players as well as benchwarmers. For these reasons, the word *team* may actually conjure up negative images for some people. None of this is to say the concept of teamwork is negative, but rather to illustrate the importance of weighing one's words in light of the intended audience and in light of the leader's desire to adhere to biblical principles.

These cautions, notwithstanding, spiritual leaders should take confidence in the fact that when God entrusts assignments to leaders, he also equips them to communicate his message (Exod. 3:10–12; Isa. 6:5–7;

Jer. 1:9). The key to effective communication is the presence of the Holy Spirit working in the leader's life. While this does not negate the leader's need to work on developing linguistic skills, nonetheless, it is the Spirit who will ultimately guide the leader to find the right vehicle through which to convey important truths about the organization and what it is facing. Traditionally, the most effective form of communication has been the story.

Howard Gardner contends that there are several types of stories leaders tell.[14] One type includes stories about the people themselves. These stories help people answer the question, "Who am I?" People need to know that their lives have relevance, that their lives matter and that they are meaningful contributors to the world around them. Leaders tell stories that help their people make sense of their existence. Sometimes leaders will tell stories from their own lives in order to help others put their experiences into perspective. This can help authenticate the leader as a person as well as the leader's message.

A second type of story pertains to the organization. Such a story explains the reason for the group's existence. It may also describe the vision of the organization's founders and chronicle hardships people endured in the beginning in order to make the organization what it is today. The leader may also relate contemporary stories that describe ways the organization is making a positive difference today.

People need to know what is truly important in life. Therefore, leaders tell stories that address issues of value and meaning. Leaders help their people understand what is true and good through the stories they tell.

Finally, leaders tell stories about culture. This could be the culture of a church, a company, or a nation. These stories identify who the heroes are and what is considered valuable and noteworthy in that organization. According to Gardner, effective leaders will tell stories that address each of these four areas of organizational life.

Ivah Bates
A Personal Example from Henry Blackaby

Experiencing God relates the story of Ivah Bates, an elderly widow who was a member of Faith Baptist Church in Saskatoon, Canada while I was the pastor.[15] When our church began to sense God commissioning us to reach out to university students, Ivah came to visit me. She was downhearted. She grieved over the fact that there was nothing she could do to help in this endeavor, since she was poor and her health was fragile. I was aware of something Ivah could contribute, so I asked her to be the church's prayer warrior for college students. Whenever there was a Bible study or outreach activity on campus, Ivah would be notified, and she would begin praying. One day a college student named Wayne asked the church for prayer as he prepared to share his faith that week with his roommate Doug. The next Sunday Wayne walked to the front of the church with Doug to introduce him as a new believer in Christ. As I looked out on the congregation, I saw Ivah weeping with joy. She had played a major role in reaching Doug for Christ, and she had not stepped foot on the campus. Doug was one of many students who would thank Ivah for her role in helping them find Christ.

I told this story, and others like it, many times in subsequent years, and it always encouraged people in my church. What did the story convey? First, it addressed people's identity. Was it possible to be too young or too old, too rich or too poor for God to use them? Absolutely not! Did they have to possess the same skills or education as other people in the church to be valued or useful? Of course not. Every person was important in that church. The story also explained the way our organization functioned. When God commissioned us to do something, every member had a part to play, and every role was important. There were no bench sitters. When God showed our church where he wanted us to start a new mission, the members understood that every member needed to ask God what role they were to play in this assignment. Third, the story addressed the values of our church. Our church valued evangelism. In order to reach people for Christ, every member in the church would be mobilized. Prayer was highly valued. People's contributions were valued.

Obedience to God was valued. Finally, the story explained the culture of the church. Those who were faithful in prayer were heroes in the organization. People who shared their faith with their friends were heroes. People who did their part, whatever that part was, were heroes. Stories such as Ivah's addressed so many of the questions people might have concerning our church that I told them often.

Leaders need to develop the habit of telling stories such as the "Ivah" story in order to help their people see God at work in their midst. It is the leader's responsibility to clearly communicate God's activity to the people, for the leader often has the best vantage point from which to see it. For example, a pastor will see connections such as Ivah's prayers and Doug's salvation that others may miss, simply because the pastor knows more of what happened. Leaders who assume their people will automatically see what they see and make the connection, are short-changing their followers.

With today's technology it is irresponsible for leaders to keep their people uninformed. Technology provides numerous forums for communication, many of them instantaneous and easily accessible. That having been said, there is a danger in relying too much on technology. For decades, technology has been overrated. Leaders should remember that nothing has yet been devised that has the impact of a face-to-face encounter. Leaders ought to seize every opportunity to speak directly to their people. Breakfast and lunch meetings with key employees or volunteers as well as regularly scheduled staff meetings can help build morale. Taking time to walk about work areas speaking directly to people can communicate more than a year's worth of newsletters.

Alfred Sloan, the famed CEO of General Motors, used to visit between five and ten car dealers every day. He had a special train outfitted so he could travel quickly across the country to keep in touch with those on the field. Sam Walton, founder of Wal-Mart, was famous for appearing at stores across the country unannounced to see how they were doing. Abraham Lincoln spent as much as 75 percent of his time receiving people in his office. Bennis and Nanus found that the top CEOs in their studies spent 90 percent of their time with people.[16] Leaders who think they are too busy to be regularly listening to and communicating with their people are doomed to fail.

LEADERS SERVE

Perhaps the greatest Christian influence on leadership theory has been in the area of "servant leadership." The example of Jesus has become the model not just for Christian leaders but for secular leaders as well. In all of literature there is no clearer example of servant leadership than that of Christ on the night of his crucifixion.

Now before the Feast of the Passover, Jesus knowing that His hour had come that He should depart out of this world to the Father, having loved His own who were in the world, He loved them to the end. And during supper, the devil having already put into the heart of Judas Iscariot, the son of Simon, to betray Him, Jesus, knowing that the Father had given all things into His hands, and that He had come forth from God, and was going back to God, rose from supper, and laid aside His garments; and taking a towel, He girded Himself about. Then He poured water into the basin, and began to wash the disciples' feet, and to wipe them with the towel with which He was girded. And so He came to Simon Peter. He said to Him, "Lord, do you wash my feet?" Jesus answered and said to him, "What I do you do not realize now, but you shall understand hereafter." Peter said to Him, "Never shall You wash my feet!" Jesus answered him, "If I do not wash you, you have no part with Me." Simon Peter said to Him, "Lord, not my feet only, but also my hands and my head." Jesus said to him, "He who has bathed needs only to wash his feet, but is completely clean; and you are clean, but not all of you." For He knew the one who was betraying Him; for this reason He said, "Not all of you are clean." And so when He had washed their feet, and taken His garments, and reclined at the table again, He said to them, "Do you know what I have done to you? You call Me Teacher and Lord; and you are right, for so I am. If I then, the Lord and the Teacher, washed your feet, you also ought to wash one another's feet. For I gave you an example that you also should do as I did to you. Truly, truly, I say to you, a slave is not greater than his master; neither is one who is sent greater than the one who sent him. If you know these things, you are blessed if you do them" (John 13:1–17).

Several keys to servant leadership are evident in this sacred passage. First, servant leadership flows from the love leaders have for their people. Scripture says, "having loved His own who were in the world, He loved them to the end." Leaders cannot truly serve people they do not love. They may perform acts of service but their followers will rightly perceive their actions as insincere and manipulative unless they are done because of genuine concern. Many leaders experience difficulty in this regard because they are unfamiliar with Christlike love. Many grew up in homes where love was in short supply. The result is performance-driven leaders who feel compelled to achieve at all costs, even if it means using or abusing others. Such leaders find it all but impossible to love those with whom they work. Yet it was the love Jesus showed his disciples (even Judas, whose feet he washed as thoroughly and lovingly as the other eleven) that brought him lifelong loyalty from his followers. Because of Jesus' unfathomable love for his disciples, the eleven would eventually follow Jesus unwaveringly, even when such loyalty was rewarded with martyrdom.

Even non-Christian organizations are catching on to the need for leaders to genuinely care for their people. When Kouzes and Posner studied the leadership traits of top CEOs they found only one characteristic that was common to all of them: affection. These successful leaders cared for their people and they wanted their people to like them in return.[17] It is significant that even well-paid, educated professionals will perform better when they believe their leader cares about them. In their book, *First Break All the Rules: What the World's Greatest Managers Do Differently*, Markus Buckingham and Curt Coffman ask, "Should you build close personal relationships with your employees, or does familiarity breed contempt?" To this, the authors respond: "The most effective managers say yes, you should build personal relationships with your people, and no, familiarity does not breed contempt."[18]

The old adage "the end does not justify the means" is no more appropriate in secular business than it is in religious organizations. There is both a right thing to do and a right way to do it. Leaders who equate bottom-line results with success are sadly deluded. When a company accomplishes its goals but decimates the lives of its members, it may win the battle but lose the war. Reaching organizational goals is important, but so is enriching the lives of people in the organization. Lee Iacocca guided Chrysler through an arduous time and achieved stellar results. But looking back over that period the celebrated CEO observed: "But our struggle had its dark side. To cut expenses, we had to fire a lot of people. It's like a war: we won, but my son didn't come back. There was a lot of agony. People were getting destroyed, taking their kids out of college, drinking, getting divorced. Overall we preserved the company, but only at enormous personal expense for a great many human beings."[19] Iacocca achieved his goal, but many of his employee's lives were irreparably damaged.

Ironically, while secular business grows increasingly aware of its responsibility to care for its people, many religious organizations remain oblivious to this need. Leaders come to Christian organizations filled with righteous zeal to see the Lord's work accomplished. Because they are striving to achieve *God's* goals, they can assume no price is too great. If downsizing an organization is required, they callously show long-term, loyal employees to the door in a manner that would shame secular business managers. If getting the job done calls for bullying and cajoling people into submission, these religious leaders stubbornly go toe to toe with their reluctant employees. No matter how worthwhile a religious organization's goal, it is impossible to believe Jesus would lead in this manner. When leaders stop loving their people, they stand tempted to use them, to neglect them, and to discard them.

Leaders who are unable to love their people and who are unwilling to consider their needs, are insecure in their own identity. Why was Jesus able to humble himself and wash his disciples' filthy feet? Scripture says, "Jesus, knowing that the Father had given all things into His hands, and that He had come forth from God, and was going back to God . . . ." Jesus knew where he had come from and where he was going. He was not insecure about his identity. His self worth was not on the line. He was dead center in his Father's will and he knew it. That made all the difference.

The second requirement for servant leadership, therefore, is self-knowledge. Leaders must know and accept who they are. Insecure people worry about how other people perceive them. They fear that serving others may cause people to take advantage of them or to think less of them. People who are secure in their identity are not enslaved by the opinions or affirmation of others. They are free to serve.

President Harry Truman was one of the most unpretentious presidents in U.S. history. There was a buzzer on his desk that previous presidents had used to summon aides to the oval office. Truman removed it. He refused to "buzz" people and insisted on going to the door to ask for them politely in person. During a special reception Truman held for Joseph Stalin and Winston Churchill, Sergeant Eugene List, an American soldier, prepared to play a special piece on the grand piano. When List asked for someone to turn the pages of music for him, Truman volunteered. Throughout the sergeant's brilliant performance, his commander in chief stood by his side turning pages for him. Later, List wrote to his wife and marveled, "Imagine having the President of the United States turn pages for you! . . . But that's the kind of man the President is."[20] In recalling his leadership style Truman explained, "I tried never to forget who I was and where I'd come from and where I would go back to."[21] Truman's biographer concluded that because of the way Truman related to his staff, "The loyalty of those around Truman was total and would never falter. In years to come not one member of the Truman White House would ever speak or write scathingly of him or belittle him in any fashion."[22] Comfort with one's identity is mandatory for servant leaders.

Third, Christlike servant leaders must understand whom they serve. On the topic of servant leadership, there is some confusion about whom leaders actually serve. Spiritual leaders are not their people's servants; they are God's. The account of Jesus washing his disciples' feet is often cited in discussions of servant leadership, and rightly so. But Scripture only records an account of Jesus doing this once. If Jesus had been a servant to his disciples, he would have washed their feet every evening. If he had been his disciples' servant, he would have granted Peter's request to be excluded from the foot washing. But Jesus was not trying to give his followers what *they* wanted; he was determined to give them what his Father wanted to give them. Jesus' response to Peter, therefore, was "If I do not wash you, you have no part with me" (John 13:8). The disciples did not set the agenda for Jesus' ministry. The Father did. Jesus was the

Father's servant not theirs. Even as Jesus served his disciples, there was no question in anyone's mind that he was still their Lord.

Jesus served the twelve because that was what the Father wanted him to do that evening. Jesus was always aware that he was the teacher and Lord of his disciples (John 13:13). When Jesus finished washing their feet, he concluded: "For I gave you an example that you also should do as I did to you" (John 13:15). Jesus was not only serving his disciples; he was teaching them. Jesus was demonstrating the ethos of his kingdom.

Spiritual leaders ought to serve their people. But their acts of service should be motivated and directed by the Holy Spirit. When leaders are not afraid to roll up their sleeves and serve their people, they encourage a corporate culture in which people willingly serve one another. When people serve each other ungrudgingly, they forge a unity that enables their organization to accomplish far more than if individuals worked on their own. Servanthood breaks down barriers and eliminates turf wars. Jesus' disciples needed to understand that they were servants of the Lord and because of this, they would be called upon to serve one another. When the disciples learned this lesson, they were ready to turn their world upside down.

LEADERS MAINTAIN POSITIVE ATTITUDES

A pessimistic leader is a contradiction in terms. Leaders, by virtue of their role, are obligated to nurture positive attitudes. Leaders who doubt that success is possible and who fear the worst should immediately change their attitude or resign so a true leader can take their place. Some people in leadership positions assume they are simply being realistic when they expect the worst. The implication is that positive leaders have their heads in the clouds. However, true leaders understand that no matter how difficult the task before them, a group of people being led by the Holy Spirit can accomplish anything God asks of them (Rom. 8:31).

It is a natural inclination for people to get discouraged in the midst of adversity, but a fundamental role of leaders is to maintain a positive attitude under every circumstance. When George Marshall became the U.S. Secretary of State, he was informed that spirits were low in the State Department. Marshall advised his staff, "Gentlemen, enlisted men may be entitled to morale problems, but officers are not . . . . I expect all officers in this department to take care of their own morale. No one is taking care of my morale."[23] If leaders cannot manage their own attitudes, they cannot be entrusted with the morale of others. When leaders believe anything is possible, their followers will come to believe that too. The Duke of Wellington claimed that the effect of Napolean's presence on his troops' morale was worth forty thousand men. General Stonewall Jackson was said to have been so inspiring to his Confederate troops that if a group of his soldiers in camp suddenly let out a yell, this could mean one of two things: either the beloved General Jackson had just ridden into camp, or someone had spotted a rabbit! Winston Churchill has been similarly honored: it was said that that no one left his presence without feeling a braver man. Leaders inspire confidence, not fear or pessimism.

Good morale is intrinsically linked with a good sense of humor. Depree suggests: "Joy is an essential ingredient of leadership. Leaders are obligated to provide it."[24] Joy was an inherent part of Jesus' ministry (John 15:11). Biographies of great leaders credit many of them with a good sense of humor. Abraham Lincoln reveled in telling humorous stories. Winston Churchill was famous for his quick wit. During World War I, Churchill lectured his officers in the trenches saying, "Laugh a little, and teach your men to laugh . . . If you can't smile, grin. If you can't grin, keep out of the way until you can."[25] Churchill believed, "You cannot deal with the most serious things in the world unless you also understand the most amusing." Great leaders know when to laugh and they know how to make others laugh. In 1984, Ronald Reagan was seeking reelection for a second term as United States president. Reagan was seventy-three years old, and his opponents had been deriding him for what they labeled the "senility factor." If elected, Reagan would be the oldest president in U.S. history. During a televised debate with his opponent, former Vice President Walter Mondale, a reporter asked Reagan whether his age would be a handicap in the campaign. Reagan responded: "I am not going to exploit for political purposes my opponent's youth and inexperience."[26] Reagan's quick rejoinder even forced a chuckle out of his opponent on national television and helped diffuse a potential landmine on his path back to the White House. While Reagan was serving his first term as president, John Hinckley Jr.

shocked the nation by attempting to assassinate him as he left the Hilton Hotel. Reagan kept his humor even with a bullet lodged less than an inch from his heart. Upon seeing his wife Nancy after the shooting, Reagan quipped, "Honey, I forgot to duck."[27] A good sense of humor is essential to effective leadership because leaders set the tone for their organizations. Many times when the situation becomes tense or difficult, leaders with a healthy sense of humor help others gain a new perspective. It is easier to follow people who know how to laugh and who make working with them enjoyable.

Spiritual leaders understand the importance of a positive attitude as an effective leadership tool, but they remain optimistic not because doing so is a vital leadership practice but because they are in touch with God. This is why spiritual leaders need to spend much time in the conscious presence of God. Only after clearly understanding who God is, can leaders gain a proper perspective on their situation. A glimpse into the Scriptures provides ample support for a positive attitude:

> Who has measured the waters in the hollow of his hand, And marked off the heavens by the span, and calculated the dust of the earth by the measure, and weighed the mountains in a balance, And the hills in a pair of scales? Who has directed the Spirit of the Lord, Or as His counselor has informed Him? With whom did He consult and who gave Him understanding? And who taught Him in the path of justice and taught him knowledge, and informed Him of the way of understanding? Behold, the nations are like a drop from a bucket, and are regarded as a speck of dust on the scales; behold, he lifts up the islands like fine dust. Even Lebanon is not enough to burn, nor its beasts enough for a burnt offering. All the nations are as nothing before Him, They are regarded by Him as less than nothing and meaningless. To whom then will you liken God? Or what likeness will you compare with Him? As for the idol, a craftsman casts it, a goldsmith plates it with gold, and a silversmith fashions chains of silver. He who is too impoverished for such an offering selects a tree that does not rot; He seeks out for himself a skillful craftsman to prepare an idol that will not totter. Do you not know? Have you not heard? Has it not been declared to you from the beginning? Have you not understood from the foundations of the earth? It is He who sits

above the vault of the earth, and its inhabitants are like grasshoppers, who stretches out the heavens like a curtain and spreads them out like a tent to dwell in. He it is who reduces rulers to nothing, who makes the judges of the earth meaningless. Scarcely have they been planted, scarcely have they been sown, scarcely has their stock taken root in the earth, but he merely blows on them, and they wither, and the storm carries them away like stubble. "To whom then will you liken me that I should be his equal?" says the Holy One. Lift up your eyes on high and see who has created these stars, the one who leads forth their host by number, He calls them all by name; Because of the greatness of His might and the strength of His power Not one of them is missing. Why do you say, O Jacob, and assert, O Israel, "My way is hidden from the Lord, and the justice due me escapes the notice of my God"? Do you not know? Have you not heard? The everlasting God, the Lord, the Creator of the ends of the earth does not become weary or tired. His understanding is inscrutable. He gives strength to the weary, and to him who lacks might He increases power. Though youths grow weary and tired, and vigorous young men stumble badly, Yet those who wait for the Lord will gain new strength; they will mount up with wings like eagles, they will run and not get tired, they will walk and not become weary (Isa. 40:12–31).

Everyone faces discouraging circumstances, but the Scriptures provide the vista leaders need to help them maintain or regain a positive attitude. Momentary setbacks are one thing, but many church leaders choose to live in the valley of despair. Incredibly, some leaders actually pride themselves in being pessimists! They refer to their pessimism as realism and consider it a sign of superior intelligence since they detect problems and things to worry about that the rank and file seem to miss. We have known pastors with rapidly declining churches who blamed their people, they blamed the location of their church building, they blamed former leaders, they blamed Satan and spiritual warfare, and they concluded that their situation was hopeless in the face of all that conspired against them. Some even declared that they knew their church could not possibly survive; they were staying only long enough to conduct the imminent funeral. One pastor concluded that since the last three churches he had "led" had all disbanded, God must have given

him the ministry of disbanding churches. He was serious! Such leadership is an abomination to almighty God! Such leaders need a fresh
encounter with the risen Lord so they come to believe that, with God, all
things are possible. People need leaders who believe that God can do
anything he says he can do. Henry's guiding life verse over the years has
been Daniel 3:17, ". . . our God whom we serve is able, and he will . . . ."

We know of a small church that had suffered years of decline. The
remaining members were discouraged and all but ready to give up.
Pastors had come and gone, but the church continued its skid into
oblivion. The church facility was so neglected that sections of it no
longer met civic safety codes. Two-thirds of the facility was being rented
out to an ethnic congregation in order to generate much-needed
income. The church building was difficult for visitors to find, and pastors had complained for years that its poor location had greatly
restricted church growth. Time after time, pastors would grow frustrated with the church and the lack of results, and they would leave in
discouragement. Rumor had it that the church was actually demon possessed and that this was the reason for its chronic failure! After many
years in spiritual limbo, it appeared there was little left for the church
to do but to disband.

In an act of desperation, the church called a young pastor fresh out
of seminary. There was little to offer the minister and his young family
by way of pay or benefits, but he agreed to come anyway. The newly
installed pastor refused to believe that God was finished with his church
or that God was unable to use his church to impact the community for
Christ. He encouraged the people to pray. God began working. New
people began visiting and joining the church. Renovations were made
to the buildings. Giving increased. A second staff person was added. A
sense of excitement grew among the people that God was preparing
their church for something special. The church's reputation in the
community changed. It was no longer considered dead but became
known as one of the most exciting churches in the city!

What happened? The church continued to meet in its old buildings
in the same poor location. The pastor worked with the very same people the previous pastors had castigated. The community at large was just
as hardened to the gospel as previous leaders had said it was. Everything

was the same. Except one thing. The church now had a leader who truly believed God could do anything he said he could do; and this leader convinced his people to believe it too.

When Colonel Norman Schwarzkopf arrived to take command of his battalion in Vietnam, the outgoing battalion commander met with him to brief him. This is how Schwarzkopf recalls the meeting:

> "Come on back to my hooch," he said. "I need to talk to you a little." We drove about a mile to the battalion base camp, which was at the bottom of a hill, and then walked to a little cabin halfway up the hillside. On the table sat a bottle of Johnnie Walker Black Label scotch. "This is for you," he said. "You're going to need it." I was expecting a two- or three-hour discussion of the battalion, its officers, its NCOs, its mission—but he only said, "Well, I hope you do better than I did. I tried to lead as best I could, but this is a lousy battalion. It's got lousy morale. It's got a lousy mission. Good luck to you." With that he shook my hand and walked out.[28]

Schwarzkopf's predecessor was obviously not a leader. A leader would not have called his battalion lousy; he would have made it better. He would not have accused his soldiers of lousy morale; he would have done what was necessary to improve their morale. He would not have complained about the mission; he would have done everything possible to accomplish and enlarge the mission. This man pointed the finger of blame at everyone and everything but himself. No wonder he failed.

In contrast, Schwarzkopf was a leader. He kept a positive attitude. It was not that he overlooked the problems of his situation or the shortcomings of his troops. He saw them as well as or better than his predecessor had. By the time Schwarzkopf was finished with the battalion, morale was up and casualties were down. In fact, the Vietcong concluded that a new, much tougher battalion had moved into the area and replaced the previous unit that had been so inept!

Norman Schwarzkopf gained worldwide attention for his handling of the Gulf War. But throughout his entire career he succeeded in every assignment he was given. His success was not based on easy assignments. Often he was placed in difficult situations. Yet when others might have complained and cast blame, he set out to improve each situation and to make his organization better. The reason he was the Chief of Command during the Gulf War was because he had built a career out of improving whatever organization he was assigned to command.

Great leaders don't make excuses. They make things better. They are not unrealistic or blind to the difficulties they face. They simply are not discouraged by them. They never lose confidence that the problems can be solved. They maintain a positive attitude. Great leaders don't blame their people for not being where they ought to be; they take their people from where they are to where they need to be. Great leaders never lose faith that this is possible.

The Leader's Influence

1. Spiritual leaders pray.
2. Spiritual leaders work hard.
3. Spiritual leaders communicate.
4. Spiritual leaders serve.
5. Spiritual leaders maintain positive attitudes.

Leaders should pay close attention to their attitudes, for these serve as barometers to the condition of their hearts. When leaders become pessimistic, cynical or critical, they need to evaluate the causes. Perhaps they have been focusing on what people are doing rather than on what God has promised. Maybe pride is corrupting their thoughts, or insecurity is causing them to be overly defensive. Whatever the reason, a wise leader will recognize these attitudes as symptoms of an unhealthy relationship with God. Often leaders will spend plenty of time seeking the world's advice on how to manage their organization, but little time considering the wisdom found in God's Word. Busy leaders neglect their prayer life and wind up overwhelmed with anxiety. Such people need a fresh encounter with God. A wise practice for those in leadership roles is to invite a few trusted friends and associates to help monitor their attitudes. Making oneself accountable to a small group of trusted people can ensure that unhealthy attitudes and actions are dealt with before they harm both the leader and the organization.

Effective leadership does not happen by chance. It happens on purpose. There are certain leadership practices that anyone can exercise if they are serious about becoming an effective leader. Those who diligently follow these five guidelines are well on their way to becoming influential spiritual leaders.

STEWARDSHIP OF INFLUENCE

Influence is a powerful thing. With influence comes a tremendous responsibility. Therefore a weighty issue for leaders is their management of influence. When people trust their leaders, they give them the benefit of the doubt. Such power can seduce unwary leaders into using people to achieve their own selfish ends. Influence used for selfish purposes is nothing more than crass manipulation and political scheming. People need to know their leaders have their best interests at heart.

Leaders should realize that even when they say things casually, their people can take them seriously. Such was the case with David. David was camped outside Bethlehem with his men while a Philistine garrison occupied Bethlehem. In an unguarded moment, David remarked wistfully, "Oh that someone would give me water to drink from the well of Bethlehem which is by the gate!" (2 Sam. 23:15). Immediately, three of his loyal men set out for the well. David's friends fought their way through a garrison of Philistine soldiers until they reached the well. When they returned with the water, David was appalled at what he had done. By his selfish wish, three of his most loyal soldiers had endangered their lives. David had been careless with his influence as a leader.

Are leaders' moral failures anyone's business but their own? A great deal of controversy surrounds this issue. Some contend that (1) everyone fails at some point and (2) personal failure does not affect one's administrative skills and effectiveness. But when leaders experience moral failure, the repercussions are devastating. Leaders are symbols of their organizations. They are the repositories of their people's trust. When they prove untrustworthy, they shatter the faith and confidence of their people. People need to know they can trust their leaders. Leaders assume a higher level of accountability because there is more at stake if they fail. When God entrusts spiritual leadership to people, he also holds those leaders accountable for their stewardship of influence. Spiritual leaders should never accept new leadership positions without much prayerful consideration. Modern society is reeling under the incessant scandals of leaders who have abused their positions of influence. People trust leaders less than ever because so many leaders have abused their influence.

The responsibility of leading people carries with it a frightening sense of accountability (2 Cor. 5:9–11). Failing to lead well not only affects the leader but it also can cause irreparable harm to many other people both inside and outside the organization. On the other hand, influencing people to achieve God's best for them and for their organization brings an irrepressible joy and a sense of satisfaction that makes all the efforts to lead others a worthwhile endeavor. Paul knew that if he led well: "in the future there is laid up for me the crown of righteousness, which the Lord, the righteous Judge, will award to me on that day . . ." (2 Tim. 4:8).

Concepts and Scriptures for Consideration

- Leadership begins with "being" but ultimately turns to "doing."
- The single most important thing leaders should do is pray.
- Without the Spirit's activity, people may be leaders but they are not spiritual leaders.
- There are times when even the most powerful CEOs in the world can do nothing but retreat to the privacy of their executive office, pray, and let God work.
- People may not understand why certain dynamics are happening in the workplace, but the leader will know.
- Being a leader does not mean one has "made it" and is now exempt from hard work. Rather, leaders should set the pace for others.
- Leaders should ask themselves, "If the people in my organization worked with the same intensity as I do, would they enhance the operations of this organization or would they reduce it to a crawl?"

- A leadership position does not provide immunity from sacrifice; rather it often provides occasions for an even greater effort.
- The bottom line is this: *leadership is hard work*. There are no shortcuts.
- The reason there are not more great spiritual leaders in our day is that there are not more men and women willing to pay the price.
- Effective leaders are sensitive to the nuances of their words.
- Traditionally, the most effective form of communication has been the story.
- It is significant that even well-paid, educated professionals will perform better when they believe their leader cares about them.
- A pessimistic leader is a contradiction in terms.
- Leaders should pay close attention to their attitudes, for these serve as barometers to the condition of their hearts.
- Leaders are symbols of their organizations. They are the repositories of their people's trust. . . . Leaders assume a higher level of accountability because there is more at stake if they fail.

John 15:5

Jeremiah 29:13

Jeremiah 33:3

Matthew 7:7

1 Peter 5:7

Matthew 11:28–30

Exodus 32:31–32

Exodus 4:10–12; Isaiah 6:5–7; Jeremiah 1:9

John 13:1–17

Isaiah 40:12–31

2 Samuel 23:15

Romans 8:31

2 Timothy 4:8

Chapter Eight

The Leader's Decision Making

DECISION MAKING IS A FUNDAMENTAL responsibility of leaders. People who are unwilling or unable to make decisions are unlikely leadership candidates. Leaders may consult counselors; they may seek consensus from their people; they may gather further information; but ultimately they must make choices. Leaders who refuse to do so are abdicating their leadership role. People need the assurance that their leader is capable of making wise, timely decisions. The fear of making a wrong decision is the overriding impetus behind some people's leadership style. Such people become immobilized by their fear of making a mistake. It is true that all decisions have ramifications, and leaders must be prepared to accept the consequences of their decisions. Those without the fortitude to live with this reality should not take on leadership roles.

In direct contrast to irresolute leaders are those who make decisions too casually. These leaders come to conclusions flippantly without giving serious consideration to the possible outcomes of their decisions. When a decision proves disastrous, the leader does an about-face, adding a second, equally reckless course of action to the first one. Such foolhardy decisions, made in rapid succession, are often contradictory, creating confused organizations with bewildered employees scrambling helter-skelter, never quite sure which direction the organization is going next. Decision making is the cornerstone of an organization's effectiveness. Decisions must be reached carefully because, as Peter Drucker observes, "Every decision is like surgery. It is an intervention into a system and therefore carries with it the risk of shock."[1]

WHEN LEADERS MAKE A DECISION

A single leadership decision has the potential to significantly impact employees and their families as well as the organization, so it is critical that leaders base their decisions firmly on biblical principles that will protect them from mistakes. There are several principles spiritual leaders should follow when making decisions.

Leaders Make Decisions by Seeking the Holy Spirit's Guidance

Spiritual leaders make two choices every time they make one decision. First, they choose whether to rely on their own insights or on God's wisdom in making their decision. Their second choice is the conclusion they reach, or the action they take. People don't naturally do things God's way, because people don't think the way God does (Ps. 118:8).

The world's way of decision making is to weigh all the evidence, compare pros and cons, and then take the course of action that seems most sensible. If spiritual leaders make their choices this way, they could easily lead their organization in the opposite direction of God's will (Prov. 14:12). God doesn't want people to do what they think is best: he wants them to do what he knows is best, and no amount of reasoning and intellectualizing will discover that. God himself must reveal it. God's Holy Spirit reveals his will to those who are seeking his mind and his heart. God's Spirit will do this through four avenues: prayer, Scripture, other believers, and circumstances. Our study *When God Speaks* covers these in detail, but for our purposes we will touch on them briefly.[2]

The Holy Spirit Guides Through Prayer. Prayer is the leader's connection with the one who promised: "Call to Me, and I will answer you, and I will tell you great and mighty things, which you do not know" (Jer. 33:3). The prayer described here is not the variety that is done in haste just before a nervous leader makes an important presentation before a skeptical audience. Prayer should always be a leader's first course of action. Spiritual leaders must spend time in prayer daily, asking God to guide them in each decision they will make, not just when they are facing a situation but also before the fact. Neglecting their prayer life is foolhardy presumption by leaders who assume they already know God's agenda and who believe calling upon God as a last resort is a legitimate function of leadership.

Pastors and leaders of Christian organizations are not the only ones God guides through prayer. God responds as readily to the sincere prayers of Christian business and political leaders. People tend to draw distinctions between secular and spiritual matters. God is not restrained by such artificial boundaries. He is as powerful in the business world as he is in the church. God's wisdom applies as much to mergers, or investments, or hiring personnel, as it does to church matters. Decisions made in the political arena can have far-reaching ramifications and require prayer for God's guidance. At times doing business can force leaders into situations where they face moral dilemmas with no apparent solutions. God is pleased to direct his people to choices that will bring him the greatest honor. At times the profit motive dictates one course of action while the desire to bring honor to God suggests another. Prayer will guide leaders to solutions that honor God while maintaining their integrity in the workplace. Prayerless leaders are like ship captains without compasses—they can make their best guess at which direction to go, but they have no assurance they are heading the right way. Prayer keeps leaders focused on the one absolutely consistent factor in their lives—God.

One of the grave realizations of many fallen leaders is that they neglected their relationship with God. Numerous men and women have testified, often in tears, that they became so consumed with fulfilling their official responsibilities they inadvertently spent less and less time with the Lord. After it was too late, these devastated leaders discovered that life seldom affords the luxury of putting off important decisions while people neglect their relationship with God. Leaders often overlook their spiritual life because they are too busy doing their jobs on a day-to-day basis. How tragic when leaders face a major decision that desperately calls for God's wisdom but they have grown unfamiliar with his voice. Even more painful is the reality that, in wandering away from God and missing his guidance, they have cost others dearly as well.

Leaders are busy, and many say there just are not enough hours in the day to maintain a vibrant prayer life. Daniel had enormous government responsibilities, yet he made it his habit to pray at least three times a day. When his rivals sought to use political intrigue to oust him from his position and have him executed, Daniel faced imminent and mortal danger (Dan. 6). What he did in the next few hours meant life or death. Daniel prayed, as was his custom. Daniel's situation looked bleak, but God faithfully guided and protected him, giving him not only victory over his enemies but even greater prominence in the government. In his moment of crisis, Daniel had complete confidence in his rich relationship with God, and he overcame a crisis that would have destroyed most people in his position.

When Job entered a dark valley of tragedy, losing his children, his health, as well as everything he owned, that was not the time for him to hastily seek a closer relationship with God so he would have strength for his trials. In those tumultuous moments, either Job had a healthy relationship with God or he did not. When it appeared that Abraham would lose his only son, when Hannah desperately longed for a child but could not have one, and when David's son rebelled against him, each of them sought solace from God, and their vibrant relationship with him sustained them. Their walk with God was already a vital part of their lifestyle, so they were able to overcome incredible adversities. These biblical heroes were secure in the knowledge they could trust God implicitly.

There have been leaders who entered difficult situations after neglecting their spiritual life. They eventually turned to God, and he restored them to fellowship with himself—but not before they, their families, and their organizations suffered grievously. How much better it would have been for them if they had nurtured their relationship with the Lord and avoided calamity in the first place. Just as good leaders know to keep their organizations prepared for whatever contingency the future might bring, so leaders ought to zealously maintain a close relationship with God today so they are prepared to make the necessary decisions of tomorrow.

The Holy Spirit Guides Through God's Word. God's Word is the plumb line for Christian living. When people give leaders advice, leaders compare their counsel with God's Word. When leaders sense God is saying something to them in prayer, they confirm it with what he says in his Word. The problem for many leaders is that they are unfamiliar with the Bible. They don't know what it says, so it doesn't guide them. They don't read it regularly, so it doesn't influence their thinking. When a crucial decision is required, leaders have no alternative but to do what makes sense to them and hope it does not violate the teachings of Scripture.

True spiritual leaders recognize their utter dependence on God. So they regularly fill their heart and mind with his Word. When leaders' minds are filled with Scripture, they find themselves thinking according to biblical principles. When a difficult situation arises, the Holy Spirit will bring appropriate Scriptures to mind. When they prepare to make a decision, the Holy Spirit will bring to memory a Scripture verse that provides relevant guidance.

The Holy Spirit Guides Through Other Believers. It is said the difference between genius and stupidity is that genius has its limits! The Book of Proverbs candidly describes the enormity of suffering that results from foolish choices. Proverbs is also peppered with safeguards against unwise decision making. One of these safeguards is enlisting the aid of wise counsel. The confirmation of other believers is a third way the Holy Spirit will guide leaders' decision making. Proverbs enjoins, "Where there is no guidance, the people fall, but in abundance of counselors there is victory" (Prov. 11:14). "Without consultation, plans are frustrated, but with many counselors they succeed" (Prov. 15:22). The essence of these Scriptures can be summed up in two truths: (1) leaders should recruit a variety of godly counselors; and (2) leaders should give their advisors the freedom to express their opinions.

Enlisting advice can help guard leaders against foolish decisions, but leaders should recognize that not all counselors are equally wise. Good leaders choose their counselors carefully. The Scriptures advise people to seek the guidance of several counselors, thus avoiding the disastrous trap of merely duplicating the mistakes of one person. Because people have expertise in different areas, leaders need counselors who represent many areas of concern.

Warren Bennis suggests that the downfall of President Richard Nixon came after he surrounded himself with clones of himself. Observes Bennis, "They couldn't tell him anything he didn't already know and so were useless to him."[3] The key to effective counselors is not that they agree with their leaders and always support their decisions but that they tell their leaders things they would not know or recognize otherwise.

Leaders should seek the best possible people to work with them and to advise them. These people must know how to think for themselves. They must be well qualified with expertise the leader lacks. They should have a consistently successful track record of demonstrating wisdom when working with others—some people want to be consultants but their track record gives them no credibility. They ought to be able to look at situations from a perspective different from the leader's. If, for example, a CEO is a rational, cognitive thinker who accepts guidance only from other rational, cognitive thinkers, they will consistently recommend the most logical direction for the company. If, on the other hand, the leader also conscripts counselors who are emotional thinkers, the counselors will be more sensitive to interpersonal issues and will direct the leader away from actions that could appear callous and might needlessly antagonize people.

Good leaders ensure they have varied perspectives available to them before they make important decisions. The one common qualification of counselors should be a close walk with God. Just being a professing Christian is not qualification enough to be considered credible. Advisors should demonstrate competence as well as a mature faith. Counselors who are not oriented to God can only offer their own advice. Spiritual leaders need counselors who walk closely with God and who take their counsel from him. Having a mind and character that are being molded by the Holy Spirit gives godly counselors a great advantage over those who do not have God as a frame of reference for their decision making. Admittedly, it is not possible in every situation to enlist the advice of fellow believers, especially in narrow fields of expertise. In such cases leaders should seek the counsel of colleagues who demonstrate honesty and integrity in their character.

John Gardner comments, "Pity the leader who is caught between unloving critics and uncritical lovers."4 One of the great downfalls of leaders is letting their egos hinder their effectiveness. They shield themselves from any form of criticism, so they foolishly quarantine themselves from wise counselors who could give healthy advice.

Throughout history, great leaders have encouraged diversity in their organizations. Despite their forceful personalities, leaders such as Winston Churchill and Martin Luther King Jr. invited their people to be honest with them even if it meant voicing disagreement. Napoleon welcomed debate among his generals. Billy Graham developed a team in which each person was encouraged to honestly share concerns with the others. Harry Truman liked to gather a variety of people around him who would provide diverse viewpoints for making decisions. Great leaders have become great by seeking out great people and learning from their insights (Prov. 11:14).

Some leaders have suffered monumental disaster, not because there was no one to warn them, but because they would listen only to counselors who told them what they wanted to hear. Often at the root of this problem is an insecure person who cannot bear dissent. The king of Judah had the prophet Jeremiah available to give him direct messages from God, but he refused to listen to him or to believe things were as ominous as the prophet said (Jer. 42–44). As a result of the king's unwillingness to heed Jeremiah's warnings, the stubborn monarch was eventually captured by the Babylonians, blinded, and led away to a lifetime of captivity. Once leaders have carefully chosen wise counselors and received advice that is borne out by the Scriptures, they would be foolish to ignore such counsel.

The Holy Spirit Guides Through Circumstances. Leaders are never simply the victims or pawns of their circumstances. Wise leaders watch for God's activity in the midst of their experiences. Just as God speaks by his Holy Spirit through prayer, the Bible, and other believers, so God can send clear messages to leaders through their experiences. A chance encounter with someone at the airport, an unexpected check in the mail, a surprise phone call are all viewed by leaders in light of what they have been praying about and reading in Scripture. Spiritual leaders astutely evaluate "coincidences" to see if these are God's answers to their prayers. Spiritual leaders are not discouraged by their circumstances—they are informed by them. Through circumstances and events in leaders' lives, God leads them forward in his will.

Leaders Strive to Be Teachable

The Holy Spirit will reveal God's agenda to leaders who seek his guidance, but it is then up to the leader to respond appropriately to the guidance God gives. A major aspect of a leader's wise decision making is having a teachable spirit. There is little reason for unteachable leaders to seek out wise counsel. Unteachable leaders intentionally or unintentionally muzzle others from saying anything that appears to thwart their own designs. Leaders can stymie input by the way they ask questions. For example, "No one has a problem with this, do they?" is not really a question; it is a statement. Another effective way to quench discussion is simply to do all the talking. When leaders spend all their time waxing eloquent about the virtues of their proposal, they are essentially squelching any thoughts of raising objections from others. Leaders who truly want feedback will give ample opportunity for it. Leaders can also stifle feedback by a defensive posture. When someone raises a question or challenges an assumption, leaders must be careful not to immediately begin arguing their point. Defensive leaders learn nothing. Listening leaders are constantly learning and growing. The apostle James sagely cautions everyone to be "quick to hear, slow to speak and slow to anger" (James 1:19). Leaders learn nothing by vehemently arguing their case. Leaders who take criticism personally or who immediately get defensive are announcing that they really are not open to feedback, even if they say they want it. It is said that despite his strong personality, Winston Churchill received criticism very meekly. No doubt he understood there was too much at stake for him to allow his ego to blind him to the best possible course of action.

Effective leaders make a concerted effort to invite discussion and constructive feedback from associates. When they find that no one raises any questions or suggestions, they recognize they may have inadvertently created an atmosphere where contributions are not considered welcome. Leaders do not needlessly promote negative or divisive thinking; but they are careful not to inadvertently discourage much-needed feedback by the way they conduct their meetings. Kouzes and Posner encourage leaders to habitually ask for a second opinion. They cite studies demonstrating that two-thirds of the time, the second solution offered is preferable to the first option suggested.[5] Wise leaders recognize the value of gathering ideas from their people, and so they create a climate in their organizations where people feel free to contribute.

Leaders Master Their History

One of the first things new leaders should do, preferably even before arriving on the field, is to study the history of the organization. This is important in any organization, but it is particularly crucial in the case of spiritual organizations such as churches, schools, and charities. The reason many new leaders are called is often because a new focus is necessary, but wise leaders resist the urge to move immediately in new directions before they understand how they arrived where they are today.

Biblical leaders functioned with a keen awareness of what God had done before they arrived on the scene. Isaac knew the same God who was leading him had also led his father Abraham (Gen. 26:24). Jacob realized his God was also the "God of Abraham and Isaac" (Gen. 35:12). Joseph understood that God's activity in his life was building upon what God had already done through his forefathers "Abraham, Isaac and Jacob" (Gen. 48:15). When God commissioned Moses to deliver the Israelites, Moses did not assume God was just beginning to implement his plan (Exod. 3:15). When Moses prepared his people to finally enter the Promised Land, he recalled with them all that God had done for them over the previous forty years.

When Stephen was arrested, his defense was an appeal to God's activity through history (Acts 7:1–50). Whenever Paul explained why he was leading people the way he was, he reviewed the story of how God had worked in his life (Acts 22:1–21; 24:10–21; 26:1–23). Over and over again, biblical leaders would use spiritual benchmarks as the framework for their decisions. They knew that God always builds on what he has done before. Biblical leaders understood this, but modern leaders often do not. Today, leaders often assume they unpack God's plan, along with their office furniture, when they arrive.

God does not work in a vacuum. He has been unfolding his plan since he began time. Much history has preceded the leader's arrival at the organization. Leaders are remiss if they make decisions as if there were no track record or history to their organization. It is no coincidence that many famous world leaders were avid students of history. Winston Churchill was a diligent history student. Robert E. Lee studied military history voraciously. Napoleon had an insatiable appetite for history. These leaders saw their lives not as an isolated entity but as a link in the chain of world history. Spiritual leaders should recognize with an even greater sense of accountability that their lives have a purpose for the particular time that God has led them to their organization; and that purpose is a part of his greater plan.

As soon as possible the new leader should seek out evidence of God's previous activity in the church or institution to which the leader has been called. For example, a new pastor would be wise to go through the minutes of previous business meetings to get an idea of what the people sensed God leading them to do up until the present. Reading written histories of the church, as well as talking with longtime members, would also lend perspective to the ways God has been leading the church thus far. Doing these things would also signify to the people that their new leader is not going to blithely discard all that has already been accomplished. For several reasons pastors often feel they must come into new situations and make immediate, sweeping changes. This is especially true when a pastor is called to a declining church and wants to give the impression of renewed vibrancy. Sometimes a new pastor seeks to develop an approach to ministry different from his predecessor's, just to be different. These pastors arrive with a comprehensive set of plans and directions for the church, without ever considering how their agenda integrates with all God has done in the church already. This is not to say that God will not lead the congregation to make significant modifications under the new leadership. In fact, God may have brought in the new leader specifically to effect change. The church leader, however, should be careful that any innovations are on God's agenda and that they are done for the right reason.

Many new leaders can develop a subtle, unconscious need to prove they are as capable as their predecessors, especially in cases where the leader is replacing a more experienced and much-loved predecessor. Leaders must diligently guard their hearts from pride-driven insecurity that motivates them to cancel good initiatives of previous leaders. Former leaders should not direct how their successor does things, but they could provide invaluable history and counsel that would help the new leader discern God's will for the future.

God is purposeful and progressive in the way he leads people and organizations. He does not change his mind every time a new leader arrives. God does not rescind everything he has said once a new leader is installed. Leaders come and go over the years but God's plans, purposes, and presence remain constant. Wise leaders understand their place in God's overall plan and are content to lead on God's agenda, setting aside any selfish or ungodly motives that may tempt them to "show what they can do."

The book *Experiencing God* discusses spiritual markers as a way for individuals to discern God's leading.[6] This involves recording instances that demonstrate God's clear direction in one's life. By reviewing God's activity, people can see patterns and gain a sense of the overall direction in which God has been guiding them. The practice of identifying spiritual markers can certainly be applied to leading an organization as well. When making decisions and seeking direction for their organization, leaders should review their organization's history, taking careful note of every event they recognize as God's activity. This helps them to know if a new decision is consistent with God's guidance in the past. Leaders have a greater assurance of making the right decision when they understand how God has led in the past. If a decision seems completely out of character with everything God has said to the organization thus far, then leaders are wise to cautiously reconsider the decision.

Leaders Give an Account to God

Secular media have become something of a moral watchdog for well-known leaders and celebrities. Decades ago, politicians and other public figures enjoyed an unspoken relationship with the press that shielded their personal lives from public scrutiny. Not so today. The moral failures of public persons are announced worldwide, including graphic details. The fear of every flaw being exposed in an ugly way has discouraged many people from pursuing political careers. Public accountability, although disheartening at times, has forced people to exercise discretion. Having your life laid bare before the public and open to misinterpretation can be disconcerting, even for those with nothing to hide.

Spiritual leaders are visible to the probing eyes of the media. In fact, the press takes particular delight in exposing the failures of Christians. But spiritual leaders must not shun public accountability. In fact, they should welcome it as a safeguard against the temptation to abuse their power and influence. They lead with integrity not only because they are accountable to public opinion or the judicial system, but more importantly because they know that God is observing and assessing their thoughts and actions all the time and because one day they will give an account to almighty God for everything they have done (Job 7:17–18). The writer of Proverbs observes: "By the fear of the Lord one keeps away from evil" (Prov. 16:6).

The apostle Paul was one of the greatest saints in history. His spiritual resumé is lengthy and impressive. He started churches all across the Roman Empire, shared his faith with kings, and performed amazing miracles. He was a respected leader among Christians, and the Holy Spirit inspired his writings that compose a large portion of the New Testament. Yet even Paul knew his stature in God's kingdom would not exempt him from the same accountability that every other servant of God would undergo. Paul said, "Therefore also we have as our ambition, whether at home or absent, to be pleasing to Him. For we must all appear before the judgment seat of Christ, that each one may be recompensed for his deeds in the body, according to what he has done, whether good or bad. Therefore knowing the fear of the Lord, we persuade men, but we are made manifest to God; and I hope that we are made manifest also in your consciences" (2 Cor. 5:9–11).

According to Paul's words, it will not just be unbelievers who stand before Christ on judgment day: everyone will give an account. Paul enjoyed a close relationship with Christ, yet he knew the awesome and terrifying God he served. Paul had raised the dead back to life in the name of Christ, yet the thought of standing before the risen Christ and giving an account of all his actions made him tremble.

It is this sobering realization, far more than the fear of public exposure, that compels true spiritual leaders to act with integrity toward their peers, their staff, their families, and the public. *Spiritual leaders make every decision with the awareness that one day they will give an account to God.* Leaders of Christian organizations who choose not to lead their organizations to take a step of faith will eventually answer to God for their unbelief. Christian CEOs who mistreat their staff will one day be required to explain their actions to the righteous, eternal judge. Spiritual leaders will be held accountable for what they could have done if only they had obeyed what God was directing them to do (James 4:17). Because of this knowledge, decision making is a much graver matter for spiritual leaders than for those who believe they are only responsible to a governing board. The good news is that spiritual leaders are forewarned and, therefore, forearmed. They are also equipped with the Holy Spirit to make wise, blameless decisions.

Guidelines for Decision Making

- Leaders allow the Holy Spirit to guide them.
- Leaders are teachable.
- Leaders know their history.
- Leaders know they are accountable to God.

AFTER LEADERS MAKE A DECISION

As important as decision making is for leaders, making the decision is only half of the process. Living with the decision is the other half. Some leaders find making decisions rather easy. It is sticking with choices and accepting the consequences that they find difficult. The benefit of hastily made decisions is, of course, negated when those decisions are constantly being amended or cancelled. Leaders who make decisions must truly decide. The following are three guidelines for handling decisions once they have been made.

Leaders Accept the Consequences

Decision making would be much easier if there were no consequences, but the reality is that every decision carries inevitable results. A good and timely decision can solidify a leader's reputation as a success. A bad decision can overshadow many years of hard work, especially when left uncorrected. It is the potentially devastating or career-making effect of choices that makes decisions a central part of the leadership role.

Harry Truman has been called a great leader because he had the ability to decide. But more than that, he was willing to accept the consequences of his decisions. Truman's famous dictum, "The buck stops here," encapsulated his belief that leaders cannot shirk their responsibility to make decisions or bear the consequences of their decisions. Truman repeatedly modeled this philosophy during his presidency.

It is at this point that true leaders separate themselves from mere office-seekers. When there are negative consequences to leaders' decisions, they refuse to blame their followers. They do not cause others in their organization to suffer the consequences for their decisions. True leaders accept the ramifications of their decisions.

Leaders Admit Their Mistakes

Because leaders make so many decisions, they are particularly vulnerable to making mistakes. Moreover, the results of their actions are often magnified because of the public nature of their jobs. Most mistakes are not terminal in nature, however, and they can actually provide the greatest moments of personal growth that leaders experience. Success can become intoxicating and can easily blind leaders to their own shortcomings. In contrast, mistakes expose leaders' inadequacies. Successful leaders are not successful because they never err in judgment, but because they continually learn from their mistakes. Mistakes made once become catalysts for personal growth and future success. The same mistakes, made repeatedly, are inexcusable.

People who are unable to admit their errors are not qualified to be leaders. Mistakes are inevitable; true leaders understand this fact and are not devastated by it. The only leaders who never make mistakes are those who never try anything, which is in itself a mistake. Mistakes are often opportunities in disguise. They are opportunities for followers to see that, though their leader is not perfect, he or she is honest. Honesty, not infallibility, has repeatedly been listed as the most important quality followers desire in their leaders. Failures are part of God's highway to personal growth. When spiritual leaders make a mistake, they need to begin by confessing it to God, receiving his forgiveness, and then moving forward in faith. Mistakes are not to be dreaded with paralyzing fear; they should be seen as learning tools to be thoroughly analyzed so leaders are better prepared for similar situations in the future. Moreover, admitting a mistake to followers is an opportunity for leaders to demonstrate how mistakes will be dealt with in their organization. If leaders readily admit their own errors, learn from them, and perform their job more effectively as a result, then followers will know that they, too, can make mistakes without being criticized. Mistakes do not make people failures. Failure is an event, not a character trait. Covering up a mistake or refusing to accept responsibility for failure is a character issue—making a mistake is not.

Leaders Stand by Their Decisions

If leaders are meticulous in making their decisions, they will not waver once they have made them. This confident ability to stand firmly behind a decision does not make a leader an unyielding tyrant. It is a characteristic of good leadership. Leaders who change their minds every time they encounter someone who holds a different view are agonizing to follow because people never know for sure whether their leaders are still going in the same direction they were yesterday or if they have changed their minds again. Obviously if circumstances alter significantly, or if leaders discover new information that shows their present approach is in error, they must adjust their decision, but these scenarios are usually the exception. More often, leaders who continually change their minds do so because they have no clear sense of direction or because their interest has shifted to a new venture. Such vacillations greatly damage their organizations' morale.

The best insurance against inconsistency is, of course, to be careful in making the right decision in the first place. Christian leaders do not have to be indecisive if they will learn how to know when God is speaking to them. Surprisingly, many spiritual leaders, despite all their rhetoric about hearing from God, do not know how to clearly understand God's will for their lives or for their organizations. Scripture provides the unmistakable pattern of God speaking to his people and guiding them in their decisions. Yet many leaders' actions demonstrate they do not believe God will guide them. Some leaders offer a token prayer and then compile a list of pros and cons from which to make their decision just like an unbeliever would do. While God can guide the thinking of leaders as they consider the ramifications of an important decision, leaders must be cognizant of the fact that determining God's will is not a matter of merely compiling a list of pros and cons; it is a matter of relating to a personal God who is more than willing to guide his people.

Indecisiveness on the part of leaders may reflect that they are overly concerned with pleasing people. People-pleasing is not the driving force of spiritual leadership. Spiritual leaders move people with them in their decisions but ultimately leaders are concerned with pleasing God, not people. There will sometimes be those whose spiritual maturity is not at a level to respond to all God is saying to the organization. While leaders need to help these people understand how to respond to God's directives, they should never be allowed to set the pace for the organization. Good leaders do not abandon their weaker members, but neither do they allow them to set the agenda for the organization. Jesus didn't forsake Judas, but neither did Jesus allow Judas to sidetrack him from his mission. When a mountain hike becomes too difficult for the children who are accompanying their parents, the adults do not abandon the children along the trail, but neither do they allow the children to lead the expedition. It is this fine balance of leadership that often reveals the most skilled leaders.

A clear sense of direction for the organization will prevent leaders from chasing after every fad that comes along. When leaders understand God's plans and purposes for their organizations, decision making becomes more straightforward. When a new opportunity arises, leaders ask, "Will this opportunity take us closer to where God is leading or will this hinder us?" When leaders have no God-given vision, one option can appear as attractive as another. Anyone can decide between good and bad options, but choosing between two equally good options can be frustrating for leaders unless they know which one is consistent with the vision God has given. Leaders who are constantly waffling reveal that they do not know where they are going.

It takes courage to stand behind a decision in the face of resistance or opposition. Some leaders simply lack the fortitude to take a stand or to make unpopular decisions. Such leaders often delay, hoping a difficult issue will go away. Unfortunately, it is usually the opportunities and rarely the difficulties that vanish over time. Spiritual leaders need not lack courage because God has promised to give it to them if they will ask for it (Isa. 41:10).

King Jehoshaphat was a godly king, ruling his small nation in a turbulent and dangerous time. When he was told that the armies of the Moabites, Ammonites, and Meunites were preparing to attack Jerusalem, Jehoshaphat knew that he lacked the resources to repel the invaders. The commonly accepted practice at that time would have been to sue for peace and accept whatever terms his oppressors demanded. The king knew that the wrong decision on his part could cause the suffering and death of thousands of his subjects as well as the end of his rule and maybe his life. Jehoshaphat turned to God for guidance.

He cried out, "'O our God, will You not judge them? For we are powerless before this great multitude who are coming out against us; nor do we know what to do, but our eyes are on You.' All Judah was standing before the LORD, with their infants, their wives and their children" (2 Chron 20:12–13).

God spoke to the people through his prophet Jahaziel, saying, "Do not fear or be dismayed because of this great multitude, for the battle is not yours but God's" (2 Chron 20:15). Despite seemingly insurmountable challenges, Jehoshaphat took courage from God's word to him. In an incredible move, the king ordered the choir to proceed the army out of the city into battle. No king had ever before given such an unorthodox order to his people at the outset of a battle. The only reason the king could make such a difficult and unusual decision was that God's word to him had given him courage. When Jehoshaphat's forces came upon the enemy, they found the enemy had turned on themselves and destroyed each other. Corpses of enemy soldiers were strewn across the land. The choir had already been singing praises to God. Now they redoubled their efforts!

Once again, we find ourselves back to the core principle of spiritual leadership: trusting God. Leaders who know what God has said and who have a clear sense of God's purpose for their organization can have the resolve to be steadfast in their leadership, regardless of whether everyone agrees with them. As long as God agrees, they should proceed.

There comes a time when leaders must decide to decide. After they have sought God's guidance and confirmed what God is saying through the Scriptures, through prayer, through the affirmation of other believers, and through an evaluation of their circumstances, after they have gathered all the pertinent information and after they have consulted with trusted advisors, the time comes for leaders to make an informed, Spirit-led decision. To delay further would be an abdication of leadership. Essential leadership skills include the ability to make a decision, to stick to it, to admit mistakes along the way, and finally to accept the consequences for the decision.

When Leaders Make a Decision

- Leaders accept the consequences.
- Leaders admit their mistakes.
- Leaders stand by their decisions.

IMPROVING DECISION MAKING

Leaders who realize they are struggling in their decision making can take specific actions to address this problem. Whether the issue is that they regularly make the wrong decisions or whether they are indecisive, leaders cannot afford to neglect this problem. Here are several steps they can take to strengthen their decision-making skills.

Leaders Evaluate the Decisions They Are Making

Leaders need to monitor the quantity of decisions they are making. One reason they may struggle is that they are bombarded by too many decisions to make. If this is the case, leaders who are deluged with decisions are taking responsibility for things that they should be delegating to someone else. If responsibility has been assigned to someone to make certain decisions, wise leaders will not unduly concern themselves with those issues. Effective leaders continually give away routine work to others and use their time to concentrate on the critical issues that leaders cannot delegate. Leaders should restrict themselves to making only the most important decisions for their organization.

Leaders Cultivate Their Relationship with God

When spiritual leaders struggle to make decisions, they need to immediately examine their relationship with God. God wants to guide them. God is perfectly capable of communicating with them. If leaders are not hearing from God, they need to discover the reason. Do they really know how to recognize God's voice? One of the most difficult things for pastors and other spiritual leaders to admit is that they struggle to know when God is speaking. Instead, many of these people simply take the direction that makes the most sense to them and then pray for God to stop them if they are making a mistake. The most important thing leaders can do in such situations is to get alone with God in an unhurried, uninterrupted time until they clearly know that God has spoken and what he wants them to do. Waiting on God is not a passive activity. It is one of the most strenuous, agonizing, faith-stretching times in a leader's life. Modern leaders have been socialized to think that unless they are constantly in motion they are unproductive. There is no reason to be embarrassed or apologetic about the need to retreat for an hour, a day, or even a week. Taking adequate time to spend with God at the front end of a decision can save leaders years of painful regret after a decision has been made (Ps. 19:13).

King Rehoboam inherited an enviable position. He ascended the throne after his illustrious father Solomon, the wealthiest king in Israel's history. Immediately upon inheriting the kingdom, however, Rehoboam faced a critical decision. His people asked him to reduce the oppressive tax rate his father had levied upon them. Rehoboam maintained two sets of counselors; one group consisted of ambitious young men like him. Wise counselors from his father's era comprised the other group. The young executives counseled toughness; the more experienced consultants recommended leniency. Rehoboam listened to his peers—and split the kingdom in two (1 Kings 12:1–17). One of the gravest blunders of any Israelite king occurred under a leader with not one but two sets of counselors! What went wrong? Why was Rehoboam susceptible to worldly, unwise counsel? Was it simply because he was young and prone to listen to youthful counselors? No. Scripture indicates: "He did evil because he had not set his heart on seeking the LORD" (2 Chron. 12:14 NIV). Rehoboam was unfamiliar with God's ways because he did not choose to cultivate his relationship with God. When he was presented with godly, wise counsel that could have preserved his kingdom, he didn't recognize the advice as coming from God. When leaders are not oriented to God, all their decisions—political, business, and religious—are vulnerable to poor advice.

Leaders Seek God's Vision

Leaders who have trouble making decisions may be struggling because they have no clear picture of where they are leading their organization. It's surprising how many leaders settle into managing the day-to-day operations of their organization with no comprehensible idea where God wants to take their people. Every decision is a step toward a destination, so it is inevitable that leaders who do not know where they are going will falter in their decisions. A leader who is unable to identify the organization's purpose needs to stop and seek God's direction. There is no value in making great progress in the wrong direction!

When leaders have received God's vision for the future, they will have a clear sense of direction from which to make decisions. Then options will eliminate themselves because they are obviously contrary to, or a deviation from, the organization's God-given purpose.

Leaders Seek God's Wisdom

The complexity of today's world is enough to make anyone indecisive! Yet while the task of leadership has not become easier over time, God continues to provide the wisdom necessary to make the right choices. When Solomon's father, King David, was approaching death, the kingdom was filled with political intrigue. Although David wanted Solomon to be his successor, Solomon's older half brother, Adonijah, was maneuvering politically to gain influential supporters for his quest for the throne. Abiathar, the high priest, had given his support to Adonijah. Joab, the commander of the army, also backed Adonijah's bid for the kingdom. Solomon did ultimately gain the throne. Perhaps it was facing such powerful opponents that helped Solomon realize he would need wisdom beyond his own in order to maintain his leadership. When God asked him what he desired most of all, Solomon asked, not for wealth, or a long life, or security, but for wisdom (1 Kings 3:9).

The world has not become any less complex since Solomon's time. The contrary is true. Yet God continues to encourage leaders to seek his wisdom (James 1:5). Political intrigue is nothing new to God. God has been helping his people overcome aggressive lobbyists, deceit, bribes, false accusations, and every manner of sinful behavior since the beginning of history, and he stands ready to assist leaders today. When leaders seek God's wisdom, he gives it to them.

Decision making does not have to be an ominous task. God has provided everything necessary for people to make good choices. With so much at stake in leaders' decisions, it is imperative that leaders make use of every resource God offers them so they can wisely and effectively lead their organizations, and most important, lead people on to God's agenda.

CONCEPTS AND SCRIPTURES FOR CONSIDERATION

- God doesn't want people to do what they think is best: he wants them to do what he knows is best, and no amount of reasoning and intellectualizing will discover that.
- Throughout history, great leaders have encouraged diversity in their organizations.
- Spiritual leaders astutely evaluate "coincidences" to see if these are God's answers to their prayers. Spiritual leaders are not discouraged by their circumstances—they are informed by them.
- God does not rescind everything he has said once a new leader is installed.
- Spiritual leaders make every decision with the awareness that one day they will give an account to God.

- It is at this point that true leaders separate themselves from mere office-seekers. When there are negative consequences to leaders' decisions, they refuse to blame their followers.
- Success can become intoxicating and can easily blind leaders to their own shortcomings. In contrast, mistakes expose leaders' inadequacies.
- Honesty, not infallibility, has repeatedly been listed as the most important quality followers desire in their leaders.
- Christian leaders do not have to be indecisive if they will learn how to know when God is speaking to them.
- Leaders need to monitor the quantity of decisions they are making.
- Leaders who have trouble making decisions may be struggling because they have no clear picture of where they are leading their organization.
- Every decision is a step toward a destination, so it is inevitable that leaders who do not know where they are going will falter in their decisions.
- Unfortunately, it is usually the opportunities and rarely the difficulties that vanish over time.

Psalm 118:8

Proverbs 14:12

Jeremiah 33:3

Job 7:17–18

Proverbs 16:6

2 Corinthians 5:9–11

James 4:17

Isaiah 41:10

Joshua 1:6–9

2 Chronicles 2:14

Isaiah 11:2–3

James 1:5

Psalm 19:13

CHAPTER NINE

The Leader's Schedule
Doing What's Important

THE LONGER HARRY TRUMAN SERVED
as president of the United States, the more time-conscious he
became. Over the years, Truman's aides noticed an increasing number of clocks on his desk in the oval office. Every time Truman sat at
his desk he faced a barrage of timepieces. With so many significant
decisions to make, Truman knew, as do all great leaders, that time
was a precious resource. Leaders' effectiveness is commensurate
with their ability to manage their time. Even the most gifted leaders
will struggle if they squander their time. Good leaders are keenly
aware of how valuable their time is. Spiritual leaders also understand
that God has granted them enough time to accomplish any assignment he gives them. The key to successful leadership is not creating
more time in one's life or packing more activities into one's day, but
staying on God's agenda.

Scientists proclaim that modern timesaving devices mean the average workers' greatest challenge will be to find sufficient activities to fill
their free time. Yet even as new timesaving gadgets are rolling off
assembly lines, life gets busier and more stressful every generation. *U.S.
News & World Report* notes that between 1977 and 1997 the average
work week of salaried Americans rose from 43 to 47 hours. Americans
are working two weeks longer each year than the notoriously hard-
working Japanese—ten more than Europeans.[1]

Kouzes and Posner observed that the harried nature of the modern office means the average executive has only nine minutes of uninterrupted time to devote to any one item.[2] If executives have such limited time, the way they manage their available time is critical. The term *time management* may be misleading. Time will proceed second by second, minute by minute, hour by hour despite leaders' best efforts to manage it. Time rolls on in an unrelenting journey toward the climax when God will bring an end to time and usher humanity en masse into eternity. What leaders can manage is themselves. Despite the pervasive and unrelenting pressures on their time, leaders ultimately choose how they perform second by second, minute by minute, hour by hour. Good leadership hinges on making the best choices with one's time.

The most inefficient and unproductive leaders have as much time as history-making leaders. Each is constrained by the need for sleep, food, exercise, and family concerns. Everyone encounters financial issues, unforeseen circumstances, and daily pressures. The difference is that wise leaders refuse to allow life's demands to control their schedule or their priorities. Unwise leaders succumb to extraneous pressures and enticements surrounding them and never accomplish all God intends for them. Great leaders don't allow their busy lives or their vast responsibilities to overwhelm them. Rather, they become the masters of their schedules through determined and conscientious effort.

TAKING CONTROL OF TIME

Peter Drucker offers many helpful suggestions for leaders and their time in his book *The Effective Executive*. He notes, "Effective executives, in my observation, do not start with their tasks. They start with their time."[3] It is not unusual for leaders to have more jobs to do than they have time to do them. This is business as usual. Earlier time management experts focused on how leaders might pack more activity into their day. Like business travelers sitting on their overstuffed suitcases attempting to cram in one more pair of pants, so earlier theory provided schemes to insert one more activity into an already-crowded schedule. Leaders who subscribed to this approach were often able to attend more meetings, write more letters, and complete more projects. But like a house of cards, one activity that ran late, or one missed flight, or one day with the flu and leaders' intricately woven schedules would crumble down around them. Such leaders would arrive home having accomplished enormous amounts of work, but they would be exhausted and left wondering what difference their Herculean efforts had made in the grand scheme of things. Simply squeezing more tasks into a day is not the answer to an effective schedule. The answer is doing the right things. In other words an effective schedule is preferable to an efficient schedule.

Leaders can avoid becoming slaves to their time by following several important practices.

Leaders Seek to Understand God's Will

It is important for leaders to realize they are surrounded by other people's agendas. These are in addition to the leader's own agenda. No two agendas are alike: The board of directors has an agenda; the leader's family has another; employees ask for certain things from their leaders; clients and competitors demand other things; governing agencies require certain commitments from leaders as do leaders' friends and churches. Each group is motivated differently. Employees' livelihoods are intrinsically linked with the leader's performance. Family members love them and want to spend time with them. Often people seek the leader's involvement in order to make their program or event successful. Others know a job will get done if the leader is involved.

Wise leaders realize there is no way they can satisfy the desires of all the people who clamor for their time. Astute leaders determine to invest themselves in those activities and projects that are most important for them to accomplish. In other words, they seek God's will.

God has a plan for each person that is uniquely suited to that individual. Unlike people, God never piles on more than someone can handle. God never overbooks people. God never drives his servants to the point of breakdown. God never burns people out. God never gives people tasks that are beyond the strength or ability he provides.

If this is true, why do so many people struggle with too much to do? Why are Christian leaders burning out from overwork and exhaustion?

Is God responsible? No. When people become overwhelmed by their commitments and responsibilities, they are operating on their own agenda. Ministers of religion are particularly susceptible to assuming responsibility for things they should not. They do this because their work is never completed. There is always another phone call to make, a Scripture passage to study, a person who needs visiting, a prayer to be offered. The key for overworked leaders is to examine each of their current responsibilities to determine whether they have inadvertently assumed ownership for things God has not intended them to carry.

The apostle Paul instructed early Christians: "Therefore be careful how you walk, not as unwise men, but as wise, making the most of your time, because the days are evil. So then do not be foolish, but understand what the will of the Lord is" (Eph. 5:15–17). Jesus was the consummate leader. No other person in history has been in higher demand than he was. Jesus' disciples had their opinions on how he should invest his time (Luke 9:12, 33; Mark 10:13, 37). Religious leaders had other designs for Jesus (Matt. 12:38; Luke 13:14). The sick, the poor, and the hungry had definite ideas on how Jesus should spend his day (Mark 1:37; Luke 18:35–43; John 6:15). Jesus' family had opinions about what he should do. Some people wanted Jesus to stay and teach them. Others wanted to travel with him (Mark 5:18). Satan planned to sidetrack Jesus from his Father's will. Jesus was besieged with opportunities to help other people, and he had the power to make a difference in every situation. It was only as Jesus kept his Father's will continually before him that he was able to stay focused on doing what was most important: obeying God's will.

Why did Jesus rise early to pray? He knew that maintaining an intimate relationship with his Father was the single most important thing he could do. Why did Jesus occasionally escape the crowds in order to spend time teaching his disciples? He knew it was important to invest time training his disciples. Why did Jesus associate with outcasts and sinners such as Zaccheus and the woman at the well? He knew it was for the spiritually needy that he had come. Why did Jesus spend time with friends such as Mary, Martha, and Lazarus in Bethany? He knew it was good to have close friends. Jesus enjoyed such a close relationship with his Father that he always recognized what his Father considered to be important. Since Jesus understood what was critical, he knew how and where to invest his time.

Once leaders clearly understand God's will, deciding how to invest their time becomes much simpler. If God confirms to a leader that she should stay with her current organization for the present, she does not need to spend weeks in agonizing prayer when a job offer comes the following week. When God convicts a leader that he should stay close to home during the next month, while his teenager is going through a tumultuous time, he knows he should decline extended business trips during that month. When leaders see God's activity and recognize it as his invitation to join him, decisions become more straightforward. It is when people do not understand God's will that their schedules get out of control. Then, every opportunity to take on another project becomes hard to reject, because harried leaders are never sure whether they will be making a mistake if they decline to become involved.

Spiritual leaders ask questions such as: What is God's will? In light of his will, what are the important things? What are the tasks he's asking me to do? Leaders always begin by investing their time in the most important things. If anything must be neglected in leaders' lives, it should always be the less critical activities. If leaders never take time to determine their priorities, however, they will invariably spend inordinate amounts of time on projects that are extraneous to their main purpose. Knowing God's will is indispensable for spiritual leaders.

Leaders Say No

General George Marshall's effectiveness as a leader of the American army during World War II is attributed in part to his ability to distinguish between the important and the unimportant. Marshall always invested his time in critical leadership issues. Leaders understand that their daily schedule primarily reveals two things: those things they have chosen to do and those things they have chosen not to do. Every decision to do one thing is at the same time a choice not to do a dozen other things.

Many leaders find that saying no is one of the hardest things they do. Leaders are generally susceptible to the "messiah complex." They can easily come to believe that only their involvement can guarantee the

success of an activity. They feel compelled, therefore, to immerse themselves in as many projects as they possibly can, so they run from meeting to meeting and appointment to appointment, trying to guarantee
the success of every enterprise their organization undertakes. They
need to understand that their success as leaders is not based on how
much they personally accomplish but on how wisely they perform their
leadership role. By spending too much time on less significant issues,
leaders invariably neglect the more important ones. They would be wise
to make it a practice to "sleep on it" before committing themselves to a
new responsibility. What seemed possible or appealing at the moment
can fade in importance once the whole picture is considered.

Some leaders have difficulty saying no because their sense of self-
worth demands that they make themselves indispensable to their organization. These leaders take pride in the fact that they are in great
demand and that their calendars are brimming with places to be and
things to do. The busier they are, the more indispensable they feel.
Declining to serve on a committee threatens their sense of self-worth.
What if, by declining this invitation, they are overlooked the next time
the organization needs committee members? What if, by not getting
involved in this project, they are not consulted on subsequent matters?
So these overwhelmed zealots trudge off to their next meeting and,
while they complain of their overwork, they really would have it no
other way.

Healthy leaders, on the other hand, graciously, yet regularly, say no
to many opportunities presented to them. They say no far more often
than they say yes. By declining to become involved in a project, these
leaders are not belittling the activity, as if it were beneath them to participate. Saying no is simply the leaders' way of acknowledging that they
are human beings, with human limitations, and thus they must make
choices with their time. Leaders who are deluged by their schedules are
leaders who have failed to say no when they should have. It's that simple. God does not give people more than they can handle, but people
regularly assume responsibility for things they should not be doing.

Many times, overburdened leaders have no idea how they became so
busy. The condition crept up on them. The problem is that leaders are
often tempted to take on just one more thing because doing so seems

easier than saying no. The axiom, "If you want to get something done—ask a busy person" is true. Too often busy people reason, "Well, I am already going to be at home doing these projects over the weekend. I guess I can squeeze in one more job." Responsibilities gradually pile up as they valiantly try to force one more job into their crowded lives. Leaders with overwhelming schedules need to ask themselves: "What things are currently in my schedule that I should have declined or delegated?" Commitments spring up in leaders' schedules like weeds in a garden. At first they appear sporadically, in spots where they don't call much attention to themselves. Gradually, however, they multiply and reproduce until they threaten to take over the entire garden. Jobs, at first undertaken out of a desire to please others, can demand ever-increasing amounts of time in leaders' schedules. As leaders meet daily with the Father, he will set their agenda. Superfluous activity must be weeded out so those activities on God's agenda can flourish.

It is a wise practice for leaders to audit their commitments annually. They should ask, "Is it still beneficial for me to serve on this committee for another year? Do I need to be responsible for this project again next year, or have I contributed all I can? What commitments did I fulfill last year that I do not need to assume again this year?" By asking such questions, leaders prune their schedules of activities and responsibilities that are extrinsic to their primary purpose.

Leaders Cultivate Healthy Routines

Routine is to some leaders like eating broccoli is to children—an unpleasant, albeit necessary, task. Some leaders go to great extremes to avoid being locked into routines. Yet wise leaders use routines to ensure that priorities are not overlooked. Drucker says that routine "makes unskilled people without judgment capable of doing what it took near genius to do before."[4] Routine allows people to work at a steady pace without having to race through the day in order to ensure that every task is accomplished. Drucker observes: "Effective executives do not race. They set an easy pace but keep going steadily."[5] Life is a marathon, not a sprint.

Routines ensure that leaders have scheduled their most important responsibilities into their calendars. Some leaders enjoy the exhilaration of responding to events spontaneously. They covet the freedom that comes with not being locked in to a daily timetable. The problem with this approach is that it does not produce freedom but slavery. If you do not make a plan for your time, someone else will. Every phone call, or person who stops by your office, will determine your schedule. Generally people who seize leaders' unscheduled time are not concerned with the most critical issues but the superfluous. Better for leaders to identify the crucial tasks of their role and then to schedule those activities into their calendars than to submit themselves by default to the whims of the people around them. The latter is crisis management; the former is self-management.

Some people are wary of routines because they fear being stifled or getting into ruts. Routines, however, can be as unique as the individuals who employ them. Some perform better under stringent routine. Churchill, for example, meticulously followed the same schedule every week, including an afternoon nap every day. Churchill observed that by napping when he did, he was able to stay up late going over reports and preparing for the next day in the quiet hours while others slept. By morning he was fully briefed and ready for the events of the day. Churchill claimed that by following his unusual regimen he was far more productive than if he kept more conventional hours.

Many of history's greatest leaders were early risers. While others were still sleeping, they were previewing their day, reading reports, and plotting a course of action. This does not necessarily mean these leaders slept less than others did, but rather they arranged their schedule to be most effective for them.

Jesus' life seemed to follow a different schedule every day, but he, too, was governed by an unwavering routine. Scripture indicates that Jesus habitually prayed late at night and early in the morning (Luke 6:12; 21:37; 22:39; Mark 1:35). Leaders must establish routines that fit their particular responsibilities as well as their health needs, but it is paramount for all spiritual leaders to schedule regular and frequent times alone with their heavenly Father. To simply attempt to seize a few moments with God as opportunities present themselves is totally ineffective for busy leaders. Such opportunities rarely come. Spiritual leaders must do what Jesus did and set times when they can regularly meet with God. Because

Jesus made it his custom to spend time regularly with his Father, he was never caught off guard by the day's events, no matter how diverse they were. The Gospels never portray Jesus as being in a hurry or experiencing stress. Despite the enormous pressures on him, Jesus never appeared to be overwhelmed or behind schedule. There has never been a person with as many important things to accomplish as Jesus, yet he displayed serenity throughout his ministry. Why? Because he was careful to let the Father schedule his life.

The axiom says, "To fail to plan is to plan to fail." Those who fail to schedule the important responsibilities of their lives into their routines invariably plan to neglect them. Routine saves time. If leaders habitually spend time with God first thing in the morning, they don't waste time each morning considering what they should do first. Their schedule has already decided that. Leaders with routines are protected from trivial interruptions. When leaders schedule regular meetings with their staff, they know that those crucial meetings will not be preempted by less important activities.

Finally, routine also protects leaders from becoming lopsided in their schedule. Some activities crave every moment of leaders' time. Leaders are naturally drawn to invest time in enjoyable activities while they tend to shun less fulfilling tasks. Only by carefully scheduling diverse activities into their schedules can leaders ensure that they have covered the broad spectrum of their responsibilities.

There is one important qualifier in the matter of routine. Although routines can be extremely freeing for leaders, when abused, they can become unyielding taskmasters. Spiritual leaders understand that God has the right to intervene in their schedule anytime he chooses. Leaders warily protect their schedules from those who want to usurp them, but spiritual leaders welcome God's intervention into their calendars. Leaders who are impervious to God's insertion of his agenda into their routines are in danger of making idols of their schedules. God is supreme even over the most meticulous leader's regimen. Spiritual leaders often find that what might appear to be an interruption at first is, in fact, a divine invitation. Wise leaders watch for God's activity, and they recognize it when they see it.

Leaders Delegate

The quantity of work leaders can accomplish is in direct proportion to their ability to delegate work to others. Leaders who refuse to delegate limit their productivity to the amount of work they can accomplish themselves. When leaders delegate, the magnitude of production they can achieve is unlimited. When leaders refuse to delegate, they limit the productivity of their organization to the level of their own physical stamina, creativity, and intelligence.

One of the most famous biblical examples of delegation, or rather the lack thereof, occurred in the ministry of Moses.

Moses was a national leader. His stature among his people was unparalleled. Everyone knew Moses had spoken face to face with God. Whenever there was a dispute, people naturally wanted Moses to settle the issue. The result? Long lines of people waiting their turn with the famous leader (Exod. 18:13–26). From morning until night, Moses dealt with issues that others could easily have processed for him. It was not until the intervention of his father-in-law, Jethro, that Moses delegated much of this responsibility to others. After delegating, Moses only handled the most difficult cases and allowed others to decide the routine issues. Not only was Moses' administrative load greatly relieved, but the people received service in a much more prompt and efficient manner.

Moses' mistake was assuming that because he could do something, he should do something.

Leaders need to ask themselves continually, "Is this something someone else could do?" Leaders take delight not only in how much they are accomplishing, but also in how much those around them are getting done. There are certain things that leaders cannot delegate. Leaders have the responsibility to hear from God and to guide their organizations into his will. The onus is on the leader to see that people are equipped to accomplish their tasks. Therefore they must delegate everything they can so they have the time to focus on these crucial responsibilities.

The reasons leaders fail to delegate are legion. Some leaders are perfectionists who assume no one can do the task as well as they can. Others are task-oriented and would rather complete the job themselves than take time to equip others to do it. Still others are uncomfortable asking people to do things; they find doing the job themselves less onerous than delegating it. Then there are the leaders who are so disorganized that by the time they realize an assignment needs to be completed, it is too late to enlist someone to do it. Whatever the reason for their reluctance to delegate, leaders must understand that mastering the art of delegation is preeminent among leadership skills. It is one of the wisest uses of a leader's time.

Leaders Use Focused Concentration

Leaders who cannot concentrate will be enslaved to interruptions and fruitless diversions. Peter Drucker warns against dividing a leader's time into small segments. Drucker suggests that most leadership tasks that can be done within fifteen minutes are tasks that could often be delegated to someone else. Leaders deal with significant issues such as the organization's future and values as well as enlisting and equipping personnel. These issues cannot be randomly plugged into fifteen-minute time slots. Leaders must allow themselves significant blocks of time in order to think through crucial issues. Leaders who divide every day into fifteen-minute segments are probably involving themselves in things they should delegate. Leaders should insert one- to two-hour time blocks in their schedules to focus intently and to think deeply about the critical issues of their organization. For example, while leaders need prayer times daily, from time to time they also need a day of prayer. Both are times with the Father, but they are not the same thing. Spiritual leaders cannot rush in and out of God's presence. God does not dispense his most profound truths and deep insights of life into convenient fifteen-minute rations. Good leaders also schedule significant blocks of time with key associates. The issues of the future are not comprehended after only ten minutes of concentration. Because of this, it behooves leaders to provide their staff with regular times of extended planning. Many organizations do not develop fresh, innovative, and revolutionary ideas because their leaders have failed to budget adequate time for their people to do so. Great insights don't come from rushed thinking.

The difference between managers and leaders can be seen here. Managers often become embroiled in the daily grind of keeping the organizational machinery functioning properly. Leaders realize they must occasionally step back from the day-to-day operations in order to gain perspective on the broader issues such as the nature and future of their organizations.

One of the key differences between leaders and managers is that managers are responsible for how something is done; leaders must also consider why it is being done, and continually communicate this to their followers. Secular writers argue that strategic thinking separates organizations that fail from those that thrive. Stuart Wells comments: "How did these stumbles happen? They are not victims of excessive government regulation. They are not victims of unfair foreign competition. They are not victims of unions. These forms of corporate whining are rather tiresome. It is not their fate or their stars. What happened is quite simple and profound—they are outthought. While they stumbled, others thrived. They are victims of one thing—their own thought patterns."[6]

While brief encounters with employees and volunteers can certainly be helpful in maintaining personal contact, they are most often merely symbolic, and they should never be substituted for quality one-on-one encounters. Leaders must invest quality time with key employees and volunteers. If leaders are to truly understand their followers and to convey their appreciation to them, they will occasionally need time slots of more than a few minutes. Effective leaders regularly set aside at least an hour to invest in personnel. They arrange breakfast and lunch meetings as a way to build relationships. Wise leaders divide their time into large enough segments that they can devote sufficient time to their tasks as well as to their people. Drucker concludes: "If there is any 'secret' of

---

Leaders Take Control of Their Time

- Leaders seek to understand God's will.
- Leaders say no.
- Leaders cultivate healthy routines.
- Leaders delegate.
- Leaders use focused concentration.

effectiveness, it is concentration. Effective executives do first things first and they do one thing at a time."[7] There is a pragmatic aspect to focused concentration as well. When leaders take the time to carefully consider the right thing to do, they will not be forced to waste valuable time backtracking when they have made needless mistakes. Taking the necessary time to concentrate at the front end saves time later. In other words, it pays to think ahead!

LEADERS MAKE TIME FOR THE IMPORTANT

Warren Bennis said: "I often observe people in top positions doing the wrong things well."[8] The question for most leaders is not whether they are busy, but whether they are busy doing the right things. Good activities subtly but brazenly crowd out the most important. Careless leaders may not even notice that serious work has been displaced by less important matters. They will continue to go to work at the same time and to be busy throughout the day, but there will be an emptiness to their efforts, a sense of futility as these leaders wonder whether all their activity is making a significant difference to their organization. Wise leaders schedule important activities into their calendars. There are at least five areas of life for which effective leaders fastidiously reserve adequate time.

Leaders Schedule Unhurried Time with God

Spiritual leaders understand that if they neglect their relationship with God, they forfeit their spiritual authority. Time spent in God's presence is never wasted. Everything spiritual leaders do should flow out of their relationship with God. The vision they have for their organization comes from God. Their daily agenda comes from God. God determines the values of their organization. God guides their choice of personnel. When spiritual leaders become disoriented to God, they imperil their organizations. Unfortunately, for most leaders it is easy to allow other activities to preempt time with God. Rather than spending unhurried, quality time with the heavenly Father, many leaders quickly skim a devotional book and then throw up a frantic prayer to God as they run to their first meeting of the day. God is not mocked. What people sow, they reap (Gal. 6:7). If leaders attempt to do things in their own strength and wisdom, they will achieve the results of what their strength and wisdom can accomplish. If leaders wait upon the Lord, they will see what God can do. The problem is, most leaders are in a hurry. Their calendar is bursting with appointments, and they are desperate not to fall behind schedule. The leader's mind-set is crucial. If leaders look upon their time with God as little more than an opportunity to gain a pithy devotional thought, they will often be tempted to forgo the experience in favor of expediency. If, however, leaders view their time as a crucial consultation with the Creator of the universe, they will diligently guard it, regardless of the busyness of their day.

King Saul's great downfall came when he rushed ahead of God's agenda (1 Sam. 13:5–14). The Israelites were facing the hated Philistine army at Gilgal. The enemy had gathered thirty thousand chariots and six thousand horsemen, together with a large contingent of foot soldiers. God had instructed Saul not to engage the enemy until Samuel arrived to offer a sacrifice to the Lord. Saul waited seven days and saw his situation rapidly deteriorating. His soldiers, terrified of their vast enemy, had begun to desert him. Saul wanted God's protection and power for his army but he was impatient to wait any longer to receive it, so he offered the sacrifice himself. Samuel immediately appeared and rebuked the presumptuous monarch. Saul won the battle that day, but his lack of patience would cost him his kingdom and ultimately his life.

Hindsight affords modern readers the luxury of criticizing Saul for his foolishness, but spiritual leaders would do well to learn from his mistake. Few spiritual leaders would openly question their need to spend time in prayer. Their lifestyle, however, would indicate they resent spending much time communing with God. God does not reveal his truth on people's terms; he does so on his terms. Far too often would-be spiritual leaders have rushed in and out of God's presence before God was willing to speak. Wise spiritual leaders remain in prayer as long as necessary until they are certain they have heard from God and they know God's will. One CEO bemoaned the fact that his schedule was so grueling he was too busy for a proper quiet time with the Lord. We challenged him to make the time, and he committed to try. A month later he jubilantly reported that he kept rising earlier and earlier in the morning until he felt he had a satisfactory amount of time to spend, unhurried, with God. His alarm was going off at 4:30 each morning. Yet he declared that God had given him specific and significant guidance that month, which had greatly helped him to lead his company. The CEO discovered that rather than taking away his time, spending time with God made him more efficient throughout the remainder of his day and actually saved him time. The key is not whether leaders spend some time with God but whether the time they spend is unhurried and adequate for all God wants to say to them (Isa. 64:4). It might be that God would say more to leaders if they would give him more time to say it!

Leaders Schedule Regular, Quality Time with Their Family

One of the great indictments of today's leaders is that in their quest to be successful in their jobs, they are failing their families. Leaders become so focused on leading their organizations that they neglect the most important relationships they have. Because they carry the ultimate responsibility for their organizations, they often find it difficult to relax and to focus on their families, even when they are not at work. Unfortunately, Christian ministers often neglect their families under the misconception that serving the Lord requires them to do so.

Lee Iacocca, former CEO of Chrysler, challenged the assumption that the more responsibility leaders were given the more their families would invariably suffer. He noted: "Some people think that the higher up you are in a corporation the more you have to neglect your family. Not at all! Actually it's the guys at the top who have the freedom and the flexibility to spend enough time with their wives and kids."[9]

Iacocca was right; leaders often do have more freedom and flexibility in their schedules if they will use it. But leaders must be creative in finding ways to spend time with their families. For example, pastors who are busy most evenings could arrange to be home some mornings to have breakfast with their families and see their children off to school. They could arrange a special one-on-one lunch date with each child, as well as with their spouse. The pressure on leaders often comes not from the organization but from within themselves. It is not always the office that places inordinate demands on leaders but the leaders themselves who feel compelled to keep working and going in to their office when they should be spending time at home. Some leaders are reluctant to stay home at unconventional times because they are afraid they will be perceived as lazy or unable to handle the pressures of their job. Such leaders must determine their priorities and then make whatever adjustments are required to protect those priorities.

Astute leaders schedule regular, quality time with their families. They are intentional about planning dates with their spouse. They calendar their children's special events well in advance so they can attend, and these remain sacrosanct. They guard the privacy of their home, and they avoid bringing work home with them if at all possible. Wise leaders strive to be home at mealtimes with their family and refuse to submit to the tyranny of the telephone during occasions when they are spending quality time with their family. A ringing telephone does not take precedence over family time.

Despite Harry Truman's role as president of the United States, he never forgot what was most important to him. When Bess Truman was asked what she considered the most memorable aspect of her life she replied: "Harry and I have been sweethearts and married for more than forty years—and no matter where I was, when I put out my hand Harry's was there to grasp it."[10] Even the presidency of the United States during some of the most critical moments of history did not confuse Truman about what, and who, was most important in his life.

Perceptive leaders also understand that there are more important things in life than their jobs. When spiritual leaders are interviewing for a new job, they will ask probing questions of their prospective employer to determine what the company's stance is toward the family. Wise leaders are wary of companies that promote lifestyles that are destructive to families. Spiritual leaders know that all the career advancement they attain means nothing if their teenage son refuses to speak to them or their daughter becomes addicted to drugs. Many a shrewd leader has declined a lucrative job offer that involved increased travel because he knew his wife and children needed his presence at home. Many leaders have turned down promotions because they knew the increased responsibility would bring multiplied pressures that would erode their family life. Leaders have also resisted promotions that would put intense pressure on them to compromise their Christian convictions. Such leaders understand that some things are more important than career advancement or personal prestige, so they manage their schedules to protect and nurture what is most significant in their lives.

Leaders Manage Time for Their Health

Some leaders live antithetical lives. They lead their organizations to become strong, healthy, and vibrant while at the same time they allow their own bodies to become overweight, out of shape, weary, and vulnerable to disease. Some leaders expend so much effort revitalizing their organizations that they have no reserve energy to maintain their own health.

Dr. Richard Swenson, in his book *Margin: Restoring Emotional, Physical, Financial and Time Reserves to Overloaded Lives,* discusses a topic so simple it should be obvious to everyone, yet most leaders have not figured it out. His thesis is this: people have limits. When people live their lives to the edge of their endurance, whether it is in their finances or their time, or their sleep, or their emotional health, they run great risks. Just like a car that is continually driven at full speed and not maintained, human bodies will break down if they are continually pushed to their limit.

Swenson is a medical doctor who developed the conviction that people must build room (margin) into their lives for unexpected crises or opportunities. His formula is: Power – Load = Margin.[11] If people deprive themselves of sleep on an ongoing basis, their bodies will suffer. People cannot continually endure emotionally draining events without restoring their emotions through such things as hobbies, friendships, vacations, or laughter. People who maximize their spending to the limit every month are inviting a financial ruin. Likewise, people who saturate their schedules, leaving no room for unforeseen interruptions, are setting themselves up for a crisis. Leaders who never allow time in their annual schedules for a relaxing vacation are racing toward an inevitable breakdown. Margin is the reserve amount of time, money, energy, and emotional strength people maintain in order to remain healthy.

It's amazing how many leaders live their lives without margin. They cannot bear to be idle or unproductive; empty spots on their calendars jump out at them as ideal places to undertake new projects. God never planned it this way. Since the beginning of time, God has emphasized the need for rest (Gen. 2:2–3).

Jesus understood that there were times he needed rest and solitude. After ministering to the crowds all day, Jesus and his disciples deliberately sought restoration (Mark 6:45). At the beginning of Jesus' final week of ministry on earth, he allowed his good friends Lazarus, Martha, and Mary to minister to him (John 12:1–3). On the climactic night of his arrest and crucifixion when he could have preached to the crowds one final time, Jesus chose an intimate supper with his close friends (Luke 22:7–13).

Taking time to care for their health is a pragmatic issue for leaders. Leaders who are overweight tend to tire more easily. People who eat poorly, who don't get enough sleep, or who don't exercise get sick more often. Unhealthy people do not have the energy and strength to accomplish as much as healthy people. Leaders do not need to become obsessed with physical fitness, but leaders who ignore health issues are ultimately choosing to be less effective over time than they could be. People who fail to take care of their health face the risk of having their leadership come to a premature end.

Healthy leaders understand that a sense of humor is essential to emotional health. Leaders realize they are ultimately responsible for the positive, upbeat spirit of their organization. If they want their followers to enjoy working with them, leaders must foster a sense of joy in the workplace.

Kouzes and Posner have even given this an official name, LBFA— Leading by Fooling Around. These authors cite empirical evidence that links fun with productivity.[12] It is possible to work hard, to be productive, and yet to have fun. Leaders ought to enjoy going to work and so should those they lead (Prov. 15:13; 17:22).

Leaders Schedule Time for People

Leaders usually have people around them. They tend to enjoy people. Abraham Lincoln spent most of each day receiving people at the White House. Spiritual leaders such as James Dobson and Billy Graham have wisely involved other godly men and women in key roles in their ministries. People who prefer to work alone, or who find it difficult to relate to others, may not be suited for leadership roles.

Those in prominent positions must always remember that without followers, they are not leaders. They may be administrators who run large organizations, but they are not leaders. To be a leader one must invest time in people. This can be difficult for leaders who face a multiplicity of tasks. They can easily be tempted to look upon their people as interruptions to their work rather than as the essence of their work. *Leadership work is people work.* Whether they lead a small church or a large corporation, genuine leaders put their people high on their priority list.

In *Encouraging the Heart*, Kouzes and Posner argue that even in secular businesses it is important for leaders to recognize, encourage, and thank their people. The authors note that many times administrators know little about their employees' lives even after having worked with them for many years.[13]

A teaching popular in modern leadership theory is the Pareto Principle, or the 20–80 Principle. This theory suggests that 20 percent of people in an organization generally produce 80 percent of the results. Advocates of this principle argue that 80 percent of a leader's time should therefore be invested in the 20 percent of the people who are doing 80 percent of the work. As with most leadership principles, the Pareto Principle addresses the experience of many organizations; however, caution must be used in its application.

It is true that the investment of a leader's time in some people will produce far greater results than an equal time investment in others. People who work hard for an organization and who are teachable deserve their leader's attention. Moreover, involvement with such people will benefit both the individual and the organization. When leaders invest in people who are motivated and eager to learn, those people have the opportunity to excel and to reach their maximum potential. When some people are achieving what God has designed for them, they can inspire others in the organization as well. Sometimes pastors vainly invest many hours trying to revive carnal or apathetic church members when they could help their church far more by discipling those members who are eager to mature in their faith.

Leaders ought never to allow the least motivated members of an organization to set the pace for the others. Rather, leaders should help teachable people achieve their best so others in the organization can see what is possible and can know what is expected of them. Wise leaders also link growing and productive followers with those who need encouragement. They do this because they know the strength of any organization depends upon whether every member is successfully doing his or her part (Eph. 4:16).

The biblical record demonstrates that Jesus often narrowed his focus to a select few. Certainly there were times when Jesus delivered profound teaching to the multitudes. At other times, he took his twelve disciples aside and gave them divine teaching that was not offered to the crowds (Matt. 10; 13:10–17; Mark 7:17–23). There were still other occasions when Jesus met with his inner circle of disciples—Peter, James, and John—and went still deeper in spiritual matters (Luke 9:28; Matt. 26:37–38). Jesus sometimes invested time in a solitary disciple (John 20:27; 21:15–19). Why would Jesus be so selective with divine, life-changing truth? He knew that some people were more willing to receive his teaching and to act upon it than were others. Some were more prepared to understand deep truths than others. By investing in small groups such as the twelve disciples, Jesus was preparing for the day when people like Peter would be powerful leaders themselves. Because Jesus took time to help Peter develop as a leader, he in turn would influence many others to become followers of Christ as well.

Many leaders have experienced the frustration of investing large amounts of time in people, only to find those people unwilling or unable to do what they should do. Meanwhile, hard-working members of the organization were neglected while their leader vainly attempted to strengthen unmotivated, resistant members.

Pastors continually face this dilemma. There are chronically needy people in every church. Such people consume countless hours of their ministers' time because they ask for extensive counseling and encouragement. Yet their unhealthy attitudes and behavior often remain unchanged. Meanwhile, church members wanting to grow in their faith may receive scant attention from their pastor because they do not complain or draw attention to themselves. Leaders who allow this to happen find themselves pouring all their energy into the least responsive people in their organization, while neglecting those who would flourish with even minimal effort. When leaders allow their time to be monopolized by the weaker members, they limit their organizations by not adequately supporting their healthy members.

Yet there is a subtle danger in misapplying the 20–80 Principle. For spiritual leaders, people—not tasks—are central. The primary role of spiritual leaders is not to merely accomplish tasks, but to take people from where they are to where God wants them to be. Fulfilling this mandate requires watching to see where God is at work in people's lives and then joining God in his activity. Spiritual leaders must be sensitive to what God is doing in the lives of their people. When someone is apathetic or resistant to God, there is little a leader can do to change that person's attitude. Leaders who continually invest large amounts of time into people who refuse to do God's will are investing their time unwisely. On the other hand, when God is working in people's lives, it is their leaders' responsibility to invest time and energy into helping these people grow. Since only God knows whether a weak member will respond positively to their leader's attention, it is essential that God set the leader's agenda. It is the hope of every conscientious leader that as they invest 20 percent of their time in those who are struggling or unproductive, these people will respond positively and join the group who are most responsive and productive. Leaders never give up on their people. They simply invest their time wisely between those who are growing and productive and those who are not.

Leaders Make Time for Important Things

- Leaders schedule unhurried time with God.
- Leaders schedule regular, quality time with their families.
- Leaders schedule time for their health.
- Leaders schedule time for people.

LEADERS AVOID TIMEWASTERS

Besides making the best use of time, effective leadership also involves steering clear of timewasters. There are a host of discussions, activities, and meetings that do nothing more than absorb leaders' valuable time. Whenever leaders are seduced into investing time in the trivial, they have become disengaged from the essential. The list of time-consuming diversions is lengthy, but we will examine some of the most notorious offenders.

Novelties

Technology can enhance leaders' work exponentially and save hours of time. Technology can also be an insidious time stealer. Technology is advancing so rapidly, few people can keep up. So many timesaving programs and devices are becoming available, it would take weeks just to read about them! Some people fritter away hours on their computers every day performing nonessential tasks. One problem is that computers are instruments for work as well as for entertainment, and some people struggle to differentiate between the two. Everyone seems to know at least one zealous Internet guru who inundates them with quotes, jokes, feel-good stories, and late-breaking news about impending crises or the most current computer virus. While it's great to spread joy among friends and colleagues, some leaders who have better things to do with their time waste hours of their day searching the Internet for such trivia while their organization languishes from neglect. Incorporating new technology is obviously essential for organizations, but wise leaders monitor the amount of time they spend investigating and experimenting with new products against the potential gains in time and efficiency. Leaders must avoid becoming so enamored with technology that they are continuously swept into unproductive time-wasting activities. The key is not for leaders to shun technology; that would be foolish and shortsighted. Leaders must master technology rather than allowing technology to master them. Leaders must learn to put technology to work for them rather than squandering valuable time investigating the latest cyber-trend.

Lack of Personnel

Leaders who understaff their organizations end up diverting their own time into jobs that, important as they may be, keep them from properly doing their own work. Leaders cannot delegate to people who are nonexistent. For most leaders the most critical staff person is an administrative assistant. A large percentage of activities that would take leaders fifteen minutes or less to accomplish could easily be handled by an assistant. Leaders seeking to build large blocks of time into their day for creative thinking, planning, and problem solving need to have people around them who can handle smaller administrative tasks. For a variety of reasons, some leaders prefer to type their own letters, make their own appointments, or arrange their own travel, even though an assistant could do these more efficiently. Effective leaders view every task in light of the question: "Is this something someone else could be doing?" Jobs constantly accumulate on leaders' desks; therefore, leaders must continually be giving jobs away. Technology can help reduce the need for additional personnel, but ultimately an understaffed organization puts undue pressure on existing staff and limits the organization's potential. Leaders do not add staff haphazardly or without regard to budget constraints, but they do monitor their organization's optimum effectiveness and seek to ensure that trained personnel are available to accomplish its mission.

Idle Conversation

Idle conversation is one of the most common timewasters for leaders. It is also one of the hardest to avoid because leaders do not want to leave the impression they are too busy to keep in touch with their colleagues. In fact, most leaders enjoy their people and have a genuine desire to spend time visiting with them. However, a conversation that begins at the lunchroom coffee pot can eventually consume an hour of a leader's day. A casual conversation in the office hallway about the local sports team can erode a leader's available time until little or no time is left to focus on critical leadership issues. This does not mean leaders never have lengthy conversations with those in their organization. Sensitive leaders are willing to spend time discussing matters of substance, whether these issues involve the work or the personal life of the coworker. Sometimes discussions about the weather lead into relevant and important conversations.

Perceptive leaders will usually detect when a colleague has an underlying issue they need to discuss or whether a conversation is going nowhere. Conversations can be profitable, informative, redemptive, and mutually encouraging. Or they can swallow up valuable amounts of time that both parties could better spend elsewhere. Leaders must find the balance between keeping up with people and becoming engaged in prolonged, time-consuming, frivolous conversations.

People who stand around the workplace visiting with every passerby send the clear message that they are not occupied in matters of importance. Leaders need to be pleasant conversationalists, but there should be a sense of intentionality about them as they invest their day in those things they consider to be most important. Good leaders find appropriate moments in idle conversation to excuse themselves and get back to their work. Efficient leaders make every effort to be brief and succinct in their communication. Their memos are concise. They get to the point when they make phone calls. They make their words as well as their time count.

Excessive Hobbies

Hobbies can provide leaders with a welcome and wholesome outlet to relieve stress and to restore emotional health. They can also be part of a fitness regimen. Leaders can often use hobbies such as golf as a means to get to know clients or colleagues. Once again, the important thing is that leaders never become so absorbed in their hobbies that they neglect their families and their jobs. When a hobby consumes a leader's time to the detriment of important relationships and activities, it has ceased to serve its rightful function.

Smart leaders put their hobbies to work for them. If they enjoy golfing or jogging, they invite a client or colleague to accompany them. Many hobbies, such as skiing, hiking, or camping, are conducive to family outings, so the leader can combine relaxation and exercise with quality family time. The key word here, as in so many areas, is *balance*. Leaders are careful to ensure that by doing one important thing they do not inadvertently neglect another. If leaders realize they have no hobbies or recreational interests, this should alert them that they have been working too hard and may not know how to relax. Others may need to reevaluate the excessive amounts of time and money they invest in their recreation and recognize the adverse effect their hobbies have on their families, their work, or other priorities. Like technology and conversation, hobbies have their advantages and disadvantages. It all comes down to good choices.

Disorganization

Disorganization can be the undoing of even the best-intentioned leader. Leaders cannot afford to be disorganized, because they stand to waste not only their own time but the valuable time of their people and clients as well. Organized leaders avoid overbooking themselves by religiously keeping their calendars up to date. Better yet, they have a capable administrative assistant do this for them. They continually look ahead in their calendars to see what tasks should be delegated now in order to allow ample time for completion. They are rigorously punctual for appointments; they begin meetings on time so they are not guilty of wasting other people's time.

Wise leaders employ an effective record-keeping system so they don't waste time trying to find information they have misplaced. Again, a competent assistant is their greatest resource. Effective leaders arrive at meetings with an agenda for what they want to accomplish, not to manipulate but to organize. When appropriate, leaders make the agenda available to others in advance so they, too, can be prepared for the meeting. Skilled leaders deal with administrative matters only once. For example, they read and respond to correspondence once, take action, and file it away. They don't waste time continually shuffling through papers and documents that have been left on their desks.

Leaders of Christian organizations are among the most disorganized of professionals. There is a reason for this: most entered the ministry because they loved God and loved people, not because they felt gifted to lead. Yet when they attain positions in churches or religious organizations, they discover, to their dismay, they are primarily called upon to lead. Unfortunately they may abhor administration because it takes them away from doing what they love to do—spending time with people. If they devote most of their energy to what they know and enjoy, they fail to organize themselves or their people effectively.

These ministers grow weary and discouraged under the administrative load that accrues.

But help is just around the corner. There are many qualified people who would gladly assist them if only the leaders were organized enough to enlist them. These ministers can brighten up a life with a hospital visit, but they conduct painfully tedious meetings because they have no sense of purpose or direction for the discussion. Such leaders may be gifted evangelists, but they continually frustrate their followers because they are either unprepared or unaware of the issues facing their organization. The answer is not for these leaders to resign and become hospital chaplains or traveling evangelists. Most often, they simply need to recognize that organizing people for a common purpose is a noble enterprise. Administration can be a significant ministry. Leaders who are not proficient administrators need to enlist a competent administrator or seek training in administration themselves. Leaders need to take advantage of their qualified personnel, and we'll say it again—they need to delegate.

If leaders will do what it takes to organize themselves, they will enjoy long, productive ministries as spiritual leaders. When people organize

Leaders Avoid Timewasters
- Novelties
- Lack of personnel
- Idle conversation
- Excessive hobbies
- Disorganization

their overstuffed closets and get rid of clutter, they are usually amazed at how much space they actually have for their clothes. Getting organized holds a similar advantage for leaders. Once they arrange their time into manageable blocks and eliminate the superfluous, they find they have enough time in the day to accomplish what God is leading them to do.

LEADERS INVEST THEIR SURPLUS TIME WISELY

Why do some leaders accomplish far more than others? Why do some leaders see nothing of significance occur under their tenure, yet their successors witness a flurry of activity and progress? There are, of course, many reasons for this, and one key factor is how they use their surplus time. To busy leaders, the very idea of surplus time may seem like a dream. The truth is, however, most people have surplus time; they just don't recognize it as such. The effective leader seizes these pockets of extra time. The mediocre leader wastes them in idle frustration. Effective leaders adhere strictly to the old Boy Scout motto: "Be prepared."

Most leaders know of several books and articles that could greatly inform them and enrich their leadership. Some leaders find ways to stay current in their fields, while others complain that they never have time to read. Wise leaders seize unexpected free moments for reading. When meeting someone at a restaurant for a breakfast meeting, prepared leaders will take a book with them. If they must wait fifteen minutes while their appointment is caught in traffic, they occupy the time reading. Productive leaders know that the person they are meeting at the airport may arrive late, so they prepare themselves for possible delays by bringing reading material with them.

Margaret Truman, the daughter of Harry Truman, could not recall a time she saw her father spending an idle moment without a book in his hand.

Preparing for enforced times of waiting, such as in a doctor's or dentist's office, has a double benefit. First, a person suddenly has a half hour to read or review work-related material. Second, the prepared person finds waiting to be a productive time rather than an irritating and stressful experience. Commercial flights offer several hours of uninterrupted time during which a prepared person can accomplish a great deal. A laptop computer is invaluable for such times. A prepared leader could respond to several e-mails and preview material for a forthcoming meeting. Entire books can be read during business travel. Unprepared people are left to glance through the in-flight magazine, look at their watches, or gaze out the window. Over the course of a three-hour flight, the person who planned ahead may have read several chapters of a helpful book, answered his e-mails, and reviewed his calendar. The unprepared leader has watched a third-rate in-flight movie and viewed the cloud cover over Nebraska.

Do not misunderstand the point here. Sometimes catching an in-flight nap is the wisest thing to do, because the leader needs to be fresh for an important meeting scheduled for that evening. There will also be times when God prompts leaders to put down their book in order to share their faith with the person in the next seat. The point is not how the time is spent but that leaders are intentional about the way they choose to spend it.

Some leaders have found a goldmine of valuable time when they redirect lost hours spent watching television into enriching reading, exercising, or family time. Leaders who spend large amounts of time commuting in their cars could occupy the time by praying, or listening to informative tapes and CDs. If leaders creatively use moments of enforced idleness, they will be pleasantly surprised to find they do have time for the things that are important to them.

Elton Trueblood, the prolific Christian author, was once visiting a theological seminary. One student asked him if he ever attended social clubs. He meekly replied, "I have written books while others have attended clubs." While not devaluing people's involvement in clubs, Trueblood was confessing that he had been forced to make choices about how to invest his time. He understood that choosing to do one thing well often required him to eliminate other activities from his schedule. Trueblood chose to write well, and people continue to be blessed by his efforts decades later.

Conclusion

No one should determine leaders' schedules but themselves, as God guides them. They must understand God's will and, from this understanding, they should set their priorities. This requires identifying the most important things in their lives and arranging their schedules so that none of these priorities are neglected. Staying organized is a deliberate and ongoing process. An uncluttered schedule one month can become a schedule filled with frivolous activities the next. Wise leaders regularly prune their schedules of those things that are unnecessary.

They learn to delegate, and they learn to say no. They learn to redeem the time (Eph. 5:16). Because great leaders want their lives to count, they use their time wisely.

CONCEPTS AND SCRIPTURES FOR CONSIDERATION

- The key to successful leadership is not creating more time in one's life or packing more activities into one's day, but staying on God's agenda.
- Despite the pervasive and unrelenting pressures on their time, leaders ultimately choose how they perform second by second, minute by minute, hour by hour.
- The most inefficient and unproductive leader has as much time as history-making leaders.
- Wise leaders realize there is no way they can satisfy the desires of all the people who clamor for their time.
- Unlike people, God never piles on more than someone can handle.
- God never burns people out.
- Once leaders clearly understand God's will, deciding how to invest their time becomes much easier.
- Many leaders find that saying no is one of the hardest things they do.
- By spending too much time on less significant issues, leaders invariably neglect the more important ones.
- God does not give people more than they can handle, but people regularly assume responsibility for things they should not be doing.
- It is a wise practice for leaders to audit their commitments annually.
- Superfluous activity must be weeded out so those activities on God's agenda can flourish.
- Routines ensure that leaders have scheduled their most important responsibilities into their calendars.
- If you do not make a plan for your time, someone else will.

- Leaders who are impervious to God's insertion of his agenda into their routines are in danger of making idols of their schedules.
- The quantity of work leaders can accomplish is in direct proportion to their ability to delegate work to others.
- Leaders who cannot concentrate will be enslaved to interruptions and fruitless diversions.
- Spiritual leaders cannot rush in and out of God's presence.
- Spiritual leaders understand that if they neglect their relationship with God, they forfeit their spiritual authority.
- One of the great indictments of today's leaders is that in their quest to be successful in their jobs, they are failing their families.
- Leadership work is people work.
- Leaders must learn to master technology rather than allowing technology to master them.
- Disorganization can be the undoing of even the best-intentioned leader.

Ephesians 5:15–17
Luke 6:12; 21:37; 22:39; Mark 1:35
Exodus 18:13–26
Isaiah 64:4
Genesis 2:2–3
Proverbs 15:13; 17:22
Ephesians 4:16
Galatians 6:7
1 Samuel 13:5–14

Chapter Ten

The Leader's Pitfalls

What Disqualifies Leaders?

EVERY YEAR THOUSANDS OF LEADERS shipwreck their careers, their organizations, and their families by making careless, foolish choices. The media parades a never-ending array of tarnished, discredited, and humiliated leaders before an increasingly disillusioned society. Why is it that some leaders go from victory to victory, year after year, while others begin with great promise but eventually crash into oblivion? Certainly they did not set out expecting to fail, but sadly, their failure can usually be traced to mistakes they could easily have avoided. This chapter examines ten of the most common pitfalls that cause spiritual leaders to fail.

PRIDE

Pride may well be leaders' worst enemy, and it has caused the downfall of many. Pride is dangerous to unwary leaders because it can be subversive in the way it creeps into their lives. Pride can be couched in pious terms. It clings tenaciously to people, blinding them to the grievous consequences of their sin. Pride shows up in a variety of disguises, some of them obvious, others more subtle, but all of them lethal to leaders' effectiveness.

Pride Tempts Others to Take the Credit from Others

Kouzes and Posner claim the most common reason for employees leaving their companies is that their leaders gave limited praise and recognition for their efforts.[1] It is demoralizing for followers to labor on behalf of their organization, only to have their leader enjoy the accolades for the success. Whereas authentic leaders shoulder the responsibility for the poor performance of their organizations, wise leaders rightfully acknowledge the efforts of their followers as critical to their organization's success. Leaders cannot always be as liberal as they want with monetary rewards, but they can be generous with the genuine praise and gratitude they express to their people.

Pride, however, tempts leaders to monopolize the credit for their organization's success. Pride drives leaders to seek the limelight. Pride moves them to magnify their own involvement and to minimize the efforts of others. The writer of Proverbs urges: "Let another praise you, and not your own mouth, a stranger, and not your own lips" (Prov. 27:2), yet some leaders cannot wait for others to praise their efforts, so they blow their own horn. In conversations or public gatherings they always find a way to publicize their latest achievement.

Pride is an offensive trait in secular leaders, but it is even more repulsive in spiritual leaders. Pride causes Christian leaders to take the credit not only for what their people have done but also for what God has accomplished. Spiritual leaders are God's servants, but pride can cause them to act as if God were their servant, obligated to answer their selfish prayers and to bless their grandiose schemes. When spiritual leaders' companies succeed financially, pride can cause them to attribute the success to their good business and management skills, rather than citing God's guidance and protection. When spiritual leaders' organizations grow, pride can tempt leaders to credit their dynamic personality or their compelling vision or their marketing savvy for the success. They direct attention to themselves rather than to God. Political leaders must understand that presuming upon the glory and sovereignty of God can bring disaster. Nebuchadnezzar, king of Babylon and possessor of an overinflated ego, learned this truth the hard way: "He was walking on the roof of the royal palace of Babylon. The king reflected and said, 'Is this not Babylon the great, which I myself have built as a royal residence by the might of my power and for the glory of my majesty?' While the word was in the king's mouth, a voice came from heaven, saying, 'King Nebuchadnezzar, to you it is declared: sovereignty has been removed from you'" (Dan. 4:29–31).

God is ruler over the world's nations, and he alone dispenses sovereign power. Political figures must recognize that, despite their political acumen or widespread popularity, they ultimately rule only by God's consent. God is protective of his glory. God abhors haughtiness (Prov. 6:16–17). When people brazenly take credit for God's activity, they are offending almighty God. When leaders continually cloak the successes of their organization in terms of what they have done, they are inviting God to humble them. Leaders who fail to acknowledge God as the source of victory are leading people away from God and wrongfully causing their followers to misdirect their praise. Such leadership is contrary to biblical principles and will prove disastrous to churches, to businesses, and ultimately to nations.

During the 1948 presidential campaign, Harry Truman was seeking reelection. The Republican candidate, Thomas E. Dewey, successful governor of New York, was the clear favorite. He had been elected governor by over 700,000 votes, the largest margin in New York history. Dewey had lost to the popular Franklin Roosevelt in the 1944 presidential election, but by the narrowest margin since 1916. Now he was totally confident he could beat Truman, who was president only because Roosevelt had died in office. The nation's top fifty political journalists were polled; all fifty predicted Dewey's victory. Twice as many reporters chronicled Dewey's campaign as followed the incumbent president's since they assumed they were following the next president of the United States. Dewey brimmed over with confidence. He was disdainful of Truman, who had not attended college and who was painfully ordinary and uncultured compared to both Dewey and Roosevelt. It was said of Dewey, he "was the only man who could strut sitting down."[2] Dewey was so confident in his ability and credentials that he took his unassuming opponent for granted. The *Chicago Tribune* prematurely attributed Dewey the victory, running the front-page headline "Dewey Defeats Truman" the morning after the election before all the results were in. Then, in one of the greatest electoral upsets in American history, voters elected Truman over the heavily favored Dewey. The Dewey camp was shocked. The unthinkable had happened! Dewey had overestimated himself and grossly underestimated his opponent. Truman's secretary of state, Dean Acheson, summarized the secret to Truman's success: He was "free of the greatest vice in a leader, his ego never came between him and his job."[3]

Pride Makes Leaders Unteachable

Pride closes leaders' minds. When leaders believe their own abilities are solely responsible for their organization's success, they dangerously assume no one else could run their organization as well as they can. Their pride convinces them that they alone possess the depth of insight for success, and they become impervious to wise counsel. They grow impatient with those who do not readily accept their opinions. They rob themselves of enormous potential opportunities, all because they are unteachable.

King Ahab was a brilliant administrator and a capable military commander, except for one fatal flaw: he disdained godly counsel. When he proposed to the godly king Jehoshaphat that they combine their armies and attack the Arameans, Jehoshaphat suggested they first seek advice from counselors. Ahab had been prepared to rely upon his own cunning and military experience, but to placate his righteous colleague, he summoned his religious advisors. Zedekiah, the chief of Ahab's four hundred counselors, dutifully predicted what Ahab wanted to hear: complete victory. Still not satisfied, Jehoshaphat asked that Micaiah, the prophet of the Lord, be consulted. Ahab demurred, claiming, "I hate him, for he never prophecies good concerning me but always evil" (2 Chron. 18:7). Sure enough, Michaiah prophesied that Ahab's forces would be routed and Ahab slain. God, through his prophet, was duly warning Ahab that if he proceeded with his plans he would lose his life. Ahab's response? He threw the recalcitrant prophet in jail and marched off to battle. Ahab's pride deafened him to wise counsel, and as a result he would soon die an ignoble death on a meaningless battlefield (2 Chron. 18).

Pride's great victory is to turn otherwise brilliant leaders such as Ahab away from God's guidance, as offered through the wisdom and support of godly people. No matter how talented or how smart a leader may be, an unteachable spirit is the path to certain failure.

If there is any quality common to all effective spiritual leaders, it is a teachable spirit. The Book of Proverbs assures us, "The fear of the LORD is the beginning of knowledge; fools despise wisdom and instruction . . . For wisdom will enter your heart, and knowledge will be pleasant to your soul; discretion will guard you, understanding will watch over you" (Prov. 1:7; 2:10–11).

Pride Causes Leaders to Think They Are Self-Sufficient

In his biography of Theodore Roosevelt, H. W. Brands commented on Roosevelt's early political efforts. He noted: "It wouldn't be the last time Roosevelt resisted someone who should have been an ally. Even at this early date he showed the egotism that would chronically compel him to denigrate almost anyone who competed with him for the limelight."[4] Historians claim Roosevelt was one of America's finest presidents, yet he had an unfortunate tendency to assume his causes were always right and just and those opposing him were corrupt and evil. This caused Roosevelt to alienate fellow politicians and supporters who would have most naturally been his friends. This single-minded confidence in his own viewpoint contributed significantly to his defeat in a later reelection attempt.

History is rife with examples of people who were at the pinnacle of success one moment and tossed into the scrap heap of abject failures the next. Business leaders have been the toast of the town one day and scandalized by criminal charges the next. Coaches have won coach-of-the-year honors one year and been fired by mid-season the next. Politicians have reached the apex of power one term and been cast out of office the next. Pastors have stood at the helm of megachurches one week and resigned in shame the next. Leaders who allow pride to blind them to their total dependence upon God's grace and the support of their people will eventually be humbled. Pride exalts people to think they are self-sufficient. Just as King Saul was humbled when he presumed upon God, so God will humble leaders who act as if they are independent of God's grace (1 Sam. 13:13–14).

In contrast to proud leaders like Saul, spiritual leaders such as D. L. Moody clearly understood the source of their success. Upon meeting Moody, the evangelist known as Uncle Johnnie Vasser exclaimed, "How glad I am to see the man that God has used to win so many souls to Christ!" In response, Moody stooped down and scooped up a handful of dirt. As he let the dust pour through his fingers he confessed: "There's nothing more than that to D. L. Moody, except as God uses him!"[5] Despite Moody's international fame and the massive audiences to which he preached, he never forgot that he owed everything to Christ.

Pride targets successful leaders, convincing them they have enough talent, wisdom, and charisma to achieve whatever they set their minds to do. Pride causes leaders to believe they can be lackadaisical in their obedience to God's Word. Leaders are most vulnerable in the area of their greatest strength. Max Depree warns, "Leaders are fragile precisely at the point of their strengths, liable to fail at the height of their success."[6] Depree is right; people fall hardest from their highest points. Wise spiritual leaders never take the grace, blessing, and presence of God for granted. When they are enjoying their greatest success is when they are most vigilant against pride causing them to fall.

Napoleon's spectacular military success across Europe convinced him he could single-handedly conquer Europe. When he chose to invade Russia, he was so confident in victory that he did not research the climate or terrain of the enemy territory. As a result, he neglected to prepare his soldiers for the lethal Russian winter. Napoleon was so puffed up by his own ability he did not even entertain the notion that he might not enjoy immediate and complete success. His blind arrogance caused tens of thousands of his soldiers to lose their lives as Napoleon's empire began its steady decline. Many years later, Adolph Hitler would be blinded by the same egotism and, having learned nothing from history, would send his forces into the same Russian winter and the same debacle Napoleon had suffered before him.

Young leaders can fall into the trap of relying solely on themselves, because experience has not yet taught them otherwise. But older leaders who should know better are also vulnerable to the pitfall of self-reliance. Because of their success over the years, some grow to believe they do not need counsel and support from others in order to lead. They may particularly disdain the suggestions of younger, less-experienced colleagues. As a result, they become detached from their followers and out of touch with the reality of their situation.

Spiritual leaders must be especially careful not to presume upon God's blessings. A proud disposition is the counterpole of an intimate walk with God. Samson was a military man with enormous strength and more than enough power to defeat his enemies. His mistake was in taking that power for granted. Samson believed he could live any way he chose and still retain the robust strength God had graciously given him. When he ignored God's clear instructions and neglected his relationship with his Lord, God allowed his power to dissipate. When Samson set out to do in his own strength what he had always done before in God's, he suffered humiliating defeat (Judg. 16:15–21). Wise leaders always recognize that they can do nothing apart from their intimate relationship with Christ (John 15:5).

Pride Leads to a Loss of Compassion

Through the prophet Ezekiel, God castigated spiritual leaders who looked upon their followers as sheep to be fleeced rather than as a flock to shepherd (Ezek. 34:1–10). These would-be spiritual leaders led for what they could gain rather than for what they could give. The people were being scattered and abused by others, yet their leaders' only concern was for their own comfort and gain.

Leadership is a high calling. It is a God-given privilege. Leaders have the opportunity to enrich the lives of their followers, and they also have the influence to do so. But when leaders lose the passion to contribute to their organization and begin to focus instead on what they can receive from it, they are no longer authentic leaders. They develop a sense of superiority that regards people as mere parts of the organizational machinery. They see themselves as entitled to whatever they can get from their organization.

A sure sign that pride has taken root in leaders' lives is that they lose compassion for those they are leading. When leaders become calloused to the hardships of their people, their pride has desensitized them. When leaders impose financial cutbacks and hardships upon their people, yet they continue to shower lucrative benefits upon themselves, they forfeit their prerogative to lead. Leaders who become preoccupied with their own personal accomplishments, and are oblivious to the needs of others are not worthy of the call to lead. Pastors who are unmoved when a church member is hurting, or who are ambivalent when one of their flock falls by the wayside, are abusing the privilege of spiritual leadership. They are like Nero, the Roman emperor who, according to legend, entertained himself with music while Rome burned; or like Marie Antoinette who, when told that French peasants had no bread to eat, purportedly responded, "Let them eat cake." History shows that such insensitive leaders eventually meet their demise.

The apostle Paul, on the other hand, demonstrated the compassion leaders must have for their people. In writing to the troubled church at Corinth, he stated: "There is the daily pressure on me of concern for all the churches. Who is weak without my being weak? Who is led into sin without my intense concern?" (2 Cor. 11:28–29). True leaders never lose sight of their responsibility to care for their followers.

Pride Makes Leaders Vulnerable

Pride is a sin, and pride will do what sin does. It destroys. Leaders who allow pride to grow unchecked will eventually lose everything— their relationships, their credibility, and ultimately their position as a leader.

The writer of Proverbs sagely warns: "Pride goes before destruction, and a haughty spirit before stumbling" (Prov. 16:18). Likewise, Scripture reveals: "God is opposed to the proud, but gives grace to the humble" (James 4:6). Jesus cautioned: "Everyone who exalts himself will be humbled, but he who humbles himself will be exalted" (Luke 18:14 NIV). Proud people have God as their opponent. This reality ought to be enough to sober even the most vain leader.

Sexual Sin

If pride is the most insidious pitfall of leaders, sexual sin is the most notorious. The media have meticulously chronicled the spectacular downfalls of leaders who succumbed to sexual temptation. Sexual sin has the heinous power to destroy a career, a family, and a reputation, all in one blow. With such lethal consequences one would think that leaders would fastidiously avoid sexual temptations. Yet year after year, society recoils under the continuous barrage of public sexual scandals. This does not have to happen. Leaders can avoid this pitfall by proactively building safeguards into their lives.

Safeguard #1: Leaders Make Themselves Accountable

The time to buy the smoke alarm is when you build the house, not after the fire starts. The time to enlist friends as partners in accountability is not when sexual temptation is already a raging inferno but before the first spark. Time after time, disgraced leaders admit that, although they were surrounded by people, they had no close friends with whom they were transparent and who were in a position to hold them accountable. They rarely cite the lack of available people or the unwillingness of others to hold them accountable. Rather, they will say that once they began to stray into sin, they deliberately avoided those who could have helped. Prudent leaders are proactive; they enlist at least two people as accountability partners and give them the freedom to regularly question their moral purity.

Safeguard #2: Leaders Heed Their Own Counsel

Leaders should listen to their own counsel. There is probably not a fallen minister who did not previously warn his church members about the dangers of sexual immorality. Moral failure does not result from lack of information on the part of the fallen. Spiritual leaders know full well what sexual sin is as well as the consequences involved. In fact, most often they have counseled others who were caught in the web of adultery or other sexual transgressions, but leaders deceive themselves into believing their situation is different. They have usually witnessed firsthand the devastation of immorality, but their own sin blinds them to the reality that they, too, are on the road to self-destruction (Prov. 14:12). Spiritual leaders must understand that they are no more immune to moral failure than those they are leading. Therefore, as they share their wisdom with others, they should apply it to their own lives as well.

Safeguard #3: Leaders Consider the Consequences

Leaders carefully and regularly contemplate the consequences if they were to commit sexual sin. They guard themselves from the attitude that they are somehow exempt from the dangers that have derailed others. They reflect on the ugly reality of what their sin would do to their spouses, to their children, and to God's name. They think through the lengthy restoration process that would be necessary for them to regain the position they were in before they sinned, all the while recognizing that there really is no going back—while they might gain forgiveness, they would never be able to undo sin's painful aftermath. They remind themselves that one careless, selfish decision could cost them their job, their reputation, their friendships, their family, and it could severely damage their relationship with God. Astute leaders cultivate the habit of regularly pondering the devastating effects of sexual sin. Then, when they are tempted, they are armed with a vivid awareness of sexual sin's deadly consequences, and they will not be unwitting victims of sin's treachery (Prov. 7:24–27).

Safeguard #4: Leaders Develop Healthy Habits

Careful leaders can take practical steps to protect themselves from sexual temptation. When Billy Graham saw that several fellow evangelists were committing sexual sins, he did not simply resolve to be careful; he built specific safeguards into his life to help ensure that he and his team avoided temptation, or even the appearance of compromise. For example, he made a commitment that he would never meet with, travel with, or eat alone with a woman other than his wife. He also developed a team of friends to monitor whether he was keeping this standard. While some might consider this safeguard excessive, it kept him from scandal for over half a century of high-profile ministry.

Leaders who are married should enlist their spouses to help them develop habits that will protect them from sexual sin. Wise leaders take the concerns and warnings of their spouse seriously. Godly leaders cultivate their relationship with their spouse so they are less vulnerable to temptations that inevitably come. Many leaders who travel will set up pictures of their spouse and children in their hotel room as a reminder of the loved ones they have waiting for them at home. Astute leaders will also seek the aid of an administrative assistant to make sure they do not find themselves in compromising positions with people of the opposite sex. Leaders can make sure there are windows in their office doors to protect against even the hint of impropriety.

Safeguard #5: Leaders Pray and Ask Others to Pray for Them

No matter how many intentional safeguards a leader puts into place, sexual temptation can sometimes ambush the unsuspecting leader. The most practical step leaders can take is to pray that God will help them keep their lives above reproach. Leaders may be blindsided by unexpected events, but God never is. God, in his grace, will build a hedge of protection around leaders who earnestly desire moral purity. Leaders should also enlist the prayers of their spouses so they know that wherever they go and whatever they face, their spouse is interceding with God for them. Ultimately, leaders are not the victims of sexual sin. They do not "fall" into sin. Rather, they reap what they sow (Gal. 6:7). Temptations will come, and leaders who neglect their relationship with God and fail to build safeguards into their lives will inevitably yield to temptation. The tragedy of sexual sin is that it is just as avoidable as it is devastating. Wise leaders heed the counsel of Proverbs that says, "A sensible man considers his steps" (Prov. 14:15).

Leaders' Safeguards

- Leaders make themselves accountable.
- Leaders heed their own counsel.
- Leaders contemplate the consequences of their sin.
- Leaders develop healthy habits.
- Leaders pray and ask others to pray for them.

CYNICISM

Leadership is a people business, and people invariably let you down. Anyone who has led for very long has dealt with people who were dishonest, lazy, or incompetent. Leaders also inevitably face unfair criticism. Sometimes people even abuse them verbally. At some point, people will question leaders' motives and second-guess their decisions. People who lead will also undergo failure as a matter of course. Any one of these experiences has the potential to harden leaders' hearts and to make them cynical. Attitudes, unlike circumstances, are entirely within the control of leaders. Leaders who surrender their positive attitude have resigned themselves to be mediocre leaders at best.

If leaders always focus on their organization's problems and weaknesses, then the attention of their people will invariably be drawn there too. When people concentrate on the negative, they lose the zeal and optimism required to overcome difficult challenges. Negative leaders spawn negative organizations. Cynical leaders cultivate cynical followers. When leaders are constantly criticizing others, they are modeling a critical spirit for their people. When leaders have no faith in their people, they prevent them from reaching their potential. It is imperative that leaders not allow themselves to be consumed by a cynical spirit.

True leaders focus on that which is right and on what gives hope, not on what is wrong. Unfortunately, leaders who have been criticized in the past or who have failed in earlier attempts to lead can be skeptical about future success. After someone they trusted has lied to them, leaders can become cynical about the honesty of everyone around them. When one employee is lazy, cynical leaders can treat all their followers as if they were indolent. When a major project fails, cynical leaders can be wary of attempting anything else that involves risk. Older leaders seem particularly susceptible to cynicism. Their youthful enthusiasm has worn off, and what they consider "realism born of experience" may in essence be nothing more than a cynical attitude that has festered over time.

When leaders sense they are developing a cynical attitude, they must correct it immediately before it poisons their effectiveness and possibly their health. Without question, a critical spirit in spiritual leaders reveals that their hearts have shifted from God. Only a conscious decision to return to God will save the leader from becoming ineffective. A cynical spirit reflects a lack of belief in God and his ability to do what he says he will do. It is crucial that leaders guard their attitudes. Christian leaders have every reason in the world to be positive and optimistic for the future. They serve the King of kings.

GREED

Like many things, money and possessions can be either good or bad in a leader's life. A leadership position often brings greater material rewards. While a sizable income is not in itself wrong, the relentless pursuit of one is. The lure of material possessions has enticed many leaders to make foolish career decisions. The world's standard maintains that the more money people make, the more successful they are. As a result, some people will sacrifice almost anything in order to achieve material success. Lee Iacocca sums this sentiment up well:

"I've never had any qualms about getting a high salary. I'm not a big spender, but I appreciate the achievement a high salary represents. Why does a guy want to be president? Does he enjoy it? Maybe, but it can make him old and tired. So why does he work so hard? So he can say, 'Hey, I made it to the top. I accomplished something.'"[7] Sadly, Iacocca tells how his career struggle climbing the corporate ladders at Ford and Chrysler took its toll on his beloved, frail wife, Mary. Mary's first heart attack came immediately after Iacocca was fired at Ford in a corporate power struggle. Iacocca notes: "On each of these occasions when her health failed her, it was following a period of great stress at Ford or Chrysler."[8] Iacocca achieved mammoth success that was the envy of CEOs around the world, but at what price?

The hunger for wealth and possessions can destroy spiritual leaders. People valuing wealth above everything else will strive for jobs that pay more, regardless of whether these jobs cause great hardship to their families. Pastors can be lured to larger churches that pay higher salaries, even though their families had been content in their smaller church setting. As one person asked, "Why does God always seem to call ministers to churches that pay more money and never to churches that pay less?"

When leaders hunger for wealth, they can also be tempted to act unethically. To cite a notorious example, Jim Bakker had his conscience dulled by the giddy financial heights he reached with his PTL organization. Bakker grew up in poverty and hardship, and his success produced personal wealth he never dreamed he would enjoy. As his ministry thrived, he began to justify his increasingly lavish lifestyle, reasoning that he was the one who was largely responsible for PTL's success. He had worked hard and many peoples' lives were being changed for the good because of his efforts, so didn't he deserve the material prosperity he was enjoying? Yet as the expenses of his organization escalated, Bakker was forced to devise increasingly aggressive ways to raise funds in order to maintain his excessive tastes. In his all-consuming quest to raise more money, it was not difficult for him to cross ethical and even legal lines.

Many Christian leaders are resisting the temptation to automatically seek or accept positions simply because they offer a bigger paycheck. Christian leaders have learned that money is not the most important thing in life. Obeying God's will is. At times business leaders will turn down lucrative job transfers because they have become actively involved in ministry in their local church and they sense God wants them to stay where they are. Some pastors will resist overtures from larger urban churches because they know God has uniquely prepared them to pastor a rural congregation and their family is finding great joy in that lifestyle. Other leaders may decline jobs that require increased travel because they value time with their families. Wise leaders do not allow themselves to be enslaved to money but instead use their money to glorify God.

Alfred Sloan, the successful CEO of General Motors, made a fortune building his company and then spent the latter part of his life giving it away to worthy causes. Alfred Nobel, the inventor of dynamite, invested his fortune in the promotion of world peace and the advancement of science. Wise leaders know that the measure of their success is not the size of their bank account but the quality of their lives. Astute leaders invest their lives in things that bring the most lasting and gratifying rewards.

MENTAL LAZINESS

Today's problems are not generally solved through brute strength but through creative, inspired thinking. Problem solving is an essential function of leadership, so leaders cannot afford to become intellectually stagnant. Good leaders never stop learning. They seek the company of wise people. They read books and articles that stretch their thinking. They read the biographies of great leaders and thinkers. They don't simply read the popular, predigested books that flood the market. They find authors who challenge their presuppositions and who bring fresh insights to their field. Ask true leaders what they have read lately, and they will readily cite something they are currently studying. Spiritual leaders regularly test what they read against the eternal wisdom found in Scripture.

Spiritual leaders also allow the Holy Spirit to guide their thinking so that it is based on God's timeless truths rather than on society's latest fad.

Great leaders are always learning how to become better leaders. John Kotter observes: "Just as we don't realize the difference between a bank account earning seven percent versus four percent, we regularly underestimate the effects of learning differentials."[9]

A commitment to learn and to change produces a growing level of leadership competence. It is no longer enough to acquire an education in order to *get* a job. Additional learning is mandatory to *keep* a job. Earning a Ph.D. simply introduces someone to all they don't know. The reason some longtime employees are forced out of work has nothing to do with age. It has to do with a reluctance to learn. Methods that worked a decade ago may be ineffective today. Leaders who aren't continually growing will eventually find themselves with skills that are obsolete. Depree claims leaders respond to change by learning something.[10]

Leaders are not only readers; they are thinkers. True leaders take time to process the events around them. When a meeting goes poorly, they don't simply race off to their next meeting; rather, they take time to evaluate why the meeting was unproductive, and they consider ways to do things differently the next time. When leaders have personnel who are struggling, they do not simply fire them or grow increasingly frustrated with them. Good leaders take time to ponder what is causing their employees to struggle. Are they the right people for the job? Have they been properly trained and equipped? Have they been kept informed? Are there factors beyond the employee's control? Leaders don't jump to conclusions. They process the facts and seek to determine the truth of their situation. Spiritual leaders spend purposeful time with God, allowing him to guide their minds to the truth regarding the condition of their organization. When mature leaders receive praise or criticism, they do not accept or reject it out of hand; they contemplate what has been said so they can continue to mature as leaders. Difficult circumstances can sometimes catch leaders by surprise, but once an adverse event has occurred, leaders seek to master the situation by careful, God-inspired reflection.

One way Jesus helped his disciples grow as leaders was by teaching them how to make sense of their circumstances. In Luke's Gospel, the twelve disciples are depicted as being unable to process the events that were unfolding around them. Luke indicates that Jesus gave them authority to cast out demons and to heal diseases (Luke 9:1). The disciples experienced and witnessed incredible miracles as a result of God's power. When they returned to Jesus they excitedly reported their success, but they soon proved they did not grasp the significance of what had happened. Shortly afterward, when faced with a multitude of hungry people, they surveyed the situation and instructed Jesus to "send the crowd away" because they could not possibly feed such a large crowd (Luke 9:12 NIV). If the disciples had contemplated the power they had seen demonstrated by Jesus thus far, they would have understood that feeding a multitude would not be difficult for Jesus. Jesus miraculously fed the multitude, but the disciples did not process that event either. Thus, they would be disoriented to God the next time an opportunity came to trust him. Mark 6:45 indicates that immediately after Jesus fed the five thousand, he sent his disciples in a boat across the Sea of Galilee to Bethsaida. When the disciples encountered a storm, they were terrified. They had been given authority to cast out demons; they had recently cast out demons from other people; they had just witnessed the power of God demonstrated in feeding five thousand men and their families, yet they were afraid in the midst of a storm. Why? They had not processed the events of the past, so they were unprepared for the challenges of the present. Scripture indicates that "they had not gained any insight from the incident of the loaves, but their heart was hardened" (Mark 6:52). Because the disciples did not take time to process and learn from their earlier failures, they continued to fail when they met new challenges. Jesus rebuked them for being slow to understand the events and the teachings they were encountering (Luke 9:41).

How was it possible that the disciples could witness incredible miracles and hear profound teaching and then be unable to build on those experiences? Were they dull-witted? Of course not. Their problem was that they rushed from activity to activity without evaluating each event for truths they could incorporate into their lives. Because they were not learning from their experiences and therefore not growing in their faith, they were ineffective. Later, after Jesus had ascended to heaven, the disciples learned to process their experiences. The Book of Acts reveals that Peter and the disciples even grew to understand the shocking reality that Judas could betray their Lord (Acts 1:15–17). Once the disciples learned to process their experiences, not even the fiercest persecution could discourage them from accomplishing God's will.

At the height of D. L. Moody's success, he realized he had grown stale. He was leading enormously successful evangelistic campaigns in Great Britain and the United States, and he had become one of the most famous religious leaders of his day, but he had grown spiritually and intellectually malnourished. He had been continually preaching, but he had not been learning. Moody's biographer, John Pollock, notes, "At the moment of reaching a height of influence in the United States he stood in danger of spiritual insolvency."[11] Moody realized he had told people everything he knew and that he had nothing new to say. Moody confessed: "My lack of education has always been a great disadvantage to me. I shall suffer from it as long as I live."[12] Moody moved to Northfield and refused to accept major speaking engagements until he felt he had studied enough to have fresh, new insights from God's Word to share with people. He set a rigid schedule that included six hours of study every morning. Even after he began traveling once again, Moody carried a small library with him. He was determined that despite the press of people and responsibilities upon his time, he could not afford to stop learning and still be effective as a spiritual leader.

Wise leaders continually learn from the events of their lives as well as from their studies. They take time after major events to process what happened and to learn from the experiences. Great leaders are thinkers. They are, to paraphrase Paul's words, transformed by the renewing of their minds (Rom. 12:2). They never stop learning or evaluating, so they never stop growing.

OVERSENSITIVITY

People who cannot handle criticism need not apply for leadership positions. Being criticized, second-guessed, and having one's motives questioned are unpleasant but inevitable aspects of leadership. Great leaders are not immune to criticism; in fact, the criticism they receive is sometimes the most venomous. It is impossible for leaders to avoid being censured. If leaders take decisive action, they are open to critique for being too reactionary. If they cautiously refrain from taking action, they are chastised for their indecisiveness. Faced with the inevitability of criticism regardless of what they do, leaders must make a choice. Either they stop leading, or they do what they know is right and trust that God will vindicate them.

Jonathan Edwards was one of the most brilliant thinkers of eighteenth-century America. As pastor of the prestigious Congregational church in Northampton, he was a leading figure during the First Great Awakening. Edwards's prolific writings were studied all over the Western world. Religious leaders such as George Whitefield, the most famous preacher of that era, traveled great distances to meet with Edwards and to discuss theological matters. Yet even a man of Edwards's impressive credentials was not exempt from criticism. When Edwards sought assurance that those in his congregation had experienced genuine conversion, a group of discontented church members took exception. They initiated a slanderous campaign against him that ultimately led to his dismissal from the church he had made famous. Edwards assumed a modest pastorate in the small frontier town of Stockbridge.[13] One of the greatest theological minds and devout pastors in American history was forced out of his church by the vehement criticism of malicious detractors.

If a leader receives ten words of support for every one word of criticism, which voice will ring loudest? The critic's voice, of course. Criticism generally carries more weight with people than praise. Many leaders have actually resigned their positions despite widespread popularity because they grew weary of a handful of unrelenting critics. Sadly, leaders can let the negativity of a few abrogate the enthusiastic support of the majority.

Constructive criticism is good for leaders. They should not only receive such input graciously; they should invite those around them to give it. But backbiting and slander can quench the spirit of even the most stouthearted leader. Most leaders have a genuine desire to do the right thing. Most people also want to be liked and appreciated by their followers. When their motives are routinely questioned, or when their actions are misjudged, the joy drains out of their leadership position, and they are left questioning whether their calling is worth the pain. Whereas even the most loyal friends can be sporadic in their affirmation, opponents can be like a dripping faucet, relentlessly communicating their displeasure.

How should leaders respond to unfounded rancor from hostile critics? First, they should honestly examine their hearts to be sure the criticism is without merit. This can hurt, but attentive leaders can usually learn something, even when they are unfairly maligned. Leaders must face criticism with integrity before God and before people. True spiritual leaders know it is ultimately God's approval and not people's that matters most. When leaders know they have obeyed God, they set aside the desire to defend themselves. They find their security in God's affirmation. God promises: "'No weapon that is formed against you will prosper; and every tongue that accuses you in judgment you will condemn. This is the heritage of the servants of the Lord, and their vindication is from me,' declares the LORD" (Isa. 54:17 NIV). The wisdom of a right decision will prove itself over time. Wise leaders let God prove the purity of their motives and the wisdom of their actions.

Eventually Jonathan Edwards was vindicated before his critics. Some of his most vocal opponents publicly confessed their sinfulness in attacking their godly minister. Ultimately, Princeton University hired Edwards as its president. Historians have concluded that Edwards was one of the most influential Americans in the eighteenth century. History has nothing noteworthy to record about his former critics except their treachery. Oswald Sanders concluded: "Often the crowd does not recognize a leader until he has gone, and then they build a monument for him with the stones they threw at him in life."[14]

True leaders are more interested in doing the right thing than they are in their popularity. Sometimes, the right thing to do is not the most popular, but spiritual statesmen do not allow detractors to deter them from God's will. Criticism has its most devastating effect upon the immature and the unsure. Leaders who clearly understand God's will do not waver when misguided or virulent opponents attempt to discourage them. Politicians may do what appeals to the majority, regardless of their private convictions. Statesmen will take a stand for what is right, though it costs them friends, supporters, and possibly their jobs. While leaders are always attempting to build consensus among followers, true spiritual leaders do not ultimately lead by consensus. A leader's decisions are not always based on a majority vote. Spiritual statesmen are not driven by what people think but by what they know God has said. True spiritual leaders fear God far more than they fear people. If people are motivated by a desire to avoid criticism, they are unfit for leadership. True spiritual leaders seek God's will, and then they follow it without wavering.

While we were attending a large convention several years ago, a distinguished-looking middle-aged man approached us and told us his story: He had once been a pastor, but some people had taken exception to his leadership and had doggedly attacked his character, his family, and his ethics. So devastated was this man by their behavior that he resigned his pastorate and vowed he would never work another day in Christian ministry. Shortly thereafter, a friend invited him to join a newly formed company as vice president, and the man accepted. The company grew and enjoyed enormous success. The former pastor became a wealthy and respected administrative vice president. Then the church he was attending began a study of the discipleship course *Experiencing God.* As the man recounted this event, he was suddenly overcome with emotion. With his voice breaking, he recalled, "God got a hold of me!" As he turned to go, he smiled and through his tears he said, "I'm a pastor again!"

Spiritual leaders must keep criticism in perspective. Criticism will come, and it will hurt, but it must not be allowed to derail leaders from God's call upon their lives. Before giving in to the temptation to quit, leaders should revisit what they know God asked them to do. No amount of opposition or hardship or sacrifice is sufficient to cancel

God's call on a person's life. We have heard many pastors say, "I just can't allow my family to continue to suffer from this criticism any longer!" It is true; leaders must diligently protect their families. But leaders and their families must realize that receiving criticism does not mean they are out of God's will. It may mean just the opposite! Jesus said, "Remember the word that I said to you, 'A slave is not greater than his master.' If they persecuted Me, they will also persecute you" (John 15:20). Leaders, and those they love, are much safer being criticized for remaining in God's will than when they are being praised while living outside of it. Leaders would do well to help their families learn how to deal with criticism. Leaders who readily forfeit their calling in response to opposition do not clearly know God's will for their lives. When leaders know they are doing exactly what God is asking, no amount of animosity will move them to do anything else.

SPIRITUAL LETHARGY

For the most part, leaders are driven people. Their role is to see that things get done. Their enthusiasm to make things happen will tempt them to forgo the "passive" pursuit of spending time with God. Most spiritual leaders would list their relationship with God as number one on their priority list. At least that is where they know it should be. Yet with so many jobs to coordinate and so many people to motivate, they inadvertently relegate their spiritual life to a place of unimportance in their schedule. If leaders have an important meeting, it may seem more expedient to get their presentation in order than to make sure their hearts are right before God. Lengthy reports that require extensive reading may compel leaders to forgo reading the Bible "just this once" in the interests of good time management. Leaders in full-time Christian ministry are no less susceptible to this mind-set. They are busy people, too. The danger for them to neglect their time with God is more subtle, because their Bibles are open so often for sermon preparation, counseling, and other religious work. If they aren't careful, they'll view their Bibles as a textbook rather than as the living Word of God. They'll begin substituting their public prayer life for their personal conversations with God.

When leaders allow their daily commitments to crowd out their time with Christ, they are slowly cutting themselves off from their lifeline. No matter how much they accomplish, their lives will suffer. Their relationships will be damaged. They will cease to be the husband/wife/parent/son/daughter/friend God wants them to be. They may have an extra hour or two in their day, but their priorities will be out of line, so whatever they accomplish will be, as the writer of Ecclesiastes says, "striving after wind" (Eccles. 1:14). Life, apart from Christ, is meaningless. Wise leaders never forget that (Matt. 6:33).

Spiritual leaders are not haphazard people. They are intentional. Just as they plan thoroughly for important meetings in their work, they also plan carefully to allow substantial time for listening to their Creator. There are a few practical steps leaders can take if they find they have fallen into a rut in their devotional life. First, they should evaluate the time they set aside to spend with God. Is it enough? Is it too rushed? Does that time face too many intrusions? Would a different time or setting be more conducive to quiet Bible study, reflection, and prayer? Would a varied approach to studying God's Word be beneficial? Perhaps a different Bible translation would give familiar verses a fresh sound and an added perspective. Perhaps the leader needs to use a devotional tool that will open up the Scriptures in new and profound ways. Oswald Chambers's *My Utmost for His Highest* has been a favorite among spiritual leaders for many years. We have written a daily devotional, *Experiencing God Day-by-Day*, which many have found challenging.[15] If they do not already do so, leaders should begin using a journal to record their daily spiritual pilgrimage. An unhurried time with God is invaluable. There is no substitute for it. It is well worth the effort involved in maintaining and protecting it as first priority.

Besides the intrinsic and immeasurable value of knowing God personally, a strong relationship with God holds numerous advantages for leaders. They clearly know when God is speaking to them. When they begin to develop unhealthy habits, God speaks forcefully to them and protects them from harm. When they are making important decisions, God guides them in the best direction. When leaders are criticized and pressured to conform to worldly standards, God gives inner strength and resolve that enables them to stand firm in their convictions.

Nurturing a strong relationship with almighty God allows leaders the freedom to follow their God-given convictions and to bring glory to God through their efforts.

DOMESTIC NEGLECT

Theodore Roosevelt was once asked by a friend why he did not take a more active role in supervising his free-spirited daughter, Alice. Roosevelt purportedly replied: "I can be president of the United States, or I can attend to Alice. I can't do both."[16] Such is the quandary of many leaders.

When holding positions of influence and responsibility, they often struggle to balance their role as a leader at work and as a leader at home. Billy Graham candidly relates a troubling event. He was entering the eighth week of his 1949 evangelistic campaign in Los Angeles. When Ruth Graham's sister and brother-in-law arrived for the final week of the crusade, they had a baby with them. Graham asked them whose baby it was. It was his daughter Anne. Graham had been away from home so long he did not recognize his own daughter. That night little Anne went to sleep crying not for her father or even her mother, but for the aunt who had been giving her primary care.[17] In concluding his autobiography, Graham confessed that if he had to live his life over again he would travel less. Graham conceded that not every trip he had taken had been necessary.[18] No one could fault Graham for his work ethic or his godliness, but every leader could learn from his dispiriting experience.

Nelson Mandela sacrificed everything he had to liberate his people from subjugation. Mandela eventually achieved his goal, won the Nobel Peace Prize, and was elected president of South Africa in the first election in which black voters were allowed to participate. Yet Mandela also suffered two divorces and spent many years in prison unable to have contact with his children. Mandela confessed that although he loved his wives, his work always came first and his marriages suffered as a result.

Ronald Reagan mediated several international conflicts and made great strides in developing closer relations between the United States and the Soviet Union. Yet even his best diplomatic skills did not gain appeasement with his daughter, Patti, during his presidency. Graham,

Mandela, and Reagan all faced the enormous challenge of investing their lives in causes that were larger than they were and yet still fulfilling their responsibilities as husbands and fathers. Theirs were roles of national and international importance, yet they agonized over the same fundamental struggle every leader faces. Every leader must balance the responsibilities of their leadership role with their commitment to their families. Those who wholly sacrifice their families may achieve great success in the public eye but privately suffer tremendous personal turmoil.

Wise leaders strive to preserve their families in the midst of the pressures on their professional lives. Most leaders love their families, but many fail to apply the same prioritizing skills they use at work when relating to the most important people in their lives. Conscientious leaders take their God-given responsibilities for their families seriously. They do this because they love God; they do it because they love their families. They also recognize the crucial nature of leaders' families (Deut. 6:4–9). Leaders' children can represent the future generation of leaders. Emerging leaders at home have the potential to impact the world even more than their parents did. Wise leaders see the importance of helping their children develop as Christians and as the next generation of leaders.

As we mentioned earlier, leaders should get in the habit of marking significant events such as birthdays, anniversaries, graduations, and special events on their calendars so they do not inadvertently schedule unnecessary outside commitments on those dates. When leaders travel, they should look for ways to bring family members with them. As much as possible, leaders who value their families seek creative ways to make their jobs a blessing to their families instead of a rival for their attention. God is the family's greatest advocate—leaders who seek God's help will readily receive it.

ADMINISTRATIVE CARELESSNESS

Leaders are, by nature, visionaries. They may focus so much attention on the vision of where their organization is going that they neglect to build the kind of organization that can actually arrive at the destination. They can be like a cross-country traveler who faithfully pores over the road map and knows exactly where he is going but doesn't bother to monitor and maintain the fuel and oil levels of his vehicle. Even when warning lights flicker on the control panel and strange noises emanate from under the hood, the traveler is absorbed in thoughts of what he will do once he arrives at his destination. Leaders can end up just like this careless traveler, stranded miles away from where they want to be. Such leaders become so preoccupied by the big picture that they neglect the details, any number of which can derail their plans for the future.

Ultimately it is the leader's task to ensure that the organization is healthy. Wise leaders understand that organizations are ultimately made up, not of vision statements, or constitutions, or long-range plans, or core values—but of people. People are the driving force behind organizations. Therefore, while leaders are constantly delegating tasks to their people, they are also regularly monitoring the attitudes, effectiveness, and concerns of their people to ensure that the organization is functioning at its optimum potential.

While the CEO of a large company will not personally hire or train every employee, he is ultimately responsible for keeping the organization adequately staffed and for ensuring proper training and resources are available. The leader is responsible for regularly communicating the direction the organization is going and its progress. It falls on the leader to clearly delineate the values of the organization and to identify behaviors that are consistent with those beliefs. If leaders fail in this regard, the people who work with them cannot be faulted for inadvertently diverting the organization from its purpose.

Leaders must become adept in two areas, or their organizations will collapse from within: conflict resolution and communication.

One way to determine the health of an organization is to measure how long it takes the top leader to become aware of a problem in the ranks. If problems are allowed to metastasize for weeks or months while the leader blithely concentrates on larger issues, the leader will eventually be forced to reckon with an organizational crisis that should never have become more than an administrative glitch. Effective leaders are known for their aggressive problem solving. Leadership positions are not for those who seek to avoid conflict at all costs. Insipid leaders will avoid people they know are unhappy or upset. Effective leaders will face problems head on. Few people actually enjoy addressing conflict, but experienced leaders know that a single problem neglected today can multiply into a cluster of problems tomorrow. It is always better to deal with problems immediately and to resolve issues quickly within the organization. Spiritual leaders do not practice "conflict management." True spiritual leaders seek *conflict resolution*. While healthy organizations encourage a diversity of personalities and ideas, organizational vitality will wane in an atmosphere of constant discord. Alert leaders are quick to facilitate conflict resolution between personnel so valuable energy and time are not squandered on superfluous and distracting issues.

Clear, timely *communication* is absolutely essential to a successful organization. Leaders who are out of touch with their people will one day be flabbergasted to discover they do not really know the organization they are leading. The loyalty they took for granted will be nonexistent. The corporate values they assumed were jointly shared by followers will be summarily rejected. Their attempts to move the organization in a particular direction will be flatly resisted. The tragedy is that this doesn't have to happen. With careful attention to the vital signs of the organization, leaders can promptly address minor conflicts and prevent issues from escalating into large-scale problems. Jesus dealt with his disciples immediately and decisively whenever they needed correction. When they misunderstood their mission, when they had doubts or fears, or when they had misplaced values, Jesus always addressed the problem swiftly and directly and helped them refocus on their mission.

One of the greatest hindrances to efficient communication in an organization can be the leader's desk. Effective leaders do not allow important tasks to pile up on their desks. Large organizations have virtually ground to a halt while an important decision or piece of paperwork sat on a disorganized leader's desk. A stack of routine memos and paraphernalia can bury crucial information and needlessly delay weighty decisions. When important tasks are left unattended, this is a sure sign that the leader is ignoring the machinery of the organization. Leaders need to develop the reputation for dealing with important issues promptly and thoroughly. When leaders are slow with their responses, the entire organization can be delayed as people wait on their leader. Effective leaders also enlist key associates to oversee daily operations so that the organization does not grind to a halt every time the leader is out of town or on vacation. Organizations led by lone rangers will slow down or stop every time the leader is out of the office, but a well-managed organization will run smoothly even when the leader is absent. A wise leader will invest in developing and equipping associates. Effective leaders carefully monitor and maintain organizational machinery, and they ensure that the machinery can run smoothly in their absence. The benefit of maintaining a healthy organization is that leaders can conduct their business without constantly having a phone attached to their ear and they can enjoy time at home or on vacation without always worrying about work.

PROLONGED POSITION HOLDING

"It is better to leave them longing than loathing." Good speakers know and follow this maxim. Skilled preachers recognize that if they haven't made their point after thirty minutes, they might as well send their parishioners home to their roast beef. Popular public speakers never abuse the privilege of a captive audience. On a much larger scale, wise leaders also know when the time has come to exit graciously and allow a new leader to step in. Some leaders have greatly depreciated their effectiveness and diminished their contribution to their organizations by staying in their positions long after their effectiveness was past.

Harry Truman observed that the prominent place people held in history had a lot to do with the timing of their death. Men such as John F. Kennedy and Martin Luther King Jr. were immortalized as much, perhaps, by their dramatic, untimely deaths as by their significant contributions to society.

In his study of leaders, Howard Gardner observed: "Sooner or later, nearly all leaders outreach themselves and end up undermining their causes."[19] Gardner concluded: "Indeed, the greater the accomplishment of the leader; the greater the strain on the milieu, strong accomplishments breed strong reactions, and by and large, only those effective leaders who die at a young age are spared the disheartening sight of their accomplishments being severely challenged, if not wholly undone."[20]

The problem for some leaders is that they gradually come to see their identity as intrinsically linked to their position. They enjoy the respect and influence that comes with their position as head of the organization. As a result, they may hesitate to yield their office to younger leaders even when it becomes apparent to everyone else that a change in the organization is needed. Such leaders can become blinded to the reality that they are no longer as effective in their role as they once were. Because they were once successful, they assume they are still the one best suited for their job. Sadly, these leaders often negate much of the positive contribution they made to their organization in their early years because they refuse to make room for the next generation of leaders. Instead they hold their organization back by their reluctance to step aside. It is pathetic to watch aging leaders who heroically led their organization to triumph in years past but who have long since become ineffective and yet stubbornly refuse to vacate their leadership positions.

Ineffective leaders who refuse to retire from their positions may put forth grandiose statements about loyalty, but they are revealing a selfish side to their character. They would adamantly argue that they only want what is best for their organization, and perhaps they do. Yet they are also reluctant to give up the prestige, power, and financial benefits that their positions provide. Leaders with integrity recognize when they have made their most worthwhile contributions. Then they graciously hand over the reigns of leadership to the next generation. How does a leader know when the time has come for a changing of the guard? God will guide leaders who seek his wisdom regarding when it is time for them to leave. Sometimes the performance of the organization gives a clear message. When an organization continually struggles, when it regularly loses to the competition, when no new ideas are being generated, when key personnel are leaving, when morale is chronically low, when there is no exciting anticipation for the future—these are all indications that something needs to change. Either the leader needs a dramatic turnaround, or the time has come for a new leader with different skills to take charge.

Oswald Sanders observes: "Advance is held up for years by well-meaning but aging men who refuse to vacate office and insist on holding the reins in their failing hands."[21]

Perhaps the classic biblical example of a leader who overstayed his mandate was King Hezekiah. Hezekiah had been a good and righteous ruler of the nation of Judah. The Bible concludes of his reign, "He trusted in the Lord, the God of Israel; so that after him there were none like him among the kings of Judah, nor among those who were before him" (2 Kings 18:5). After ruling for fourteen years, Hezekiah contracted a terminal illness and the prophet Isaiah told the king to get his house in order for it was God's will that he should soon die. King Hezekiah wept bitterly and prayed for his life to be spared. God granted his request and promised him fifteen additional years of life.

Had Hezekiah accepted God's will in the first place, his period of leadership would have been unblemished. But during his extended rule, he made two major blunders. When envoys visited him from Babylon, Hezekiah vainly showed them all of his kingdom's treasures. Such foolish indiscretion would come back to haunt his successors when the Babylonian armies came to forcibly relieve Judah of those same treasures. During the additional years God granted him, Hezekiah also had a son, Manasseh, but he failed to raise Manasseh to fear God. Upon Hezekiah's death, Manasseh became king and commenced the longest, most wicked reign in Judah's history. By the time Manasseh's reign ended, Judah's immorality and idolatry were so perverse and had reached such intolerable levels that God's judgment on the nation was irrevocable. By prolonging his leadership beyond what God had planned for him, Hezekiah planted the seeds for his nation's certain demise.

Theodore Roosevelt was an enigma to many Americans. Having been elected by one of the highest popular votes in American history, he believed he carried a strong mandate to lead his nation. However, he had promised not to hold office for more than two terms, so the popular president declined to run for office a third time. Instead, he strongly endorsed his associate and friend, Howard Taft, as the Republican candidate. It did not take long for Roosevelt to become disenchanted with his successor. Taft did not govern as Roosevelt would have, and Roosevelt found it increasingly difficult to deflect the attention he received from those who wanted him to seek office again. In the 1912 presidential election, Roosevelt ran as an Independent against both the

Democratic candidate and his former friend, Howard Taft. By running against his old party, Roosevelt divided the Republican vote. Despite the fact, Roosevelt garnered more votes than Taft, he and Taft both lost to the Democratic candidate, Woodrow Wilson. The combined votes for Taft and Roosevelt would have beaten the Democratic ticket but, divided, they lost their hold on the presidency. Roosevelt's major accomplishments in running were to hurt his good friend, to divide his party, and to bring his Republican party down to defeat for the first time in sixteen years. His refusal to stay out of office and to support the next generation of leaders brought disastrous results.

Older leaders tend to have difficulty giving their blessing to the emerging generation of leaders. Senior leaders often disparage younger leaders as naïve or radical or too inexperienced to conduct the important affairs of executive office. Veteran leaders see new and different techniques and misinterpret these as new and different values. In fact, while biblical principles and values never change, methods that were appropriate in one generation may be obsolete, even counterproductive, in the next. For example, through technology, the amount of time an organization needs to spend in meetings can be reduced without forfeiting clear and timely communication. Older leaders who were accustomed to meeting every week may fear the new leadership devalues communication because they prefer monthly meetings. In reality, the younger leaders may value communication as much as their predecessors but are simply communicating through the use of new and efficient technological tools. Older leaders understand that the next generation of leaders will have to develop its own leadership style. New leaders must seek God's direction for the organization just as the generation of leaders before them did. Senior leaders should become the greatest supporters of the next generation. They could become a valuable source of wisdom and experience, if they fastidiously avoid meddling or criticizing their successors. Many aging leaders have lost the opportunity to advise the next generation because their criticism alienated those who took their place. This is a colossal waste and a sad way to end a productive career. Wise leaders, on the other hand, refrain from imposing their own prejudices on their successors. Rather, they generously express

---

The Ten Pitfalls of Leadership

1. Pride
2. Sexual sin
3. Cynicism
4. Greed
5. Mental laziness
6. Oversensitivity
7. Spiritual lethargy
8. Domestic neglect
9. Administrative carelessness
10. Prolonged position holding

---

their affirmation and their encouragement for the accomplishments of their younger colleagues.

Leaders with integrity genuinely place the well-being of the organization before their own prestige. Spiritual leaders take time to stand before God and ask whether their continued leadership in the organization is helpful or harmful. Leaders who truly care about their organization and its people may find it painful to acknowledge that the most helpful thing they can do for it is to resign, but integrity insists that leaders no longer continue collecting a paycheck when they cannot effectively lead their organization any farther. Astute leaders read the organizational signs and know when it is time to leave. They look to God as the source of their contentment in life. They also realize that although they can retire from their career, they can never retire from their calling. Those leaders who have made a commitment to continually grow and learn have no need to cling tenaciously to their position because they know God has new challenges for them and they are ready to embrace his next assignment.

CONCLUSION

Developing a healthy awareness of the pitfalls that can bring failure and disgrace to leaders is the first step to avoiding them. The second step is putting safeguards in place that will provide protection in times of temptation or indecision. Third, leaders should have before them the continual reminder that (a) their organization is more about people than it is about productivity; that (b) they are not indispensable; and that (c) the most effective, efficient thing they can do for their organization is to maintain a close, vibrant relationship with God.

Combining business effectiveness and personal faith in Jesus Christ is not only possible; it's essential. Successful Christian business leaders all over North America are meeting to encourage one another to do what is right in the business world. They pray for each other. They counsel one another about pivotal decisions. There is a growing movement for leaders to form small groups for the purposes of mutual encouragement and accountability. We are both involved in such groups. Henry leads a Bible study for business, legal, and medical leaders at 6:30 A.M. once a month to discuss relevant issues for professionals in the workplace. These studies are taped and sent out all over the world. This type of Bible study is occurring in cities across North America, providing practical, biblical help to spiritual leaders in every walk of life. Pastors are forming groups that meet regularly to challenge one another to continue growing in their relationship with God and with their families. Richard is part of a group that includes two pastors and a denominational leader. These four busy men meet every month to pray, to encourage each other, and to share with one another their progress in becoming the leaders God wants them to be. Executives meet over breakfast or lunch in order to help one another follow God's will. Through e-mail and various technologies, business leaders can stay in contact even when they are traveling around the world on assignments.

More and more leaders are recognizing that, with deliberate effort, good planning, and much prayer, they need not succumb to the pitfalls that could impair their leadership and jeopardize their personal lives. If you have not already become part of a small group, we encourage you to form one. This group should consist of three to five godly people whom you respect and with whom you will feel free to be completely honest. Group members should be of the same gender. For obvious reasons this will exclude your spouse. Here are some questions to consider both individually and as a part of your small-group discussion.

1. Do I pray regularly with at least one other leader?
2. Are there other leaders with whom I am free to be candid about my personal struggles?
3. Who holds me accountable to follow through on what I know to be God's will?
4. What safeguards have I built around my relationship with my spouse? Are they adequate to protect me from temptation?
5. How am I presently studying and applying God's Word to my life?
6. Have I built safeguards around my time with God?
7. When was the last time I clearly heard God speaking to me? How did I respond to what he said?
8. Do I have people who are willing to challenge my actions when they think they are harmful?
9. Are the fruits of the Spirit growing in me? (Gal. 5:22–23). Am I becoming more and more like Christ?

CONCEPTS AND SCRIPTURES TO CONSIDER

- Pride is dangerous to unwary leaders because it can be subversive in the way it creeps into their lives.
- Whereas authentic leaders shoulder the responsibility for the poor performance of their organizations, wise leaders rightfully acknowledge the efforts of their followers as critical to their organization's success.
- Pride drives leaders to seek the limelight.
- Spiritual leaders are God's servants, but pride can cause them to act as if God were their servant, obligated to answer their selfish prayers and to bless their grandiose schemes.
- Pride is a sin that festers in people, making them unreceptive to God's guidance and the wise counsel and support of other people.
- Leaders are most vulnerable in the area of their greatest strength.
- Sexual sin has the heinous power to destroy a career, a family, and a reputation, all in one blow.
- Leaders should listen to their own counsel.

- Leadership is a people business, and people invariably let you down.
- True leaders focus on that which is right and on what gives hope, not on what is wrong.
- Many Christian leaders are resisting the temptation to automatically seek or accept positions simply because they offer a bigger paycheck.
- Leaders don't jump to conclusions. They process the facts and seek to determine the truth of their situation.
- Leaders, and those they love, are much safer being criticized for remaining in God's will than when they are being praised while living outside of it.
- Spiritual leaders are not haphazard people. They are intentional.
- Older leaders tend to have difficulty giving their blessing to the emerging generation of leaders.

Proverbs 27:2
Daniel 4:29–31
Proverbs 6:16–17
Proverbs 1:7; 2:10–11
Judges 16:15–21
John 15:5
2 Corinthians 11:28–29
Proverbs 16:18; James 4:6; Luke 18:14
Proverbs 14:12
Proverbs 7:24–26
Galatians 6:7
Proverbs 14:15
Isaiah 54:17
John 15:20
Deuteronomy 6:4–9
Ezekiel 34:1–10

CHAPTER ELEVEN

The Leader's Rewards

MUCH HAS BEEN WRITTEN ABOUT THE skills required and the responsibilities of leadership, but little has been written about the rewards of being a leader. For leaders currently embroiled in the toil and stress of facing a major challenge, reviewing the leadership rewards can be encouraging. For leaders who feel unappreciated or taken for granted, a consideration of their rewards can bring them renewed resolve. While leaders ought to fulfill their leadership responsibilities with noble intentions and not for their personal benefit, they should be cognizant of the fact that with their responsibility also comes the opportunity to obtain unique rewards.

To even the casual observer, the immediate rewards of leadership are self-evident. The most tangible and obvious reward is monetary. Those who hold leadership positions usually garner higher pay than their subordinates. This singular factor motivates some people to seek the highest office possible, but many leaders have discovered that if the only compelling force behind their leadership aspirations is financial, the negatives of leadership often outweigh the positives. A stout bank balance does not always compensate for the increased pressure and criticism leaders shoulder.

Money isn't the only thing that drives people to become leaders. Leadership brings a second, less measurable but equally enticing reward, and that is power. Leaders in an organization have greater freedom to control and change their environment. People pay closer attention to leaders' opinions; people seek leaders' involvement in activities and their endorsement for projects; people may also seek to curry leaders' favor by showering them with praise and privileges. For some, this aspect of leadership is intoxicating. They are exhilarated when their opinions carry weight with people, and they welcome the opportunity to express their views to a wide audience. They enjoy the authority their position affords them. Nevertheless, such influence comes with a price. Influence comes with accountability. Authority includes liability. For this reason, many find that attaining a position of influence is relatively easy compared to the much harder task of maintaining it. The cost of influence, including peoples' high expectations and increased responsibilities, is simply a higher price than some are willing to pay. If having influence were easy, more people would have it! Positional influence, unlike character influence, is transitory, because when the position ends, so does the influence.

A third conspicuous reward for leadership is prestige. Leaders are usually treated with respect. The world places a premium on status, but true leaders recognize its actual value. Prestige appeals to people's egos; it can bring out the worst in people, and it is as fleeting as the morning mist. People who seek leadership positions in order to achieve status have disqualified themselves from holding such positions. They will discover, to their dismay, that prestige can be an albatross more than a reward. For, along with prestige comes close scrutiny. Celebrities know only too well that, in exchange for the public's adulation, they often forfeit their personal privacy. Over and over public personalities will, in the same interview, relate how they pursued fame, and then they will chastise the adoring public for intruding into their privacy! It can be unnerving, even to the most upright person, to have every move watched and evaluated. Prestige is therefore a third bittersweet reward for leadership.

The previous three ephemeral rewards: wealth, power, and fame are usually the goals of one-dimensional cartoon villains. There are, however, more noble rewards that make the efforts of leadership worthwhile. These rewards allow virtuous leaders to enjoy the fruit of their labors and to experience a deep sense of fulfillment. The following are the meaningful rewards leaders can anticipate when they lead their people according to God's standards.

SPIRITUAL REWARDS

At the end of his life, the apostle Paul said, "I have fought the good fight, I have finished the course, I have kept the faith; in the future there is laid up for me the crown of righteousness, which the Lord, the righteous Judge, will award to me on that day; and not only to me, but also to all who have loved His appearing" (2 Tim. 4:7–8). Paul's words epitomize the true reward for a spiritual leader who has led well. Such a leader can expect the reward of God's affirmation and the satisfaction of a calling fulfilled.

God's Affirmation

No other reward could possibly equal the joy that comes from knowing almighty God is pleased with you and what you have done with your life. To sense God's affirmation and pleasure in the present life and to know that he has eternal rewards waiting in the next life is to experience a prize of immeasurable value. No earthly treasure can compare with it.

The Scriptures provide numerous examples of men and women whose lives incurred God's blessings. Job was a businessman whose righteousness on earth brought glory to God in heaven (Job 1:8; 2:3). Daniel was a government official whose conduct in the king's court earned him high esteem in the courts of heaven (Dan. 9:23). Elizabeth was the wife of a priest. The Bible says she was "upright in the sight of God" and therefore found favor with God (Luke 1:6, 25 NIV). Likewise Mary was a young woman whose moral purity invoked God's praise (Luke 1:28). Jesus' life so pleased his heavenly Father that the Father declared, "You are my beloved Son, in you I am well-pleased" (Luke 3:22). Jesus promised his disciples that if their lives honored God, they too would be richly rewarded in this life as well as in heaven (Luke 18:28–30).

Paul could face death with confidence because of the way he had lived, always keeping before him the sobering reality of Christ's coming judgment: "Therefore also we have as our ambition, whether at home or absent, to be pleasing to Him. For we must all appear before the judgment seat of Christ, that each one may be recompensed for his deeds in the body, according to what he has done, whether good or bad. Therefore knowing the fear of the Lord, we persuade men" (2 Cor. 5:9–11).

Paul understood that worldly prestige was incomparable to pleasing God. Because he had experienced, both he clearly knew the difference.

Despite their greatest accomplishments, non-Christians face death with apprehension and uncertainty. Christians, leaders and followers alike, have peace knowing that death assures them of God's presence for eternity. Winston Churchill was one of the twentieth century's most confident, fearless leaders. He faced the full fury of Hitler's Nazi war machine without flinching. Toward the end of his illustrious life he joked: "I am ready to meet my Maker. Whether my Maker is ready to meet me is another question."[1] Yet despite his bravado, on his deathbed, at the brink of eternity, Churchill's last words were: "There is no hope." The old warrior had fought the fierce Pathans in India. He had bravely charged with 310 cavalry into a mass of over three thousand enemy dervishes in Sudan. He had escaped captivity from the Boers in South Africa. He had commanded British troops on the front lines during World War I. His apparent lack of fear for enemy bullets was mystifying. He once quipped: "There is nothing more exhilarating than being shot at without result."[2] The only enemy he could not face with confidence was death and his uncertainty of what lay beyond.

Contrast Churchill's final moments with those of the dynamic spiritual leader: D. L. Moody. Shortly before Moody's death, at age sixty-two, he declared: "Some day you will read in the papers that Moody is dead. Don't you believe a word of it. At that moment I shall be more alive than I am now."[3] Four months later, as Moody lay dying, he said: "Earth recedes, heaven opens up before me! . . . If this is death, it is sweet. God is calling me and I must go. Don't call me back! . . . No pain, no valley, it's bliss . . ."[4]

Having accomplished your personal goals in life can provide small comfort at the point of your death. On the other hand, could there be any greater satisfaction than having spent your life in obedience to God's call? Could there be any greater comfort than approaching death without fear, knowing you have invested your life in developing a relationship with the God of heaven? That is the highest reward for leaders, as it is for every believer—knowing that heaven welcomes you and, because of your relationship with Christ and your obedience to his will, your heavenly reward awaits you.

A Calling Fulfilled

There is a second reward for godly leadership, and it is closely tied to the first. It is the satisfaction of knowing you have accomplished God's will and purposes for your life. Scripture says of King David, "For David, after he had served the purpose of God in his own generation, fell asleep, and was laid among his fathers" (Acts 13:36). David was not a perfect man, yet the Scriptures say God used him to accomplish his heavenly purposes. God has a purpose for each person. There is no more worthy ambition for people than to fulfill God's purposes for their life.

God calls some people to serve him in leadership roles (Eph. 4:11). Those God calls to leadership positions, he also equips for leadership. For those people to do anything else would be to invest their lives in less than God's will. Those who resist God's will for them never experience all God had in store for them. The apostle Paul said: "I press on toward the goal for the prize of the upward call of God in Christ Jesus" (Phil. 3:14). Paul's life ambition was to follow God's will unwaveringly. Those who embrace God's will for their lives and pursue it with all their strength can say with the apostle, "I did not prove disobedient to the heavenly vision" (Acts 26:19). There is something enormously satisfying in knowing you have reached your maximum potential in life. At the close of Jesus' life he prayed to his heavenly Father, "I glorified You on earth, having accomplished the work which You have given Me to do" (John 17:4). While Jesus hung on the cross at Calvary, about to breathe his last, he shouted out in triumph, "It is finished!" (John 19:30). Jesus did not say, "I am finished." He had received the most difficult assignment ever given, and he had obeyed to the end.

Leadership is a broad term that covers a wide spectrum. Some are called to lead in smaller capacities. Others are assigned positions of great influence. No matter how grand or how seemingly small a position, those who have been called to lead will misspend their lives and squander their potential if they do not yield to God's will.

Some people know God has called them to lead, but they are apprehensive. They may be reluctant to leave the security of their present position. They may fear the criticism that inevitably comes with leadership. They may doubt their abilities, which means they question God's sufficiency. But if they will allow God to stretch them personally, he will lead them to do things they never thought possible. They will one day look back over their lives and marvel at all God did through them. There is no life more fulfilling to live than a life lived according to God's will.

Spiritual Rewards

- God's affirmation
- A calling fulfilled

THE REWARDS OF INTEGRITY

Experiencing God's affirmation and fulfilling God's call are, in themselves, reward beyond comprehension for spiritual leaders. Yet there are additional personal rewards to spiritual leadership. These benefits are the overflow of God's blessing on leaders who lead God's way.

A life of integrity is a life that is true, consistent, and genuine. Integrity brings many intrinsic rewards, but tragically some leaders forsake integrity in their quest for success. The results are disastrous. Even if they win, they lose. The following are four rewards inherent in a life lived with integrity.

Integrity at Home

If you want to know what a leader is really like, ask his family. A leader with integrity will not give his best at work and then serve emotional and physical leftovers to his family. If a leader is known at work as easy going, quick to forgive, and always willing to go the extra mile, yet she behaves like a short-tempered tyrant at home, she lacks integrity. One problem for many leaders is that they invest the greatest amounts of their emotional and physical energy on the projects they are working on for their organization. By the time they get home to their families, their reserves are depleted. Problems arise at home, and these same people who solved complex issues at work have no capacity for dealing with even simple domestic challenges. Such leaders, though they may be remarkably competent at work, are painfully inept at home.

People only have so much time and energy. If they direct all their reserves to job-related pursuits and don't pace themselves, they will have nothing left, regardless of how much they claim to love God and to love their family. Conscientious leaders know their priorities, and they order their lives accordingly.

Leaders with integrity are purposeful in leading their families just as they are diligent in their work. They understand that their greatest achievements as leaders should occur in their homes. If they are zealous in solving problems at work, they are even more earnest in problem solving at home. If they are known for their courteous and upbeat attitude at work, they are even more so in their home. If they are respectful of their coworkers, they go to even greater lengths to honor their spouse and children. Leaders who are consistently loving, patient, and kind whether at home or at work prove they are genuine spiritual leaders. Leaders can accomplish marvelous feats in the public eye and be praised as heroes. But the real heroes are the ones who go home at the end of the day to a family that loves and respects them.

At the height of D. L. Moody's public success, he faced a crisis in his personal life. His preaching ministry was enormously successful; he had founded a church, three schools, and a publishing house, yet he felt like a failure. His oldest son Will had enrolled at Yale University and had apparently rejected his parents' faith. In a letter to his wayward son Moody wrote: "The thing that shames me most is that I am preaching to others and my son does not believe in the gospel I preach."[5] Moody's ministry success meant little to him if he failed those he loved the most. To Moody's great joy, Will eventually returned to Christ and joined his father in his ministry.

True spiritual leaders move their families from where they are to where God wants them to be. Although they enjoy seeing progress and growth in their organizations, they take even greater delight in seeing growth and maturity in their families. God has clearly laid out his principles for leading families (Eph. 5:22–6:4). Those who unwaveringly follow God's instructions will experience success in the most important arena of leadership—their home (Prov. 22:6). As a result, spiritual leaders will leave behind them a "godly seed," which carries out God's purposes generations afterward (Deut. 6:4–9; Mal. 2:11–15).

Integrity at Work

There is a profound reward for people who invest themselves with integrity in their work. It makes no difference how prestigious a job is, as was demonstrated by Ervin Sievers. Sievers died of brain cancer at age 45. He was not an executive or an oil tycoon or a celebrity, but he took his work seriously. He had served as a garbage collector since he was seventeen years old. Some people disdained his occupation, but Sievers took pride in his work. He was twice recognized as his company's top employee. Paul Cronkite, an apprentice of Sievers, commented: "I was a loader on the back of Erv's truck. He taught me how to drive. It's not very glamorous. But he took a job that nobody likes, and he did it well." Sievers specified in his will that when he died, a garbage truck would be included in the funeral procession immediately following the hearse. Sievers had found his niche in life and he had done his job with excellence.[6] That's integrity.

Spiritual leaders would do well to shun the example of many "successful" leaders and instead follow Sievers's model (Eph. 6:5–9; 1 Tim. 6:1–2). Spiritual leaders carry out their jobs with integrity and they do so to honor their Lord (1 Cor. 10:31; Col. 3:17, 23). For as long as they lead an organization, spiritual leaders give their best. True leaders strive to do well, not so they will earn a higher salary or gain people's praise, but to honor God. Such leaders go home at the end of the day knowing they did their best.

Many Christians who work for secular organizations find it challenging to be effective in their work while not compromising their Christian beliefs. It can be tremendously tempting to neglect one's basic values in order to make more sales or to climb the corporate ladder. Those who travel frequently on business face unique temptations that are magnified because there is no one there to hold them accountable. Even church work can put pressures on people to use worldly methodology to accomplish God's purposes. Pastors and counselors are particularly susceptible to sexual temptation because their duties often require them to hear confidential details of the personal lives of emotionally vulnerable people. These situations are not easy, but wise leaders will remember that no matter where they are, they are in God's presence. The apostle Paul expressed integrity clearly when he said,

"For our proud confidence is this: the testimony of our conscience, that in holiness and godly sincerity, not in fleshly wisdom but in the grace of God, we have conducted ourselves in the world" (2 Cor. 1:12).

There are times when integrity requires a leader to leave a position. Christians know that their calling has priority over their career. Their obedience to Christ supercedes their obligation to their organization. Sometimes taking a stand for God's way and refusing to participate in ungodly ventures will cost Christians their leadership positions. This experience can be devastating unless leaders are secure in the knowledge that they are in God's hands. Leaders who put godliness before worldly success can take comfort in knowing their integrity is intact. Moreover, they can trust God's promise to honor those who honor him (1 Sam. 2:30). God will not abandon someone who has sought to glorify him. Christian leaders' main concern regarding their career should be: "What is God's agenda at my workplace?" Christian leaders who ignore God's agenda may be ultrasuccessful in the eyes of the business world, yet fail in God's eyes. God's primary concern is advancing his kingdom, not advancing people's careers (Matt. 6:33). When God calls leaders to new jobs, they should look back over their completed assignments and ask themselves: "While I worked there, was God's will done through my life?" (Matt. 6:9–10). If the answer to this question is yes, the leader has led with integrity. Those spiritual leaders who refuse to compromise their Christianity while leading their organization will know tremendous satisfaction at the end of their journey, and they will be able to sleep at night along the way.

Integrity in Relationships

Integrity pays some of its largest dividends in the area of relationships. Some leaders have willingly forsaken relationships through the course of their lives in order to achieve success. They have alienated friends, colleagues, and family members. Some ambitious leaders have used people as steppingstones on the path to prosperity. As a result, they have left a trail of embittered and resentful former friends behind them. Such leaders are generally lonely people. By the end of their careers they have little else but their work to occupy them because they have destroyed or neglected most of their relationships. Wise leaders know that people are never the means to an end; they are the end. No matter how eager leaders may be to achieve their goals, true leaders will do everything possible to treat others with dignity and to preserve relationships. They will be above reproach in their dealings with everyone regardless of how they are treated themselves. Pastoral leaders must understand this truth. Pastors are called to lead people who are usually less mature spiritually than they are. When these people reveal their immaturity, pastors do not give up on them or steer clear of them. They help them grow to maturity. Immature people do not prevent pastors from achieving God's purposes. The people and their spiritual growth are God's purpose.

Samuel maintained integrity in relating to those with whom he worked. As a result, when he came to the end of his tenure, he stood before all the people he had led and asked:

> "Here I am; bear witness against me before the Lord and His anointed. Whose ox have I taken, or whose donkey have I taken, or whom have I defrauded? Whom have I oppressed, or from whose hand have I taken a bribe to blind my eyes with it? I will restore it to you." And they said, "You have not defrauded us, or oppressed us, or taken anything from any man's hand." And he said to them, "The Lord is witness against you, and His anointed is witness this day that you have found nothing in my hand." And they said, "He is witness" (1 Sam. 12:3–5).

Samuel had served as a leader for his entire adult life. Those he led had seen him in every conceivable situation. He had numerous opportunities to take advantage of people and to compromise his integrity. Nevertheless, at the close of his life, when he stood before his entire nation and asked if there was even one person whom he had mistreated, no one had a complaint.

Likewise, the apostle Paul stood before the elders of the church of Ephesus at the close of his ministry to them and said: "You yourselves know, from the first day that I set foot in Asia, how I was with you the whole time, serving the Lord with all humility and with tears and with trials which came upon me through the plots of the Jews; how I did not shrink from declaring to you anything that was profitable, and teaching you publicly and from house to house, solemnly testifying to both Jews and Greeks of repentance toward God and faith in our Lord Jesus Christ" (Acts 20:18–21).

The ability to look people in the eye and to know you have nothing for which you ought to be ashamed is a reward of inestimable value. That is the reward of integrity.

Integrity with Self

Every year an alarming number of executives and Christian ministers take their own lives. Many do so because they cannot live with the shame and regret they feel for violating their morals and religious convictions. God gives clear guidance to leaders on how they should conduct themselves. Leaders generally have a code of conduct for their lives that they subscribe to, and they know when they have compromised it. While some leaders can become hardened to ethical and moral failures, most people know when they have broken their vows to God, to their family, and to themselves. No one has to prove their guilt. They stand tried and condemned by the court of their own conscience.

The notorious Judas violated his own principles. Having betrayed Jesus for a handful of silver, Judas could not bear the resulting anguish. In a desperate effort to purge his conscience of his despicable act, he took his own life (Matt. 27:3–5).

What about leaders who realize that, in their quest for success, they have compromised their Christian principles and betrayed a friend, or dishonored Jesus' name, or neglected their family? When people come to this realization, they can claim the promises of Scripture for their lives: "He who conceals his transgressions will not prosper, but he who confesses and forsakes them will find compassion" (Prov. 28:13). Leaders with integrity live in such a way that they do not have to endure the self-reproach that comes from having compromised their convictions.

In 1948, the American public was enthralled by the congressional investigation of Alger Hiss, a former friend of President Franklin Roosevelt and a suspected communist. Despite the absence of incriminating evidence, members of the congressional committee believed Hiss was guilty and they alleged a cover-up. The committee investigating the case was doggedly persistent in their accusations, insisting that the public had a right to know the truth and that justice must be served.

Leading the congressional inquiry with pious zeal was an ambitious, talented young congressman named Richard Nixon. It's ironic that the political event that launched Richard Nixon's career was his part in uncovering a high-profile political scandal. Nixon, whose name would be forever linked with government cover-up, began his career by denouncing this very thing. Those who violate their own standards of decency, morality, and Christian principles are in danger of sacrificing their personal integrity. If that is lost, nothing else will matter.

The Rewards of Integrity

- Integrity at home
- Integrity at work
- Integrity in relationships
- Integrity with self

On the other hand, those who remain true to their convictions derive great satisfaction in life. In anticipating his death, Mahatma Ghandi told one of his followers, "If someone were to end my life by putting a bullet through me . . . and I met his bullet without a groan and breathed my last taking God's name—then alone would I have made good my claim."[7] The next day, late for prayers, Ghandi hurried to a waiting crowd of five hundred people. Suddenly, thirty-five-year-old Nathuram Vinayak Godse stepped before him, bowed low as if in reverence, then shot Ghandi three times at point-blank range. Ghandi murmured, "O God" and, making the sign of forgiveness to his assassin, fell to the ground dead. Although not a Christian, Ghandi developed his own convictions of how he as a spiritual leader ought to live and how he ought to die. He remained true to those commitments even to death. How much more reason for Christian leaders to follow through with the commitments they have made to Christ. Leaders with integrity will not only know in their hearts how they ought to live; they will steadfastly live out their convictions throughout their lives.

THE REWARDS OF HAVING MADE A CONTRIBUTION

Churchill noted: "History judges a man, not by his victories or defeats, but by their results."[8] The ultimate measure of leaders' success is not that they were always successful but that they made a difference in the lives of the people they led. Leadership is a people business. Spiritual leaders move people on to God's agenda. Spiritual leaders' primary contribution is allowing God to use them in his work to transform people into Christlikeness (Rom. 8:29). The more willing leaders are to be God's instruments, the more they can celebrate their success.

Contributions to People

It has been said of D. L. Moody, "One could not be downhearted or defeated in his presence."[9] Great leaders are people who make those around them better people as well. Leaders should not underestimate the influence their character has on those who follow them. When longtime General Motors CEO Alfred Sloan retired, his employees spontaneously collected $1.5 million dollars and donated the entire amount to cancer research in his honor. It was a fitting tribute to their philanthropic leader who had invested so much in them. On the contrary, Napoleon was a vain, ambitious leader. Not surprisingly, he later lamented, "In this crowd of men I have made into kings, there is not one who is grateful, not one who has a heart, not one who loves me."[10] Leaders ought not to become too frustrated with longtime followers who demonstrate disagreeable character traits. It could easily be that they are simply modeling what they have witnessed in their leader.

Leaders who invest in people will know the deep satisfaction of seeing these people fulfill God's purposes for their lives. There is no greater experience for leaders than rejoicing with those who have matured in their faith as a result of their leader's faithfulness. Paul described the church he had established in Philippi as his joy and his crown (Phil. 4:1). Leaders' joy is multiplied as younger associates follow their example and they in turn help others to grow in Christian maturity. D. L. Moody was one who mightily impacted his generation by investing in people. The list of people who were his friends and protégés reads like a Who's Who of leading Christian leaders of the late nineteenth century. Men such as F. B. Meyer, Ira Sankey, Philip Bliss, C. T. Studd, John R. Mott, Fleming Revell, S. D. Gordon, R. A. Torrey, Robert Speer, Wilbur Chapman, G. Campbell Morgan, C. I. Scofield, Henry Drummond, and J. H. Moulton were just some of the hundreds of Christian leaders whose lives Moody impacted. At one point when his colleagues D. W. Whittle and Phillip Bliss were struggling to continue their evangelistic campaigns across the United States, Moody sent them funds and exhorted them, "If you have not got faith enough launch out on the strength of my faith."[11] By the time Moody died in 1899, there were scores of dedicated Christian leaders in every sector of society, not just in religious work, who had looked to Moody as their mentor and encourager.

Contributions to Organizations

Jean Monnet observed: "Nothing is made without men; nothing lasts without institutions."[12] Leaders understand that one of the best ways to exert an ongoing influence on people is by investing in organizations. Organizations can generally do more than individuals can. For one thing, they usually have a longer life span. D. L. Moody preached to more than one million people during his illustrious ministry, but his greatest impact was undoubtedly through the organizations he helped create. Although he was not an educated man himself, he founded the Mount Hermon School for Boys and the Northfield Seminary for Girls. He established the Chicago Evangelization Society (later renamed the Moody Bible Institute), he developed the YMCA in Chicago and the Moody Church, and he began the Northfield Conferences from which sprang the Student Volunteer Movement. Through this movement, hundreds of college graduates went out as foreign missionaries around the world. Moody also played a part in founding the Fleming H. Revell publishing company as well as the Moody Press. All of these organizations continue to function effectively over one hundred years after Moody's death.

Leaders may not always know the full extent of their influence upon people, but their impact upon an organization is more easily measured. Kouzes and Posner define leadership success as "leaving the area a better place than when you found it."[13] Leaders should expect that the organization they lead will one day be stronger because of their leadership. Mahatma Ghandi saw the day when his nation of India was liberated from Great Britain. After three decades of personal sacrifice, Nelson Mandela witnessed South Africa's first free election by black voters. Winston Churchill took a demoralized nation and led it to defeat the seemingly invincible Nazi war machine.

Christian leaders can know tremendous satisfaction when God leads them to a weakened, directionless organization and through them brings renewed strength and purpose. Many pastors have known the fulfillment of helping a declining church become revitalized. Truly one of the most satisfying experiences for leaders is leaving their organization stronger than they found it. Robert Greenleaf observes: "The secret of institution building is to be able to weld a team of . . . people by lifting them up to grow taller than they would otherwise be."[14] This is certainly one of the unique rewards of leadership.

Contributions to a Successor

One of the most important, yet often overlooked, responsibilities of leaders is that of leaving a successor. The Bible reveals God's pattern of working through successive generations. God gave his people specific instructions concerning how they were to train and prepare the emerging generation of leaders (Deut. 6:6–9; 20–25). One of the primary reasons Scripture gives for God's disdain of divorce is that it disrupts the lives of the children God is preparing as his "godly seed" (Mal. 3:15–16). God's people always stand just one generation away from being in the center of God's will, or completely out of it. For God's purposes to continue, each generation must be prepared to embrace a fresh relationship of love for him and obedience to his word. That is why true spiritual leaders are always investing in the next generation of leaders. It's no coincidence that great spiritual leaders follow in the footsteps of great spiritual leaders. Joshua succeeded the revered Moses and even surpassed his accomplishments by conquering the land Moses had been unable to overcome. Elisha not only followed the mighty Elijah as prophet; he was given a double portion of Elijah's spirit (2 Kings 2:9–10). Jesus made this incredible statement to his disciples: "Truly, truly, I say to you, he who believes in Me, the works that I do, he shall do also; and greater works than these he shall do; because I go to the Father" (John 14:12).

Many times God will bless one faithful generation with the privilege of seeing their children carry on the ministry begun through their parents. Often leaders do not carefully consider their successor until they come to the end of their time as leader. Many leaders give little thought to the conclusion of their leadership and so they do little to prepare for it. However, when suddenly faced with leaving their office, they realize that much of their work will have been in vain unless there is a capable successor. Margaret Thatcher came face to face with this reality when she was forced from office as prime minister of Great Britain. When it became clear she must relinquish her office, she observed: "But there was one more duty I had to perform, and that was to ensure that John Major was my successor. I wanted—perhaps I needed—to believe that he was the man to secure and safeguard my legacy and to take our policies forward."15

It is a grievous experience to labor to build up an organization or a ministry only to watch it disintegrate under an ineffective successor. Former leaders have been forced to watch in horror as subsequent leaders dismantled everything they worked so hard to build. Much of leaders' joy and satisfaction in a job well done can be diminished when they are forced to witness an incompetent successor at work.

True joy comes in knowing that one's work has been preserved and is continuing due to the leader's careful preparation of a successor. While Ronald Reagan was president, he met with Vice President George Bush every Thursday for lunch. Although American presidents historically neglected and marginalized their vice presidents, Reagan would review the week and the pressing issues they were facing with his associate. To Reagan's delight, Bush was elected president after Reagan's two terms came to an end. During Reagan's last moments in the Oval Office, he left a note to the new president on stationary with the heading, "Don't let the turkeys get you down." On it he wrote:

Dear George,

You'll have moments when you want to use this particular stationary. Well, go for it. George, I'll treasure the memories we share and wish you all the very best. You'll be in my prayers. God bless you and Barbara. I'll miss our Thursday lunches.

Ron[16]

This note was waiting for President Bush when he sat at his desk in the Oval Office for the first time. Reagan had the satisfaction of knowing his efforts would not come to an abrupt end at the close of his last term. While leaders cannot always choose their successors, they can prepare their organizations for the next leader and they can invest in emerging leaders who will be capable of eventually taking their place. Leaders always have an eye on the future and that includes preparing their organization for its next leader. The rewards for this responsibility of leadership are threefold. Not only do the leaders benefit, but so do their successors and their organizations.

THE REWARDS OF RELATIONSHIPS

Leaders know that of the many rewards available to them, one of the most treasured is the pleasure that comes from their relationships. While leaders may help to liberate nations, build enormous corporations, and win Nobel prizes, the reward that often brings the greatest satisfaction is knowing they have developed deep, meaningful, and abiding relationships.

Family

Family relationships have the potential to bring leaders both their greatest joy and their deepest grief. Much depends on how leaders nurture their family relationships. Leaders who neglect their families in favor of achieving organizational goals may experience outward success but suffer abysmal failure in their home. Richard heard a sad testimony of this when he was leading a conference for pastors. At the close of one of the services, a handsome young man approached him in tears. He shared that five years earlier he had taken a half-dozen people and started a new church. Now, five years later, the church was flourishing and attendance had surpassed 800 people. From a church growth perspective, he had been a resounding success. But, through his tears, he explained that when he was first considering starting the church, his wife had pleaded with him not to do it. She had warned: "I know what you're like. You're driven. You'll give everything you have to grow your church, and your family will lose you." The young pastor had vehemently denied the possibility. He prized his family. He would never allow anything to come between him and his family. Then, this brokenhearted pastor admitted, "She was right! She was right! How did I ever get to this place?" Two weeks earlier his wife had gently told him that he could go his way, with the church, and she and the kids would go theirs. He had sacrificed that which meant the most to him for the sake of growing his church. In that moment of agonizing self-realization, this young man would gladly have forfeited all of his "success" in order to regain the close relationship he had once enjoyed with his wife and children.

King David suffered similar anguish. As a general, a king, and an overall administrator, his leadership of Israel was considered commendable. However, his remarkable accomplishments were tarnished by his failure as a leader in his home. David's wife Michal ridiculed him for praising God (2 Sam. 6:20–23). David committed adultery with one of his soldier's wives and arranged the soldier's murder (2 Sam. 11). David's son Amnon raped Amnon's half-sister Tamar (2 Sam. 13:1–22). David's son Absalom murdered Amnon and launched a rebellion against his father that threw the nation into civil war (2 Sam. 15–18). Even while David lay upon his deathbed, his sons Adonijah and Solomon were plotting against each other for their father's throne (1 Kings 1:5–53). David's son Solomon, born out of his adulterous relationship, would prove susceptible to the influence of pagan women and would allow his heart to turn away from the Lord during his reign (1 Kings 11:1–8). David's grandson, Rehoboam, foolishly listened to unwise counsel and saw the kingdom handed down to him from his grandfather David torn in two (1 Kings 12:1–15). David's inability to lead his family robbed him of much of the joy he should have experienced for leading his nation well and ultimately cancelled much of what he had accomplished.

Wise leaders cherish their relationships with their family. They find solace in their homes when their world is so hectic. Wise leaders are diligent to apply godly leadership skills in their homes. Just as leaders move their organizations to follow God's will, they also seek God's agenda for their families. Just as leaders evaluate their performance as leaders in their organization, they also reflect on their performance as a loving parent and a faithful spouse. Just as conscientious leaders give their best effort to lead their organization, so leaders do all they can to provide a godly role model in their homes. Leading a home is not a haphazard venture. Leading one's family to Christlikeness takes prayer, deliberate choice, and conscientious effort.

The rewards for intentional, godly leadership in one's family are directly proportional to the efforts involved. Leaders derive a rich dividend of joy and contentment when their families are intact and serving God as he intended. Long after a task is done or a project is finished or even a career has ended, the leader's family will continue to provide a deep source of fulfillment. Leaders who invest in their families enjoy the rewards that come from a spouse and children and grandchildren who love and respect them. Spiritual leaders who have led their families well can generally look for their children to enjoy following their God just as they have. People who lead their families wisely can often set in motion a heritage of several generations who know how to lead their own families as well as others effectively. Knowing that one has led well both at work and at home brings tremendous satisfaction.

Friends

Leadership is not about positions but about relationships—with God and with people. Since leadership involves working closely with people, deep and lasting friendships can and should develop. True leaders value people. They don't neglect them or manipulate them in order to accomplish their goals. One quality that characterized many of history's great leaders was the number of close, loyal friends they enjoyed. Close friendships are the leader's reward for investing in the lives of people.

Kouzes and Posner note: "A managerial myth says we can't get too close to our associates. We can't be friends with people at work. Well, set this myth aside."[17] The role of a leader cannot be fulfilled unless the leader invests in people. As leaders invest in people, friendships develop. Leaders must show concern for those they lead. People need to know that their leader cares for them. Leaders need friends. The responsibility of leadership can become overwhelming unless leaders are strengthened by strong friendships. Friendship is an effective stress reliever. Being able to relax and share one's feelings with concerned friends is critical to a person's mental and emotional health. Leaders who insulate themselves from others and choose to bear their burdens single-handedly are destined for loneliness and burnout. Leaders, like everyone else, need friends, and perhaps in light of the load they carry, even more so.

Some of the most enjoyable byproducts of leadership are close, loyal and abiding friendships. Once work is done, or retirement has come, those friendships continue. Often it is not until retirement that leaders see clearly what type of friends they have. Once people no longer hold positions of power and influence, they have an unobstructed view of who their true friends are. Those who failed to cultivate true friendships will find this time can be revealing and disheartening, but those who used their leadership to genuinely invest in people will find the experience supremely rewarding. Friendships do not come haphazardly. They come intentionally. For leaders who love their people, friendships are inevitable.

David is known for many things, but one obvious characteristic is that he endeared himself to his friends. David and Jonathan's friendship is a model of genuine devotion and loyalty. David gathered close friends around him throughout his life. The group of "mighty men" who accompanied him is legendary (1 Chron. 11:10–47). Even as David lay dying, his close friends continued to protect him and to strive to see that his will was done.

The apostle Paul made many close friends who stood with him and ministered to him. Barnabas, Timothy, Titus, Luke, Priscilla, Aquila, and many others were dear to Paul. The ability to attract so many high-caliber friends says much about Paul's character. Though Jesus was the Son of God and could have lived self-sufficiently, he too enjoyed close friendships (John 15:14). Few things provide more joy than good friends, and leaders have the opportunity to make many over the course of their careers.

THE REWARDS OF INFLUENCE

There is a final reward that has potential for bringing great satisfaction to leaders, and that is the reward of influence. This influence does not come from position, but from personhood. It is based on who leaders are, not on the positions they hold. It is founded on what leaders have done, not on what they promise to do. It is an influence that comes from an impeccable track record. Leaders are symbols. During their time as leader, they represent the vision of their organization. At the close of their formal period of leadership, leaders symbolize all that God did during their time of leadership. George Washington, Winston Churchill, and Martin Luther King Jr. were all symbols for their people while they led them; now they are symbols of history that still inspire those who identify with them.

Many people desire such lasting influence, but few achieve it. Many look for it in a position, but they won't find it. Mahatma Ghandi was never the president of his country, but his life exerted an enormous and lasting influence upon people. He did not have to lobby for a job or impose his opinions on others; people came to him asking his advice. Mother Teresa became world-renowned for her humble service to others. She was physically diminutive and she shunned position and wealth, yet she was an honored guest among world leaders and carried a moral authority around the world that few could match.

Personal Rewards of Leadership

- The rewards of integrity
- The rewards of having made a contribution
- The rewards of relationships
- The rewards of influence

Positive, enduring influence comes from ending a leadership career as well as it was begun. In other words, it comes through integrity. Often leaders lose their influence because of the poor way they end their official leadership positions. Leaders who overstay their welcome or who alienate themselves from the next generation of leaders forfeit their opportunity to continue exercising influence in their senior years. The younger generation looks for mentors and consultants. If all they find is criticism and resistance, they will seek counsel elsewhere. On the other hand, *leaders who graciously encourage the next generation and help them assume leadership roles will continue to make valuable contributions long after the name plate comes off their office door.* Leaders who have spent their careers learning and growing can find rich contentment sharing their wisdom with others and having their life encourage those who come after them. Psalms 92:12–14 declares: "The righteous man will flourish like the palm tree, he will grow like a cedar in Lebanon. Planted in the house of the LORD, they will flourish in the courts of our God. They will still yield fruit in old age."

CONCLUSION

Spiritual leadership is a noble undertaking, but it is something God must assign. Moving people on to God's agenda is an exhilarating endeavor. Helping people grow, mature, and gain new skills is immensely gratifying. Taking weak, ineffective organizations and transforming them into robust, productive enterprises brings tremendous satisfaction. Nevertheless, such leadership does not come arbitrarily. People do not become spiritual leaders haphazardly. They become leaders through the opportunities the Holy Spirit provides as they strive to become the kind of people God desires them to be. Effective leadership results from hard work and a continuing effort to learn. Ultimately, spiritual leadership comes as a result of the working of the Holy Spirit. It is the Holy Spirit who reveals God's will to people. It is the Holy Spirit who equips people to lead others. It is the Holy Spirit who guides leaders and authenticates their leadership before people. It is, therefore, essential that leaders cultivate a deeply personal and vibrant relationship with God as they strive to become the kind of leader God wants them to become.

Where do leaders begin when they want to improve their leadership skills? They begin with God. They stand before God and ask him to reveal his evaluation of their character and leadership. Leaders search God's Word to see if their leadership is in keeping with the standards God has clearly established for leaders. Leaders also take responsibility for what is presently happening in their organizations. If there are problems, leaders ask, "What is it about my leadership that has allowed this to happen?" When organizations struggle, genuine leaders don't blame their people; they ask God to show them how to make a positive difference. Finally, leaders grow. They learn. They continue to change until they have the character and walk with God that is required to lead their organization effectively. Leaders who are willing to make the effort will experience the joy and satisfaction of being used by the Lord to make a significant difference in their world.

What if you have failed in your attempts to be a leader thus far? Is there any hope? Yes. If you sense that God has called you to be a leader but you have failed to lead according to biblical principles, there may still be the opportunity for you to become the leader God wants you to be. If you know you have neglected areas in your personal growth in your pursuit to lead others, ask God to take you back to those places in your character in order to develop you properly into the kind of leader that pleases him. If you have disregarded personal holiness, don't waste another day displeasing God. You may need immediately to get alone with God and your Bible and allow God to speak to you about changes that must take place in your life before he will use you for his service once again. If you have broken relationships, or if you have not been leading your family properly, ask God to help you put those areas back in place before you ask him for a new opportunity to lead. If you have children who have rejected God's Word, daily allow God to mold you into the kind of domestic leader you must be if you are to exert a godly influence upon your family. The biblical pattern suggests God is sequential in the way he develops leaders. He will undoubtedly take you back to the steps you bypassed before he will develop you further as a leader. Don't give up! Be patient. Allow God to take all the time he wants to build your character. If God has called you to lead, he is perfectly capable of developing you into the leader he wants you to be. No person, no demon, no circumstance, no obstacle can prevent God from accomplishing his will in your life. It only takes your willingness to obey him and to do what he asks you to do next.

CONCEPTS AND SCRIPTURES FOR CONSIDERATION

- No other reward could possibly equal the joy that comes from knowing almighty God is pleased with you and what you have done with your life.

- There is something enormously satisfying in knowing you have reached your maximum potential in life.
- True spiritual leaders move their families from where they are to where God wants them to be.
- Some ambitious leaders have used people as stepping-stones on the path to prosperity. As a result, they have left a trail of embittered and resentful former friends behind them.
- Wise leaders know that people are never the means to an end; they are the end.
- Those who violate their own standards of decency, morality, and Christian principles are in danger of sacrificing their personal integrity.
- Spiritual leaders' primary contribution is allowing God to use them in his work to transform people into Christlikeness.
- Leaders should expect that the organization they lead will one day be stronger because of their leadership.
- Great leaders are people who make those around them better people as well.
- Sooner or later people become an expression of those who lead them.
- The reward of seeing your life being reproduced in the lives of the next generation is truly an awesome experience. The reward of knowing that the next generation of leaders wants to emulate you is a reward only few leaders enjoy.
- Leadership is not about positions but about relationships—with God and with people.
- Leaders who insulate themselves from others and choose to bear the burdens single-handedly are destined for loneliness and burnout.
- Friendships do not come haphazardly. They come intentionally. For leaders who love their people, friendships are inevitable.
- At the close of their formal period of leadership, leaders symbolize all that God did during their time of leadership.

- Leaders who graciously encourage the next generation and help them assume leadership roles will continue to make valuable contributions long after the name plate comes off their office door.
- Spiritual leadership is a noble undertaking, but it is something God must assign.
- Ultimately, spiritual leadership comes as a result of the working of the Holy Spirit.

Job 1:8; 2:3; Daniel 9:23; Luke 3:22; Luke 18:28–30
2 Corinthians 5:9–11
Acts 13:36
Philippians 3:14
Acts 26:19
John 17:4
John 19:30
Ephesians 5:22–6:4
Ephesians 6:5–9; 1 Timothy 6:1–2
1 Corinthians 10:31; Colossians 3:17, 23
2 Corinthians 5:9
Matthew 6:33; Matthew 6:9–10
1 Samuel 12:3–5
Acts 20:18–21
Romans 8:29
John 15:12
1 Chronicles 11:10–47
Psalm 92:12–14
Proverbs 22:6

Notes

Chapter 1, "The Challenge of Leadership"

1. Gordon R. Sullivan and Michael V. Harper, *Hope Is Not a Method: What Business Leaders Can Learn from America's Army* (New York: Broadway Books, 1997), 48.

2. Warren Bennis, *Why Leaders Can't Lead* (San Francisco: Jossey Bass, 1989), 36.

3. Ibid., 33.

4. Charles Handy, *The Age of Paradox* (Boston: Harvard Business School Press, 1995), 36.

5. Daniel Goleman, *Working with Emotional Intelligence* (New York: Bantam Books, 1998), 58.

6. Robert K. Greenleaf, *Servant Leadership* (New York: Paulist Press, 1977), 156.

7. *Calgary Herald*, 9 December 1997, C6.

8. George Barna, *Leaders on Leadership* (Ventura: Regal Books, 1997), 18.

Chapter 2, "The Leader's Role: What Leaders Do"

1. James MacGregor Burns, *Leadership* (New York: Harper Torchbooks, 1978), 2.

2. Warren Bennis and Burt Nanus, *Leaders: Strategies for Taking Charge* (New York: HarperCollins, 1997), 4.

3. John Gardner, *On Leadership* (New York: The Free Press, 1990), 1.

4. Burns, *Leadership*, 18.

5. Oswald Sanders, *Spiritual Leadership* (Chicago: Moody Press, 1967; reprint ed., 1994), 31.

6. George Barna, *Leaders on Leadership* (Ventura, Calif.: Regal Books, 1997), 25.

7. Robert Clinton, *The Making of a Leader* (Colorado Springs: NavPress, 1988), 203.

8. In recent discussions on leadership, John Maxwell has popularized the approach that "leadership is influence." See John Maxwell, *Developing the Leader Within You* (Nashville: Thomas Nelson, 1993).

9. Robert K. Greenleaf, *Servant Leadership* (New York: Paulist Press, 1977), 45.

10. Peter F. Drucker, foreword to *The Leader of the Future*, edited by Francis Hasselbein, Marshall Goldsmith, and Richard Beckhard (San Francisco: Jossey Bass, 1996), vii.

Chapter 3, "The Leader's Preparation: How God Develops Leaders"

1. George Barna, *Today's Pastors* (Ventura, Calif.: Regal Books, 1983), 122, 125.

2. William Manchester, *Winston Spencer Churchill: The Last Lion, Visions of Glory 1874–1932* (New York: Dell Publishing, 1983), 17.

3. Howard Gardner, *Leading Minds: An Anatomy of Leadership* (New York: Basic Books, 1995), 186.

4. Peter Senge, *The Fifth Discipline: The Art and Practice of the Learning Organization* (New York: Currency Doubleday, 1994), 359.

5. Peter Drucker, *The Effective Executive* in *The Executive in Action* (New York: HarperBusiness, 1996), 525.

6. Manchester, *Winston Spencer Churchill*, 117.

7. Winston S. Churchill, *My Early Life* (Glasgow: Fontana Books, 1930; reprint ed. 1963), 13.

8. Ibid., 27.

9. Ibid., 70.

10. Homer G. Ritchie, *The Life and Legend of J. Frank Norris: The Fighting Parson* (Fort Worth: Homer G. Ritchie, 1991), 22–23.

11. Gary L. McIntosh and Samuel D. Rima, *Overcoming the Dark Side of Leadership* (Grand Rapids: Baker Books, 1997), 22.

12. H. W. Brands, *TR: The Last Romantic* (New York: Basic Books, 1997), 162–63.

13. *Calgary Herald*, February 21, 2000, A11.

14. Gardner, *Leading Minds*, 37.

15. Calvin Kytle, *Ghandi: Soldier of Nonviolence* (Washington, D.C.: Seven Locks Press, 1969), 43.

16. John Pollock, *Moody* (Grand Rapids: Baker Books, 1963), 31.

17. Billy Graham, *Just as I Am* (New York: HarperPaperbacks, 1998), 62.

18. Donald T. Phillips, *Lincoln on Leadership: Executive Strategies for Tough Times* (New York: Warner Books, 1992), 109.

19. Senge, *The Fifth Discipline*, 154.

20. J. Oswald Sanders, *Spiritual Leadership* (Chicago: Moody, 1967), 33.

Chapter 4, "Vision: Where Do Leaders Get It and How Do They Communicate It?"

1. Max Depree, *Leadership Jazz* (New York: Dell Publishing, 1992), 47.

2. Peter Drucker, *The Effective Executive* in *The Executive in Action* (New York: HarperBusiness, 1996), 628.

3. Donald T. Phillips, *Martin Luther King Jr. on Leadership: Inspiration and Wisdom for Challenging Times* (New York: Warner Books, 1999), 185.

4. Felix Markham, *Napoleon* (New York: New American Library, 1963), 264.

5. Warren Bennis, *On Becoming a Leader* (Reading, Mass.: Addison-Wesley, 1989), 22.

6. Warren Bennis, *Why Leaders Can't Lead* (San Francisco: Jossey Bass, 1989), 178.

7. Bennis, *On Becoming a Leader,* 178.

8. George Barna, *Turning Vision into Action* (Ventura, Calif.: Venture Books, 1996), 75.

9. Burt Nanus, *Visionary Leadership* (San Francisco: Jossey Bass, 1992), 34.

10. James M. Kouzes and Barry Z. Posner, *The Leadership Challenge* (San Francisco: Jossey Bass, 1995), 109.

11. James C. Collins and Jerry I. Porass, *Built to Last: Successful Habits of Visionary Companies* (New York: HarperBusiness, 1994), 91–114.

12. Mike Huckabee, *Character Is the Issue* (Nashville: Broadman & Holman, 1997), 105–106.

13. See John Beckett, *Loving Monday: Succeeding in Business Without Selling Your Soul* (Downers Grove: InterVarsity Press, 1998).

14. Nanus, *Visionary Leadership,* 3.

15. James Champy, *Reengineering Management: The Mandate for New Leadership* (New York: HarperBusiness, 1995), 55.

16. George Bernard Shaw, *Man and Superman* (Baltimore: Penguin Books, 1903), xxxii.

17. Peter Senge, *The Fifth Discipline: The Art and Practice of the Learning Organization* (New York: Currency Doubleday, paperback ed., 1994), 218.

18. Howard Gardner, *Leading Minds: An Anatomy of Leadership* (New York: Basic Books, 1995), ix.

19. Depree, *Leadership Jazz,* 100.

Chapter 5, "The Leader's Character: A Life That Moves Others to Follow"

1. H. W. Crocker, *Robert E. Lee on Leadership: Executive Lessons in Character, Courage, and Vision* (Rocklin, Calif.: Forum, 1999), 4.

2. Oswald Sanders, *Spiritual Leadership* (Chicago: Moody Press, 1967; reprint ed., 1994), 11.

3. Max Depree, *Leadership Is an Art* (New York: Dell Publishing, 1989), 28.

4. Watchman Nee, *Spiritual Authority* (New York: Christian Fellowship Publishers, 1972), 12.

5. Ibid., 97.

6. Ibid., 71.

7. James C. Collins and Jerry I. Porass, *Built to Last: Successful Habits of Visionary Companies* (New York: HarperBusiness, 1994), 7.

8. Charles G. Finney, *The Autobiography of Charles Finney*, ed. Helen Wessel (Minneapolis: Bethany House, 1977), 124–25.

9. Billy Graham, *Just as I Am* (New York: HarperCollins, 1997), 692–95.

10. Finney, *Autobiography*, 21–22.

11. John Pollock, *Moody* (Grand Rapids: Baker Books, 1963), 89.

12. Graham, *Just As I Am*, 163–64.

13. Kouzes and Posner, *The Leadership Challenge*, 21.

14. Kouzes and Posner, *Encouraging the Heart: A Leader's Guide to Rewarding and Recognizing Others* (San Francisco: Jossey Bass, 1999), 131.

15. Kouzes and Posner, *Credibility: How Leaders Gain and Lose It, Why People Demand It* (San Francisco: Jossey Bass, 1993), 185.

16. Max Depree, *Leadership Jazz* (New York: Dell Publishing, 1992), 10.

17. Crocker, *Robert E. Lee on Leadership*, 34.

18. Warren Bennis and Burt Nanus, *Leaders: Strategies for Taking Charge* (New York: HarperCollins, 1997), 24.

19. Graham, *Just as I Am*, 150.

20. Kouzes and Posner, *Credibility*, 17.

21. Kouzes and Posner, *Encouraging the Heart*, 145.

22. L. R. Scarborough, *With Christ After the Lost* (Nashville: Broadman Press, 1952), 79.

23. Bennis, *Why Leaders Can't Lead*, 40.

24. Crocker, *Robert E. Lee on Leadership*, 147.

25. Graham, *Just as I Am*, 852.

26. Bennis, *Why Leaders Can't Lead*, 48.

Chapter 6, "The Leader's Goal: Moving People On to God's Agenda"

1. Peter F. Drucker, foreword to *The Leader of the Future*, edited by Francis Hasselbein, Marshall Goldsmith and Richard Beckhard (San Francisco: Jossey Bass, 1996), xii.

2. Peter Senge, *The Fifth Discipline: The Art and Practice of the Learning Organization* (New York: Currency Doubleday, paperback ed., 1994), 4.

3. Max Depree, *Leadership Jazz* (New York: Dell Publishing, 1992), 23.

4. Ibid., 24.

5. Ibid., 91.

6. Max Depree, *Leadership Is an Art* (New York: Dell Publishing, 1989), 60.

7. Ibid., 62.

8. Ibid., 11.

9. Felix Markham, *Napoleon* (New York: New American Library, 1963), 233.

10. Ibid., 143.

11. Peter Drucker, *The Effective Executive* in *The Executive in Action* (New York: HarperBusiness, 1996), 637.

12. David McCullough, *Truman* (New York: Touchstone, 1992), 564.

13. John Beckett, *Loving Monday: Succeeding in Business Without Selling Your Soul* (Downers Grove: InterVarsity Press, 1998), 22–23.

Chapter 7, "The Leader's Influence: How Leaders Lead"

1. James MacGregor Burns, *Leadership* (New York: Harper Torchbooks, 1978), 427.

2. Oswald Sanders, *Spiritual Leadership* (Chicago: Moody Press, 1967; reprint ed., 1994), 31.

3. Ronald Reagan, *Ronald Reagan: An American Life* (New York: Pocket Books, 1990), 693–94.

4. Basil Miller, *George Muller: The Man of Faith*, 3d ed. (Grand Rapids: Zondervan: 1941), 145–146.

5. J. R. Hamilton, *Alexander the Great* (Pittsburgh: University of Pittsburgh Press, 1973), 120.

6. Norman H. Schwarzkopf and Peter Petre, *It Doesn't Take a Hero* (New York: Bantam Books, 1992), 169–72.

7. Sanders, *Spiritual Leadership*, 180.

8. Howard Gardner, *Leading Minds: An Anatomy of Leadership* (New York: Basic Books, 1995), 34.

9. David McCullough, *Truman* (New York: Touchstone, 1992), 162.

10. Steven F. Hayward, *Churchill on Leadership: Executive Success in the Face of Adversity* (Rocklin, Calif.: Forum, 1997), 98.

11. William Manchester, *Winston Spencer Churchill: The Last Lion, Visions of Glory 1874–1932* (New York: Dell Publishing, 1983), 32.

12. Robert K. Greenleaf, *Servant Leadership* (New York: Paulist Press, 1977), 17.

13. Ibid., 300.

14. Gardner, *Leading Minds*, 41–65.

15. Henry T. Blackaby and Claude V. King, *Experiencing God: How to Live the Full Adventure of Knowing and Doing the Will of God* (Nashville: Broadman & Holman, 1994), 15.

16. Warren Bennis and Burt Nanus, *Leaders: Strategies for Taking Charge* (New York: HarperCollins, 1997), 52.

17. James M. Kouzes and Barry Z. Posner, *Encouraging the Heart: A Leader's Guide to Rewarding and Recognizing Others* (San Francisco: Jossey Bass, 1999), 9.

18. Marcus Buckingham and Curt Coffman, *First, Break All the Rules: What the World's Greatest Managers Do Differently* (New York: Simon & Schuster, 1999), 202.

19. Lee Iacocca, *Iacocca: An Autobiography* (Toronto: Bantam Books, 1984), 230.

20. McCullough, *Truman*, 427–28.

21. Ibid., 927.

22. Ibid., 559.

23. Ibid., 560.

24. Max Depree, *Leadership Is an Art* (New York: Dell Publishing, 1989), 146.

25. Manchester, *Winston Spencer Churchill*, 591.

26. Ronald Reagan, *Ronald Reagan: An American Life* (New York: Pocket Books, 1990), 329.

27. Ibid., 260.

28. Schwarzkopf and Petre, *It Doesn't Take a Hero*, 152.

Chapter 8, "The Leader's Decision Making"

1. Peter Drucker, *The Effective Executive* in *The Executive in Action* (New York: HarperBusiness, 1996), 679.

2. Henry and Richard Blackaby, *When God Speaks: How to Recognize God's Voice and Respond in Obedience* (Nashville: Lifeway Press, 1995).

3. Warren Bennis, *Why Leaders Can't Lead* (San Francisco: Jossey-Bass, 1989), 92.

4. John Gardner, *On Leadership* (New York: Free Press, 1990), 135.

5. James M. Kouzes and Barry Z. Posner, *The Leadership Challenge* (San Francisco: Jossey Bass, 1995), 85.

6. Henry T. Blackaby and Claude V. King, *Experiencing God: How to Live the Full Adventure of Knowing and Doing the Will of God* (Nashville: Broadman & Holman, 1994), 196–201.

Chapter 9, "The Leader's Schedule: Doing What's Important"

1. James Lardner, "World-class Workaholics," *U.S. News & World Report*, December 20, 1999.

2. James M. Kouzes and Barry Z. Posner, *The Leadership Challenge* (San Francisco: Jossey Bass, 1995), 250.

3. Peter Drucker, *The Effective Executive* in *The Executive in Action* (New York: HarperBusiness, 1996), 549.

4. Ibid., 565.

5. Ibid., 627.

6. Stuart Wells, *Choosing the Future: The Power of Strategic Thinking* (Woburn, Mass.: Butterworth-Heinemann, 1998), 4.

7. Drucker, *The Effective Executive*, 624.

8. Warren Bennis, *Why Leaders Can't Lead* (San Francisco: Jossey Bass, 1989), 18.

9. Lee Iacocca, *Iacocca: An Autobiography* (Toronto: Bantam Books, 1984), 288–89.

10. David McCullough, *Truman* (New York: Touchstone, 1992), 564.

11. Richard A. Swenson, *Margin: Restoring Emotional, Physical, Financial, and Time Reserves to Overloaded Lives* (Colorado Springs: NavPress, 1992), 92.

12. Kouzes and Posner, *The Leadership Challenge*, 300, 309.

13. James M. Kouzes and Barry Z. Posner, *Encouraging the Heart: A Leader's Guide to Rewarding and Recognizing Others* (San Francisco: Jossey Bass, 1999).

Chapter 10, "The Leader's Pitfalls: What Disqualifies Leaders?"

1. James M. Kouzes and Barry Z. Posner, *Encouraging the Heart: A Leader's Guide to Rewarding and Recognizing Others* (San Francisco: Jossey Bass, 1999), 13.

2. David McCullough, *Truman* (New York: Touchstone, 1992), 564.

3. Ibid., 755.

4. H. W. Brands, *TR: The Last Romantic* (New York: Basic Books, 1997), 146.

5. John Pollock, *Moody* (Grand Rapids: Baker Books, 1963), 163.

6. Max Depree, *Leadership Jazz* (New York: Dell Publishing, 1992), 48.

7. Lee Iacocca, *Iacocca: An Autobiography* (Toronto: Bantam Books, 1984), 146.

8. Ibid., 285.

9. John P. Kotter, *Leading Change* (Boston: Harvard Business School, 1996), 181.

10. Depree, *Leadership Jazz*, 84.

11. Pollock, *Moody*, 169.

12. Ibid., 187.

13. Ian H. Murray, *Jonathan Edwards: A New Biography* (Edinburgh: Banner of Truth Trust, 1987; reprint ed., 1992), 313–70.

14. Oswald Sanders, *Spiritual Leadership* (Chicago: Moody Press, 1967; reprint ed., 1994), 180.

15. Henry and Richard Blackaby, *Experiencing God Day-by-Day* (Nashville: Broadman & Holman, 1997).

16. H. W. Brands, *TR: The Last Romantic* (New York: Basic Books, 1997), 521.

17. Billy Graham, *Just as I Am* (New York: HarperCollins, 1997), 183.

18. Ibid., 852.

19. Howard Gardner, *Leading Minds: An Anatomy of Leadership* (New York: Basic Books, 1995), 262.

20. Ibid., 289.

21. Sanders, *Spiritual Leadership*, 232.

Chapter 11, "The Leader's Rewards and Results"

1. William Manchester, *Winston Spencer Churchill: The Last Lion, Visions of Glory 1874–1932* (New York: Dell Publishing, 1983), 177.

2. Ibid., 228.

3. John Pollock, *Moody* (Grand Rapids: Baker Books, 1963), 271.

4. Ibid., 272.

5. Ibid., 238.

6. *Calgary Herald*, 19 September 1998, A18.

7. Calvin Kytle, *Ghandi: Soldier of Nonviolence* (Washington, D.C.: Seven Locks Press, 1969), 185.

8. Manchester, *Winston Spencer Churchill*, 44.

9. Pollock, *Moody*, 248.

10. Felix Markham, *Napoleon* (New York: New American Library, 1963), 137.

11. Pollock, *Moody*, 118.

12. Howard Gardner, *Leading Minds: An Anatomy of Leadership* (New York: Basic Books, 1995), 280.

13. James M. Kouzes and Barry Z. Posner, *Credibility: How Leaders Gain and Lose It, Why People Demand It* (San Francisco: Jossey Bass, 1993), 261.

14. Robert K. Greenleaf, *Servant Leadership* (New York: Paulist Press, 1977), 21.

15. Margaret Thatcher, *Margaret Thatcher: The Downing Street Years* (New York: HarperCollins, 1993), 860.

16. Ronald Reagan, *Ronald Reagan: An American Life* (New York: Pocket Books, 1990), 722.

17. James M. Kouzes and Barry Z. Posner, *Encouraging the Heart: A Leader's Guide to Rewarding and Recognizing Others* (San Francisco: Jossey Bass, 1999), 84.

Bibliography

Barna, George. *Today's Pastors*. Ventura, Calif.: Regal Books, 1993.

Barna, George, ed. *Leaders on Leadership*. Ventura, Calif.: Regal Books, 1997.

———. *Turning Vision into Action*. Ventura, Calif.: Venture Books, 1996.

Beckett, John D. *Loving Monday: Succeeding in Business Without Selling Your Soul*. Downers Grove, Ill.: InterVarsity Press, 1998.

Bennis, Warren. *On Becoming a Leader*. Reading, Mass.: Addison-Wesley, 1989.

———. *Why Leaders Can't Lead*. San Francisco: Jossey Bass, 1989.

Bennis, Warren, and Burt Nanus. *Leaders: Strategies for Taking Charge*. New York: HarperCollins, 1997.

Blackaby, Henry T., and Claude V. King. *Experiencing God: Knowing and Doing the Will of God*. Nashville: Lifeway Press, 1990.

Blackaby, Henry T., and Richard Blackaby. *Experiencing God Day-by-Day*. Nashville: Broadman & Holman, 1997.

———. *When God Speaks: How to Recognize God's Voice and Respond in Obedience*. Nashville: LifeWay Press, 1995.

Brands, H. W. *TR: The Last Romantic*. New York: Basic Books, 1997.

Buckingham, Marcus, and Curt Coffman. *First, Break all the Rules: What the World's Greatest Managers Do Differently*. New York: Simon & Schuster, 1999.

Burns, James MacGregor. *Leadership*. New York: Harper Torchbooks, 1978.

Cathy, S. Truett. *It's Easier to Succeed than to Fail*. Nashville: Thomas Nelson, 1989.

Champy, James. *Reengineering Management: The Mandate for New Leadership*. New York: Harper Business, 1995.

Churchill, Winston S. *My Early Life*. Glasgow: Fontana Books, 1930; reprint ed. 1963.

Clinton, J. Robert. *The Making of a Leader*. Colorado Springs: Navpress, 1988.

Collins, James C. and Jerry I. Porras. *Built to Last: Successful Habits of Visionary Companies*. New York: HarperBusiness, 1994.

Crocker, H. W. *Robert E. Lee on Leadership: Executive Lessons in Character, Courage, and Vision.* Rocklin, Calif.: Forum, 1999.

DePree, Max. *Leadership Is an Art.* New York: Dell Publishing, 1989.

———. *Leadership Jazz.* New York: Dell Publishing, 1992.

Drucker, Peter F. *The Executive in Action.* New York: HarperBusiness, 1996.

Finney, Charles G. *The Autobiography of Charles G. Finney.* Edited by Helen Wessel. Minneapolis: Bethany House, 1977.

Gardner, Howard. *Leading Minds: An Anatomy of Leadership.* New York: Basic Books, 1995.

Gardner, John W. *On Leadership.* New York: Free Press, 1990.

Goleman, Daniel. *Working with Emotional Intelligence.* New York: Bantam Books, 1998.

Graham, Billy. *Just As I Am.* New York: HarperCollins, 1997.

Greenleaf, Robert K. *Servant Leadership.* New York: Paulist Press, 1977.

Hamilton, J. R. *Alexander the Great.* Pittsburgh: University of Pittsburgh Press, 1973.

Handy, Charles. *The Age of Paradox.* Boston: Harvard Business School Press, 1995.

Hayward, Steven F. *Churchill on Leadership: Executive Success in the Face of Adversity.* Rocklin, Calif.: Forum, 1997.

Hasselbein, Francis, Marshall Goldsmith, and Richard Beckhard, eds. *The Leader of the Future.* San Francisco: Jossey Bass, 1996.

Huckabee, Mike. *Character Is the Issue.* Nashville: Broadman & Holman, 1997.

Iacocca, Lee, with William Novak. *Iacocca: An Autobiography.* Toronto: Bantam Books, 1984.

Kotter, John P. *Leading Change.* Boston: Harvard Business School Press, 1996.

Kouzes, James M., and Barry Z. Posner. *Credibility: How Leaders Gain and Lose It, Why People Demand It.* San Francisco: Jossey Bass, 1993.

———. *Encouraging the Heart: A Leader's Guide to Rewarding and Recognizing Others.* San Francisco: Jossey Bass, 1999.

———. *The Leadership Challenge.* San Francisco: Jossey Bass, 1995.

Kytle, Calvin. *Ghandi: Soldier of Nonviolence.* Washington, D.C.: Seven Locks Press, 1969.

Manchester, William. *Winston Spencer Churchill: The Last Lion, Visions of Glory, 1874–1932.* New York: Dell Publishing, 1983.

Markham, Felix. *Napoleon.* New York: New American Library, 1963.

Maxwell, John C. *Developing the Leader Within You.* Nashville: Thomas Nelson, 1993.

McCullough, David. *Truman.* New York: Touchstone, 1992.

McIntosh, Gary L., and Samuel D. Rima. *Overcoming the Dark Side of Leadership.* Grand Rapids: Baker Books, 1997.

Miller, Basil. *George Muller: The Man of Faith.* 3d ed. Grand Rapids: Zondervan, 1941.

Murray, Iain H. *Jonathan Edwards: A New Biography.* Edinburgh: Banner of Truth Trust, 1987.

Nanus, Burt. *Visionary Leadership.* San Francisco: Jossey Bass, 1992.

Nee, Watchman. *Spiritual Authority.* New York: Christian Fellowship Publishers, 1972.

Phillips, Donald T. *Founding Fathers on Leadership.* New York: Warner Books, 1997.

———. *Lincoln on Leadership: Executive Strategies for Tough Times.* New York: Warner Books, 1992.

———. *Martin Luther King, Jr. on Leadership: Inspiration and Wisdom for Challenging Times.* New York: Warner Books, 1999.

Pollock, John. *Moody.* Grand Rapids: Baker Books, 1963.

Reagan, Ronald. *Ronald Reagan: An American Life.* New York: Pocket Books, 1990.

Ritchie, Homer G. *The Life and Legend of J. Frank Norris: The Fighting Parson.* Fort Worth: Homer G. Ritchie, 1991.

Sanders, J. Oswald. *Spiritual Leadership.* Chicago: Moody Press, 1967.

Scarborough, L. R. *With Christ After the Lost.* Nashville: Broadman Press, 1952.

Shaw, George Bernard. *Man and Superman.* Baltimore: Penguin Books, 1960.

Schwarzkopf, H. Norman, and Peter Petre. *It Doesn't Take a Hero.* New York: Bantam Books, 1992.

Senge, Peter M. *The Fifth Discipline: The Art and Practice of the Learning Organization.* New York: Currency Doubleday, 1994.

Sullivan, Gordon R., and Michael V. Harper. *Hope Is Not a Method: What Business Leaders Can Learn from America's Army.* New York: Broadway Books, 1996.

Swenson, Richard A. *Margin: Restoring Emotional, Physical, Financial, and Time Reserves to Overloaded Lives.* Colorado Springs: Navpress, 1992.

Thatcher, Margaret. *Margaret Thatcher: The Downing Street Years.* New York: HarperCollins, 1993.

Wells, Stuart. *Choosing the Future: The Power of Strategic Thinking.* Boston: Butterworth-Heinemann, 1998.

Index

About the Authors

Henry Blackaby (B.A., M.Div., Th.M., D.D.) has extensive leadership experience. He has been a senior pastor for almost thirty years as well as a director of missions in Vancouver, Canada, and a special consultant to the presidents of the North American Mission Board, International Mission Board, and LifeWay Christian Resources of the Southern Baptist Convention. Henry regularly consults with CEOs concerning leadership issues. Currently Henry resides in Atlanta with his wife Marilynn. He leads Henry Blackaby Ministries, which provides ministries to leaders in Christian as well as secular organizations. Henry travels frequently with national and international speaking engagements and has written books such as *Experiencing God: Knowing and Doing the Will of God, Experiencing God Day–by–Day, The Man God Uses, Created to Be God's Friend* and *The Ways of God.*

Richard Blackaby (B.A., M.Div., Ph.D.) is the oldest son of Henry and Marilynn Blackaby. He has served as a senior pastor and currently is president of the Canadian Southern Baptist Seminary in Cochrane, Canada. Richard is a popular speaker on leadership and has coauthored books with his father, including *When God Speaks, God's Invitation, CrossSeekers, Experiencing God Day-by-Day* and *The Experience.* Richard lives in Cochrane, Canada, with his wife Lisa and their children Mike, Daniel, and Carrie.